Inner solar system : the sun, Mercury, Venus, Earth and Mars

THE INNER SOLAR SYSTEM

THE SUN, MERCURY, VENUS, EARTH, AND MARS

AN EXPLORER'S GUIDE TO THE UNIVERSE

THE INNER SOLAR SYSTEM

THE SUN, MERCURY, VENUS, EARTH, AND MARS

EDITED BY ERIK GREGERSEN, ASSOCIATE EDITOR, ASTRONOMY AND SPACE EXPLORATION

Britannica®
Educational Publishing

IN ASSOCIATION WITH

ROSEN
EDUCATIONAL SERVICES

Published in 2010 by Britannica Educational Publishing
(a trademark of Encyclopædia Britannica, Inc.)
in association with Rosen Educational Services, LLC
29 East 21st Street, New York, NY 10010.

Distributed exclusively by Rosen Educational Services.
For a listing of additional Britannica Educational Publishing titles, call toll free (800) 237-9932.

First Edition

Britannica Educational Publishing
Michael I. Levy: Executive Editor
Marilyn L. Barton: Senior Coordinator, Production Control
Steven Bosco: Director, Editorial Technologies
Lisa S. Braucher: Senior Producer and Data Editor
Yvette Charboneau: Senior Copy Editor
Kathy Nakamura: Manager, Media Acquisition
Erik Gregersen: Associate Editor, Astronomy and Space Exploration

Rosen Educational Services
Jeanne Nagle: Senior Editor
Nelson Sá: Art Director
Nicole Russo: Designer
Introduction by Greg Roza

Library of Congress Cataloging-in-Publication Data

The inner solar system: the sun, Mercury, Venus, Earth, and Mars / edited by Erik
Gregersen.—1st ed.
    p. cm.—(An explorer's guide to the universe)
"In association with Britannica Educational Publishing, Rosen Educational Services."
Includes index.
ISBN 978-1-61530-012-9 (library binding)
1. Solar system—Popular works. 2. Planetology—Popular works. I. Gregersen, Erik.
QB501.2.I56 2010
523.2—dc22

2009030575

Manufactured in the United States of America

Cover photo: © www.istockphoto.com/Mehmet Salih Guler

CONTENTS

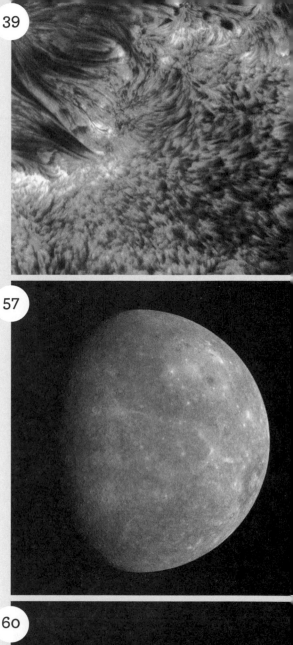

39

57

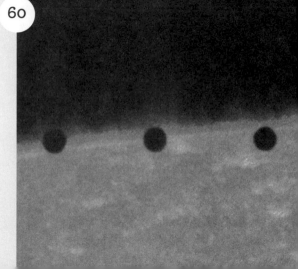

60

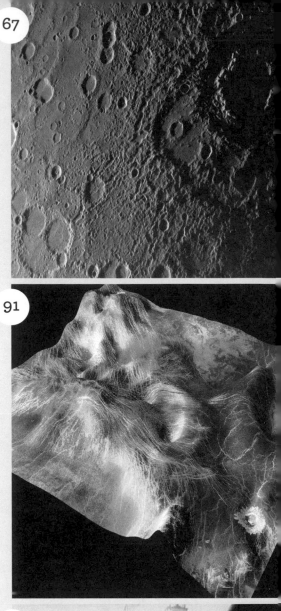

67

91

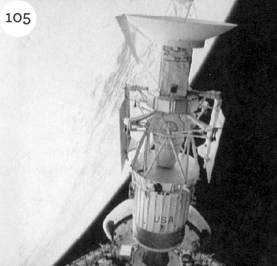

105

143

165

166

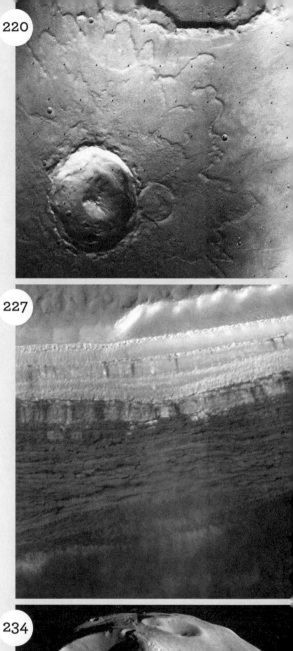

220

227

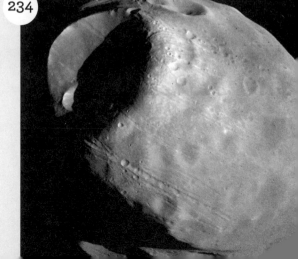

234

INTRODUCTION

Ancient people around the globe once believed the Moon, Sun, planets, and stars were gods and goddesses, demons and angels revolving around Earth, the centre of their universe. Little did they know that Earth is a mere speck in a vast universe. It took many centuries for people to realize that Earth isn't even the centre of our solar system. It is, however, one of the components of what's known as the inner solar system—comprised of the Sun, four terrestrial planets, and the moons that orbit them—which is examined thoroughly in this book.

With the development of modern astronomy and the advent of scientific tools, particularly the telescope, scientists began examining the solar system and theorizing about our place in it. The solar system and the space just beyond it form the extent of our physical reach in the universe. Even with manned and unmanned spacecraft, we may never explore farther than the outer boundary of the solar system. So scientists observe and study our solar system in order to learn more about the universe itself. Much of our knowledge comes from the celestial bodies within the inner solar system, but there is still much to learn.

Our solar system includes the Sun, eight planets (formerly nine), many moons, comets, asteroids, and traces of gas and dust known as interplanetary medium. Although the solar system still presents mysteries, scientists have made great strides over the past 400 years in explaining its origins. The commonly accepted explanation today says that billions of years ago a massive cloud of gas and dust began to collapse in on itself due to gravity. The cloud began to rotate as it collapsed, forming a disk shape. Nuclear reactions began to occur at the centre due to the immense heat and pressure, and the Sun began to form. Material in the rest of the disk slowly collided and merged together to form planets and moons.

The outer planets are much bigger than the inner planets and are largely made up of gases. From Jupiter out, the temperature is so cold that water exists mainly as ice. Large amounts of ice joined together when the outer planets formed, giving them more mass and greater gravitational pull. They drew in large amounts of hydrogen, helium, and other gases, creating "gas giants." However, water in the inner solar system remained liquid, allowing the inner planets to become much smaller and rockier. These ideas about the creation of the solar system are widely supported by many scientists.

Scientists believe the solar system was formed when a cloud of gas and dust (similar to the one in this image captured by NASA in 2004) collapsed upon itself, then compressed to form the Sun and the planets. HO/NASA/AFP/Getty Images

At the heart of the solar system is the Sun. This relatively large star makes up more than 99 percent of the solar system's total mass. The Sun's diameter is about 109 times larger than Earth's. The temperature of the surface of the Sun is about 5,500°C (10,000°F). However, that's nothing compared to the temperature at the Sun's core, which is closer to 15 million°C (27 million°F)!

Approximately 90 percent of the atoms in the Sun are hydrogen atoms. Helium makes up a much smaller amount. These amounts change very slowly over time because hydrogen is continually being converted to helium during a process called nuclear fusion in the Sun's core. The core becomes hotter as more helium is created, and the Sun becomes brighter. At its present rate, the Sun should shine for another 5 billion years, but it will eventually become much larger and brighter than it is now before its hydrogen is depleted.

The Sun's atmosphere is made up of layers. Closest to the Sun, the photosphere is the layer we see. Farther out are the chromosphere and the corona, which we can see during a solar eclipse. For centuries, scientists have observed and theorized about the Sun's many dazzling characteristics, including sun spots, prominences, and solar flares. Scientists continue to study the Sun and the many ways it affects life on Earth, including the solar wind it creates.

The innermost planet, Mercury, is the eighth largest planet in the solar system in terms of size and mass. Its small size—just 4,880 kilometres (3,032 miles) in diameter—and its closeness to the sun make it difficult to observe from Earth. Probes face nearly insurmountable forces to get close to the tiny planet. However, scientists are keen to study the planet further due to several notable differences between it and the other planets, such as its elongated orbit and peculiarities regarding the nature of gravity.

Mercury has an average orbital distance of 58 million km (36 million miles) and orbits the Sun once every 88 days. Although it is the smallest planet, it is also the densest. Its lead core makes up approximately three-quarters of the planet. The rocky, outer shell is dotted with craters caused by countless asteroid impacts. Between the larger craters are sparsely cratered surfaces called intercrater plains and smooth plains. Caloris, Mercury's largest crater, is 1,550 km (960 miles) in diameter. Space probes have detected minute traces of atmospheric gases, but they are nearly nonexistent. Mercury's magnetic field resembles Earth's bipolar field, although it is much, much weaker.

The next closest planet to the Sun, Venus, is very similar to Earth in size, mass, density, and gravity. It has an average orbital distance of 108 million km (67 million miles). Of all the planets its orbit is the most circle-shaped. Unlike most planets, Venus rotates in a clockwise direction when viewed from its north pole.

Venus is perpetually blanketed by a thick veil of clouds high in carbon dioxide, and its surface temperature approaches 482°C (900°F). NASA Marshall Space Flight Center

The planet also spins very slowly, taking 243 Earth days to complete a rotation.

Venus's dense, swirling cloud cover circles the planet in just four days. The planet has the most massive atmosphere of all the inner planets. Carbon dioxide is the most abundant gas, but it also contains highly concentrated sulfuric acid and solid sulfur, among other ingredients. The atmosphere is so thick it creates a powerful greenhouse effect similar to the one on Earth. As a result, the temperature at the surface can be about 464°C (867°F), which is higher than the melting point of lead.

Little was known about Venus's surface until the 1960s, when scientists used radar and spacecraft to study the planet. Most of the surface is rocky and sandy, dominated by vast, rolling plains. Some areas feature rifts, mountains, volcanoes, lava flows, and craters. Scientists hope for clearer images of Venus's surface as technology improves.

Earth—the only planet known to harbor life—orbits the Sun at a mean distance of 150 million km (93 million miles), completing one orbit in about 365.25 days. It makes one revolution every 23 hours, 56 minutes, and 4 seconds. Earth is the largest of the inner, rocky planets, with a diameter of 6,378 km (7,926 miles). It has one satellite, which we simply call the Moon.

Earth's atmosphere is mainly comprised of nitrogen (78 percent) and oxygen (21 percent), but contains tiny amounts of other substances, including argon, methane, carbon dioxide, and water vapour. Most of the atmosphere is contained in the troposphere, a layer that extends up to an altitude of about 10–15 km (6–9 miles). The ozone layer is found in the upper layer of the stratosphere and protects the Earth from harmful ultraviolet rays from the Sun. Above the stratosphere are the mesosphere, thermosphere, and ionosphere. Unlike the other planets, Earth also has a hydrosphere, which is a layer of water at or near the planet's surface.

Earth's crust is a rigid layer of rock that "floats" on a softer layer of hot rock called the mantle. The landmasses on Earth's surface are in constant motion, often bumping into each other or drifting apart. About one-third of Earth's mass is contained in its hot, liquid iron core. Fluid motions within Earth's core create a powerful electromagnetic field around the planet. This field, called the magnetosphere, deflects dangerous solar winds and keeps them from striking Earth.

Earth's satellite is one of the largest moons in the solar system and the brightest object in the sky other than the Sun. Some scientists consider Earth and the Moon "twin planets." It is the only object in the solar system besides Earth that human beings have visited so far. Scientific observations of the Moon and the way it acts have helped scientists make breakthroughs about the mechanics of the solar system.

The gravitational fields of Earth and the Moon have a great effect on each other. The Moon causes the cycle of tides in Earth's larger bodies of water. Because the rate at which the Moon orbits Earth matches the rate at which the Moon rotates on its axis, the same side of the Moon always faces Earth. Seen from Earth, the Moon is lighted by the Sun and takes on different shapes, called phases, depending on the day of the month.

The Moon orbits Earth at a mean distance of about 384,000 km (238,600 miles).

Sunlight illuminates specific portions of the Moon as it orbits Earth. Consequently, the Moon is visible from Earth in phases, changing from partially illuminated (top) to fully illuminated (bottom) and back again. Shutterstock.com

It has a diameter of 3,476 km (2,160 miles). Its surface features many impact craters separated by flat, rocky plains and is covered with rocks and dust caused by the countless objects that have hit it. Because of the Moon's small size and mass, its gravity is about one-sixth of Earth's. It has very little atmosphere.

Thanks to the Moon, people on Earth are treated to occasional celestial shows called eclipses. An eclipse occurs when one object in space partially or totally blocks another. Scientists have been studying eclipses for centuries and have used them to make many discoveries about the solar system.

A solar eclipse occurs when the Moon passes in front of the Sun, casting a shadow over part of Earth's surface. To someone standing in this shadow on Earth, the Sun appears to be growing dimmer. Those lucky enough to witness a total eclipse will see all but the Sun's corona totally disappear for several minutes, creating a dazzling natural light show. The diameter of the Sun is about 400 times larger than that of the Moon. However, it is also about 400 times farther away from Earth. Due to this fascinating coincidence, the Moon and the Sun appear to be about the same size from the perspective of someone standing on Earth. This coincidence is what makes solar eclipses possible. However, the Moon is slowly moving away from Earth. Millions of years from now, total eclipses will no longer be possible.

During a full Moon—when the Moon and the Sun are on opposite sides of Earth—the Moon may pass through Earth's shadow, resulting in a lunar eclipse. The Moon dims considerably but remains partially visible, often with a red glow. Although total solar eclipses rarely last more than a few minutes, a total lunar eclipse can last several hours.

Mars, the fourth planet from the Sun, is the second-smallest planet in the solar system. With a diameter of 6,792 km (4,220 miles), it is about half the size of Earth. It has an average orbital distance of 228 million km (140 million miles). One day on Mars is slightly longer than a day on Earth. One year on Mars equals 687 Earth days. Due to its elongated orbit, Mars is less than 56 million km (35 million miles) from Earth at its closest, but almost 400 million km (250 million miles) away when they are on opposite sides of the solar system.

The Martian atmosphere is comprised mainly of carbon dioxide, and is much thinner than Earth's. Water vapour in the atmosphere sometimes forms low-lying clouds and fog in valleys or craters. Some of the water vapour forms ice caps at the north and south poles. Many scientists now think water also exists beneath Mars's surface. Dust storms are common and can last for weeks. "The red planet," as it is often called, has deep rifts, some of which can be seen with the aid of a telescope. It also has the tallest volcano in the solar system—Olympus Mons. Mars has two small, irregularly shaped moons, Phobos and Deimos, which may have once been asteroids captured by Mars's gravitational field.

Mars was one of the first planets to be studied with telescopes, and it continues to intrigue scientists. Some think it once supported life and may one day be colonized by humans. More than 50 meteorites that originated on Mars have been found on Earth. We are constantly learning new things about Mars thanks to several space probes and rovers that have been sent to explore the planet.

These are the planets and moons of the inner solar system, but other objects are lurking out there. They include comets, asteroids, and meteors, many of which have their own orbits around the Sun. Scientists use the term interplanetary medium to describe thinly scattered matter drifting between the planets. Neutral hydrogen atoms and plasma come from the Sun in the form of solar wind. Cosmic rays are high-speed, high-energy atomic nuclei and electrons. Some come from the Sun itself, while most come from outside the solar system. Very small dust particles, sometimes called micrometeoroids, orbit the Sun much like the planets. This dust is probably the result of collisions between asteroids and material shed from comets.

The inner solar system is our local neighbourhood in a limitless, continually expanding universe. It provides scientists with some of the best chances for studying the forces that govern the cosmos. This book will guide you through the inner solar system and give you a close-up look at many of the topics discussed in this introduction and more. So strap in, the countdown has begun. Let's explore the inner solar system!

CHAPTER 1

COMPOSITION AND ORIGIN OF THE SOLAR SYSTEM

Our home planet, Earth, floats as a tiny oasis of life in the immensity of the universe. However, Earth does not wander space alone. From the earliest ages of history, humanity watched the skies and studied the motions of the Sun, which lit the day, and the Moon, which shone at night. The stars were thought fixed to the vault of heaven, but some stars were wanderers, or *planetes*, as the Greeks called them. Earth, the Sun, the Moon, and the planets are part of one assembly of nearby astronomical bodies called the solar system.

Located at the centre of the solar system and influencing the motion of all the other bodies through its gravitational force is the Sun, which in itself contains more than 99 percent of the mass of the system. The planets, in order of their distance outward from the Sun, are Mercury, Venus, Earth, Mars, Jupiter, Saturn, Uranus, and Neptune. The first four planets, Mercury, Venus, Earth, and Mars, constitute the inner solar system.

ORBITS

All the planets move around the Sun in elliptical orbits in the same direction that the Sun rotates. This motion is termed prograde, or direct, motion. Looking down on the system from a vantage point above Earth's North Pole, an observer would find that all these orbital motions are in a counterclockwise direction.

The shape of an object's orbit is defined in terms of its eccentricity. For a perfectly circular orbit, the eccentricity is 0; with increasing elongation of the orbit's shape, the eccentricity increases toward a value of 1, the eccentricity of a parabola. Of the four planets of the inner solar system, Venus has the most circular orbit around the Sun, with an eccentricity of 0.007. Mercury, the closest planet, has the highest eccentricity, with 0.21.

Another defining attribute of an object's orbit around the Sun is its inclination, which is the angle that it makes with the plane of Earth's orbit—the ecliptic plane. Again, of the inner planets, Mercury has the greatest inclination, its orbit lying at 7° to the ecliptic.

PLANETS AND THEIR MOONS

The eight planets can be divided into two distinct categories on the basis of their densities (mass per unit volume). The four inner, or terrestrial, planets—Mercury, Venus, Earth, and Mars—have rocky compositions and densities greater than 3 grams per cubic cm (g/cm^3; 1.73 oz/in^3). (For comparison purposes, water has a density of 1 g/cm^3.) In contrast, the four outer planets, also called the Jovian, or giant, planets—Jupiter, Saturn, Uranus, and Neptune—are large objects with densities less than 2 g/cm^3 (1.16 oz/in^3).

The eight planets of the solar system and dwarf planet Pluto, in a montage of images scaled to show the approximate sizes of the bodies relative to one another. Outward from the Sun, which is represented to scale, are the four rocky terrestrial planets (Mercury, Venus, Earth, and Mars), the four hydrogen-rich giant planets (Jupiter, Saturn, Uranus, and Neptune), and Pluto. NASA/Lunar and Planetary Laboratory.

The relatively small inner planets have solid surfaces, lack ring systems, and have few or no moons. The atmospheres of Venus, Earth, and Mars are composed of a significant percentage of oxidized compounds such as carbon dioxide. Among the inner planets, only Earth has a strong magnetic field, which shields it from the interplanetary medium. The magnetic field traps some of the electrically charged particles of the interplanetary medium inside a region around Earth known as the magnetosphere. Heavy concentrations of these high-energy particles occur in the Van Allen belts in the inner part of the magnetosphere. The moons of Earth and Mars move around their respective planets in the same direction in which those planets orbit the Sun.

THE INTERPLANETARY MEDIUM

The space between the planets of the solar system is not an empty void. It is permeated by thinly scattered matter called the interplanetary medium. The material components of the interplanetary medium consist of neutral hydrogen, the solar wind (discussed in detail in the Sun section), cosmic rays, and dust particles.

Extremely small amounts of neutral (nonionized) hydrogen have been detected throughout much of interplanetary space. At the distance of Earth's orbit from the Sun, for example, the concentration of neutral hydrogen is about one atom per 100 cubic cm (6 cubic inches).

Some of the neutral hydrogen that enters the solar system from interstellar space is ionized by sunlight and by charge exchange with the plasma of the solar wind emanating from the Sun.

Those cosmic rays detected in the vicinity of Earth comprise high-speed, high-energy atomic nuclei and electrons. Among the nuclei, the most abundant are hydrogen nuclei (protons; 90 percent) and helium nuclei (alpha particles; 9 percent). Nuclei outnumber electrons about 50 to 1. A minority of cosmic rays are produced in the Sun, especially at times of increased solar activity. The origin of those coming from outside the solar system—called galactic cosmic rays—remains to be conclusively identified, but they are thought to be produced in stellar processes such as supernova explosions.

Relatively small amounts of dust particles, often called micrometeoroids, exist in the solar system, most of which appear to be orbiting the Sun in or near the plane of the solar system. This dust consists of small grains, generally less than a few hundred micrometres in size and composed of silicate minerals and glassy nodules but sometimes including sulfides, metals, other minerals, and carbonaceous material, in orbit around the Sun. Spacecraft have detected these particles nearly as far out in space as the orbit of Uranus, which indicates that the entire solar system is immersed in a disk of dust, centred on the ecliptic plane.

The existence of interplanetary dust particles was first deduced from observations of zodiacal light, a glowing band visible in the night sky that comprises sunlight scattered by the dust. The zodiacal light is seen in the west after twilight and in the east before dawn, being easily visible in the tropics where the plane of the zodiac, or ecliptic, is approximately vertical. In mid-northern latitudes it is best seen in the evening in February and March and in the morning in September and October. The zodiacal light can be followed visually along the ecliptic from a point 30° from the Sun to about 90°. Photometric measurements indicate that the band continues to the region opposite the Sun where a slight enhancement called the gegenschein, or counterglow, is visible. There is some zodiacal light in all parts of the sky.

Every object in the solar system can produce dust by outgassing, cratering, volcanism, or other processes. Most interplanetary dust is believed to come from the surface erosion and collisions of asteroids, as well as from comets, which give off gas and dust when they travel near the Sun.

The orbits of interplanetary dust particles are easily altered by interaction with the light and charged particles (solar wind) that emanate from the Sun. The smallest particles, less than 0.5 micrometre (0.00002 inch) in size, are blown out of the solar system. Drag effects from sunlight and the solar wind cause larger particles to spiral toward the Sun, some on paths that intercept planets or their moons.

Considered in the context of their collisions with other objects in space, interplanetary dust particles are frequently called micrometeoroids. Because of their high speed (in the tens of kilometres per second), micrometeoroids as small as a few hundred micrometres in size pose a significant collision hazard to spacecraft and their payloads. An impact can, for example, puncture a vital component or create a transient cloud of ions that can short-circuit an electrical system. Consequently, protection against micrometeoroid impacts has become a necessary element of space hardware design. Components of the Earth-orbiting International Space Station use a "dust bumper," or Whipple shield (named for its inventor, the American astronomer Fred Whipple), to guard against damage from micrometeoroids and orbiting debris. Spacesuits intended for extravehicular activity, which is activity that takes place outside a module or space station, also incorporate micrometeoroid protection in their outer layers.

Analyses of micrometeoroid pitting on Earth-orbiting satellites indicate that about 30,000 tons a year of interplanetary dust strike Earth's upper atmosphere, mostly particles between 50 μm and 1 mm (0.002–0.04 inch) in size. Particles from space larger than a few hundred micrometres—i.e., meteoroids—are heated so severely during deceleration in the atmosphere that they vaporize, producing a glowing meteor trail. Smaller particles experience less severe heating and survive, eventually settling to Earth's surface. When found in Earth's atmosphere or on its surface, they are often referred to as micrometeorites or cosmic dust particles.

Using high-altitude research aircraft, the U.S. National Aeronautics and Space Administration (NASA) has collected cosmic dust particles directly from Earth's stratosphere, where the concentration of terrestrial dust is low. Particles larger than 50 μm are relatively uncommon there, however, which makes their collection by aircraft impractical. These larger particles have been collected in sediment that has been filtered from large volumes of melted polar ice. Spacecraft missions have been developed to retrieve dust particles directly from space. The U.S. Stardust spacecraft, launched in 1999, flew past Comet Wild 2 in early 2004, collecting particles from its coma (the cloud around a comet formed by evaporating ice) for return to Earth. In 2003 Japan's space agency launched its Hayabusa spacecraft to return small amounts of surface material, comprising fragments and dust, from the near-Earth asteroid Itokawa for laboratory analysis.

Some cosmic dust particles gathered from the stratosphere are the least altered samples of early solar system dust that have been studied in the laboratory. They provide clues to the temperature, pressure, and chemical composition of the nebular cloud from which the solar system condensed 4.6 billion years ago. The continuous accretion of micrometeorites on early Earth may have contributed organic compounds that were important for the development of life. A few micrometeorites are thought to contain preserved interstellar grains—samples of matter from outside the solar system. Spacecraft sample-return missions to comets and asteroids should provide scientists on Earth the opportunity to study even better-preserved material from the birth of the solar system.

There is also a nonmaterial component to the interplanetary medium. The magnetic field lines that are carried outward from the Sun by the solar wind remain attached to the Sun's surface. Because of the Sun's rotation, the lines are drawn into a spiral structure. Closely associated with the interplanetary magnetic field are electric forces that act to attract or repel charged particles.

ORIGIN OF THE SOLAR SYSTEM

As the amount of data on the planets, moons, comets, and asteroids has grown, so too have the problems faced by astronomers in forming theories of the origin of the solar system. In the ancient world, theories of the origin of Earth and the objects seen in the sky were certainly much less constrained by fact. Indeed, a scientific approach to the origin of the solar system became possible only after the publication of Isaac Newton's laws of motion and gravitation in 1687. Even after this breakthrough, many years elapsed while scientists struggled with applications of Newton's laws to explain the apparent motions of planets, moons, comets, and asteroids. Meanwhile, the first semblance of a modern theory was proposed by the German philosopher Immanuel Kant in 1755.

THE KANT-LAPLACE NEBULAR HYPOTHESIS

Kant's central idea was that the solar system began as a cloud of dispersed particles. He assumed that the mutual gravitational attractions of the particles caused them to start moving and colliding, at which point chemical forces kept them bonded together. As some of these aggregates became larger than others, they grew still more rapidly, ultimately forming the planets. Because Kant was highly versed in neither physics nor mathematics, he did not recognize the intrinsic limitations of his approach. His model does not account for planets moving around the Sun in the same direction and in the same plane, as they are observed to do, nor does it explain the revolution of planetary satellites.

A significant step forward was made by Pierre-Simon Laplace of France some 40 years later. A brilliant mathematician, Laplace was particularly successful in the field of celestial mechanics. Besides publishing a monumental treatise on the subject, he wrote a popular book on astronomy, with an appendix in which he made some suggestions about the origin of the solar system.

Laplace's model begins with the Sun already formed and rotating and its atmosphere extending beyond the distance at which the farthest planet would be created. Knowing nothing about the true source of energy in stars, Laplace assumed that the Sun would start to cool as it radiated away its heat. In response to this cooling, as the pressure exerted by its gases declined, the Sun would contract. According to the law of conservation of angular momentum, the decrease in size would be accompanied by an increase in the Sun's rotational velocity. Centrifugal acceleration would push the material in the atmosphere outward, while gravitational attraction would pull it toward the central mass. When these forces just balanced, a ring of material would be left behind in the plane of the Sun's equator. This process would have continued through the formation of several concentric rings, each of which then would have coalesced to form a planet. Similarly, a planet's moons would have originated from rings produced by the forming planets.

Laplace's model led naturally to the observed result of planets revolving around the Sun in the same plane and in the same direction as the Sun rotates. Because the theory of Laplace incorporated Kant's idea of planets coalescing from dispersed material, their two approaches are often combined in a single model called the Kant-Laplace nebular hypothesis. This model for solar system formation was widely accepted for about

100 years. During this period, the apparent regularity of motions in the solar system was contradicted by the discovery of asteroids with highly eccentric orbits and moons with retrograde orbits. Another problem with the nebular hypothesis was the fact that, whereas the Sun contains 99.9 percent of the mass of the solar system, the planets (principally the four giant outer planets) carry more than 99 percent of the system's angular momentum. For the solar system to conform to this theory, either the Sun should be rotating more rapidly or the planets should be revolving around it more slowly.

MODERN IDEAS

In the early decades of the 20th century, several scientists decided that the deficiencies of the nebular hypothesis made it no longer tenable. The Americans Thomas Chrowder Chamberlin and Forest Ray Moulton, as well as James Jeans and Harold Jeffreys of Great Britain, independently developed variations on the idea that the planets were formed catastrophically—i.e., by a close encounter of the Sun with another star. The basis of this model was that material was drawn out from one or both stars when the two bodies passed at close range, and this material later coalesced to form planets. A discouraging aspect of the theory was the implication that the formation of solar systems in the Milky Way Galaxy must be extremely rare, because sufficiently close encounters between stars would occur very seldom.

The next significant development took place in the mid-20th century as scientists acquired a more mature understanding of the processes by which stars themselves must form and of the behaviour of gases within and around stars. They realized that hot gaseous material stripped from a stellar atmosphere would simply dissipate in space; it would not condense to form planets. Hence, the basic idea that a solar system could form through stellar encounters was untenable. Furthermore, the growth in knowledge about the interstellar medium indicated that large clouds of such matter exist and that stars form in these clouds. Planets must somehow be created in the process that forms the stars themselves. This awareness encouraged scientists to reconsider certain basic processes that resembled some of the earlier notions of Kant and Laplace.

The current approach to the origin of the solar system treats it as part of the general process of star formation. As observational information has steadily increased, the field of plausible models for this process has narrowed. This information ranges from observations of star-forming regions in giant interstellar clouds to subtle clues revealed in the existing chemical composition of the objects present in the solar system. Many scientists have contributed to the modern perspective, most notably the Canadian-born American astrophysicist Alistair G. W. Cameron.

FORMATION OF
THE SOLAR NEBULA

The favoured paradigm for the origin of the solar system begins with the gravitational collapse of part of an interstellar cloud of gas and dust having an initial mass only 10 to 20 percent greater than the present mass of the Sun. This type of collapse could be initiated by random fluctuations of density within the cloud, one or more of which might result in the accumulation of enough material to start the process, or by an extrinsic disturbance such as the shock wave from a supernova. The collapsing cloud region quickly becomes roughly spherical in shape. Because it is revolving around the centre of the Galaxy, the parts more distant from the centre are moving more slowly than the nearer parts. Hence, as the cloud collapses, it starts to rotate, and, to conserve angular momentum, its speed of rotation increases as it continues to contract. With ongoing contraction, the cloud flattens, because it is easier for matter to follow the attraction of gravity perpendicular to the plane of rotation than along it, where the opposing centrifugal force is greatest. The result at this stage, as in Laplace's model, is a disk of material formed around a central condensation.

This configuration, commonly referred to as the solar nebula, resembles the shape of a typical spiral galaxy on a much reduced scale. As gas and dust collapse toward the central condensation, their potential energy is converted to kinetic energy (energy of motion), and the temperature of the material rises. Ultimately the temperature becomes great enough within the condensation for nuclear reactions to begin, thereby giving birth to the Sun. Meanwhile, the material in the disk collides, coalesces, and gradually forms larger and larger objects, as in Kant's theory. Because most of the grains of material have nearly identical orbits, collisions between them are relatively mild, which allows the particles to stick and remain together. Thus, larger agglomerations of particles are gradually built up.

DIFFERENTIATION INTO
INNER AND OUTER PLANETS

At this stage the individual accreting objects in the disk show differences in their growth and composition that depend on their distances from the hot central mass. Close to the nascent Sun, temperatures are too high for water to condense from gaseous form to ice, but, at the distance of present-day Jupiter (778 million kilometres [km], 5.2 astronomical units [AU], or 483 million miles) and beyond, water ice can form. The significance of this difference is related to the availability of water to the forming planets. Because of the relative abundances in the universe of the various elements, more molecules of water can form than of any other compound. (Water, in fact, is the second most abundant molecule in the universe, after molecular hydrogen.) Consequently, objects forming in the solar nebula at temperatures at which water can condense to ice are able to acquire much more mass in the form of solid material than objects forming closer to the Sun.

Once such an accreting body achieves approximately 10 times the present mass of Earth, its gravity can attract and retain large amounts of even the lightest elements, hydrogen and helium, from the solar nebula. These are the two most abundant elements in the universe, and so planets forming in this region can become very massive indeed. Only at distances of 5 AU or more is there enough mass of material in the solar nebula to build such a planet.

This simple picture can explain the extensive differences observed between the inner and outer planets. The inner planets formed at temperatures too high to allow the abundant volatile substances—those with comparatively low freezing temperatures—such as water, carbon dioxide, and ammonia to condense to their ices. They therefore remained small rocky bodies. In contrast, the large low-density, gas-rich outer planets formed at distances beyond what astronomers have dubbed the "snow line"—i.e., the minimum radius from the Sun at which water ice could have condensed, at about 150 K (Kelvin; -120 °C, or -190 °F). The effect of the temperature gradient in the solar nebula can be seen today in the increasing fraction of condensed volatiles in solid bodies as their distance from the Sun increases. (See the table of compositional data for selected objects.) As the nebular gas cooled, the first solid materials to condense from a gaseous phase were grains of metal-containing silicates, the basis of rocks. This was followed, at larger distances from the Sun, by formation of the ices. In the inner solar system, Earth's Moon, with a density of 3.3 g/cm^3 (1.91 oz/in^3), is a satellite composed of silicate minerals. In the outer solar system are low-density moons such as Saturn's Tethys. With a density of about 1 g/cm^3 (0.58 oz/in^3), this object must consist mainly of water ice. At distances still farther out, the satellite densities rise again but only slightly, presumably because they incorporate denser solids, such as frozen carbon dioxide, which condense at even lower temperatures.

Despite its apparent logic, this scenario has received some strong challenges since the early 1990s. One has come from the discovery of other solar systems, many of which contain giant planets orbiting very close to their stars. Another has been the unexpected finding from the Galileo spacecraft mission that Jupiter's atmosphere is enriched with volatile substances such as argon and molecular nitrogen. For these gases to have condensed and become incorporated in the icy bodies that accreted to form Jupiter's core required temperatures of 30 K (-240 °C, or -400 °F) or less. This corresponds to a distance far beyond the traditional snow line where Jupiter is thought to have formed. On the other hand, certain later models have suggested that the temperature close to the central plane of the solar nebula was much cooler (25 K [-248 °C, or -415 °F]) than previously estimated.

COMPOSITIONAL DATA FOR SELECTED SOLAR SYSTEM OBJECTS

OBJECT	DISTANCE FROM SUN (AU)*	MEAN DENSITY (g/cm³)	GENERAL COMPOSITION
Sun	—	1.4	hydrogen, helium
Mercury	0.4	5.4	iron, nickel, silicates
Venus	0.7	5.2	silicates, iron, nickel
Earth	1	5.5	silicates, iron, nickel
Moon	1	3.3	silicates
Mars	1.5	3.9	silicates, iron, sulfur
asteroids	2–4.5 (main and outer belts)	typically 2–4	silicates, iron, nickel
Jupiter	5.2	1.3	hydrogen, helium
Io	5.2	3.6	silicates, sulfur
Europa	5.2	3.0	silicates, water ice (crust)
Ganymede	5.2	1.9	water ice, silicates
Callisto	5.2	1.8	water ice, silicates
Saturn	9.5	0.7	hydrogen, helium
Tethys	9.5	1.0	water ice
Titan	9.5	1.9	water ice, silicates, organics
Centaur objects	5–30 (mainly between orbits of Jupiter and Neptune)	possibly less than 1	presumed similar to that of comets: water ice, other ices, traces of silicates
Uranus	19.2	1.3	ices, silicates, hydrogen, helium
Neptune	30.1	1.6	ices, silicates, hydrogen, helium
Triton	30.1	2.0	water ice, silicates, organics
Pluto	39.5	2.0	water ice, silicates, organics
Kuiper belt objects	30–50 (main concentration)	possibly less than 1	presumed similar to that of comets: water ice, other ices, traces of silicates, organics
Oort cloud objects	20,000–100,000	possibly less than 1	presumed similar to that of comets: water ice, other ices, traces of silicates, organics

*One astronomical unit (AU) is the mean distance of Earth from the Sun, about 150 million km.

Although a number of such problems remain to be resolved, the solar nebula model of Kant and Laplace appears basically correct. Support comes from observations at infrared and radio wavelengths, which have revealed disks of matter around young stars. These observations also suggest that planets form in a remarkably short time. The collapse of an interstellar cloud into a disk should take about one million years. The thickness of this disk is determined by the gas it contains, as the solid particles that are forming rapidly settle to the disk's midplane, in times ranging from 100,000 years for 1-micrometre (0.00004-inch) particles to just 10 years for 1-cm (0.4-inch) particles. As the local density increases at the midplane, the opportunity becomes greater for the growth of particles by collision. As the particles grow, the resulting increase in their gravitational fields accelerates further growth. Calculations show that objects 10 km (6 miles) in size will form in just 1,000 years. Such objects are large enough to be called planetesimals, the building blocks of planets.

LATER STAGES OF PLANETARY ACCRETION

Continued growth by accretion leads to larger and larger objects. The energy released during accretionary impacts would be sufficient to cause vaporization and extensive melting, transforming the original primitive material that had been produced by direct condensation in the nebula. Theoretical studies of this phase of the planet-forming process suggest that several bodies the size of the Moon or Mars must have formed in addition to the planets found today. Collisions of these giant planetesimals—sometimes called planetary embryos—with the planets would have had dramatic effects and could have produced some of the anomalies seen today in the solar system; for example, the strangely high density of Mercury and the extremely slow and retrograde rotation of Venus. A collision of Earth and a planetary embryo about the size of Mars could have formed the Moon. Somewhat smaller impacts on Mars in the late phases of accretion may have been responsible for the present thinness of the Martian atmosphere.

Studies of isotopes formed from the decay of radioactive parent elements with short half-lives, in both lunar samples and meteorites, have demonstrated that the formation of the inner planets, including Earth, and the Moon was essentially complete within 50 million years after the interstellar cloud region collapsed. The bombardment of planetary and satellite surfaces by debris left over from the main accretionary stage continued intensively for another 600 million years, but these impacts contributed only a few percent of the mass of any given object.

SOLUTION TO THE ANGULAR MOMENTUM PUZZLE

The angular momentum problem that defeated Kant and Laplace—why the planets have most of the solar system's angular momentum while the Sun has most of the mass—can now be approached in a cosmic context. All stars having masses that range from slightly above the mass of the Sun to the smallest known masses rotate more slowly than an extrapolation based on the rotation rate of stars of higher mass would predict. Accordingly, these sunlike stars show the same deficit in angular momentum as the Sun itself.

The answer to how this loss could have occurred seems to lie in the solar wind. The Sun and other stars of comparable mass have outer atmospheres that are slowly but steadily expanding into space. Stars of higher mass do not exhibit such stellar winds. The loss of angular momentum associated with this loss of mass to space is sufficient to reduce the rate of the Sun's rotation. Thus, the planets preserve the angular momentum that was in the original solar nebula, but the Sun has gradually slowed down in the 4.6 billion years since it formed.

CHAPTER 2

THE SUN

At the centre of the solar system is the Sun, the star around which Earth and the other components revolve. It is the dominant body of the system, constituting more than 99 percent of its entire mass. The Sun is the source of an enormous amount of energy, a portion of which provides Earth with the light and heat necessary to support life.

The Sun is classified as a G2 V star, with G2 standing for the second hottest stars of the yellow G class and the V representing a main sequence, or dwarf, star, the typical star for this temperature class. (G stars are so called because of the prominence of a band of atomic and molecular spectral lines that the German physicist Joseph von Fraunhofer designated G.) The Sun exists in the outer part of the Milky Way Galaxy and was formed from material that had been processed inside a supernova. The Sun is not, as is often said, a small star. Although it falls midway between the biggest and smallest stars of its type, there are so many dwarf stars that the Sun falls in the top 5 percent of stars in the neighbourhood that immediately surrounds it.

PHYSICAL PROPERTIES

The radius of the Sun, $R_\odot$, is 109 times that of Earth, but its distance from Earth is 215 $R_\odot$, so it subtends an angle of only ½° in the sky, roughly the same as that of the Moon. By comparison, Proxima Centauri, the next closest star to Earth, is 250,000 times farther away, and its relative apparent brightness is reduced by the square of that ratio, or 62 billion times. The temperature of the Sun's surface is so high that no solid or liquid can exist there; the constituent materials are predominantly gaseous atoms, with a very small number of molecules. As a result, there is no fixed surface. The surface viewed from Earth, called the photosphere, is the layer from which most of the radiation reaches us. The radiation from below is absorbed and reradiated, and the emission from overlying layers drops sharply, by about a factor of six every 200 km (124 miles). The Sun is so far from Earth that this slightly fuzzy surface cannot be resolved, and so the limb (the visible edge) appears sharp.

The mass of the Sun, $M_\odot$, is 743 times the total mass of all the planets in the solar system and 330,000 times that of Earth. All the interesting planetary and interplanetary gravitational phenomena are negligible effects in comparison to the force exerted by the Sun. Under the force of gravity, the great mass of the Sun presses inward. To keep the star from collapsing, the central pressure outward must be great enough to support its weight. The density at the Sun's core is about 100 times that of water (roughly six times that at the centre of Earth), but the temperature is at least 15 million K, so the central pressure is at least 10,000 times greater than that at the centre of Earth, which is 3,500 kilobars. The nuclei of

atoms are completely stripped of their electrons, and at this high temperature they collide to produce the nuclear reactions that are responsible for generating the energy vital to life on Earth.

While the temperature of the Sun drops from 15 million K (27 million °F) at the centre to 5,800 K (5,500°C, 10,000°F) at the photosphere, a surprising reversal occurs above that point. The temperature drops to a minimum of 4,000 K (3,700°C, 6,700°F), then begins to rise in the chromosphere, a layer about 7,000 km (4,300 miles) high at a temperature of 8,000 K (7,700°C, 13,900°F). Above the chromosphere is a dim, extended halo called the corona, which has a temperature of 1 million K (1.8 million °F) and reaches far past the planets. Beyond a distance of $5R_\odot$ from the Sun, the corona flows outward at a speed (near Earth) of 400 km per second (km/sec; 250 miles/sec); this flow of charged particles is called the solar wind.

The Sun is a very stable source of energy. Its radiative output, called the solar constant, is 137 ergs per square metre per second (ergs/metre^2/sec), or 1.98 calories per square cm per minute (cal/cm^2/min), at Earth. The solar constant is defined as the total radiation energy received from the Sun per unit of time per unit of area on a theoretical surface perpendicular to the Sun's rays and at Earth's mean distance from the Sun. It is most accurately measured from satellites where atmospheric effects are absent. The solar constant does increase, but only by 0.2 percent at the peak of each solar cycle.

ENERGY GENERATION AND TRANSPORT

The energy radiated by the Sun is produced during the conversion of hydrogen (H) atoms to helium (He). The Sun is at least 90 percent hydrogen by number of atoms, so the fuel is readily available. Since one hydrogen atom weighs 1.0078 atomic mass units, and a single helium atom weighs 4.0026, the conversion of four hydrogen atoms to one helium atom yields 0.0294 mass unit, which are all converted to energy, 6.8 million electron volts (MeV), in the form of gamma (γ) rays or the kinetic energy of the products. If all the hydrogen is converted, 0.7 percent of the mass becomes energy, according to the Einstein formula $E = mc^2$, in which E represents the energy, m is the mass, and c is the speed of light. A calculation of the time required to convert all the hydrogen in the Sun provides an estimate of the length of time for which the Sun can continue to radiate energy. In only about 10 percent of the Sun are the temperatures high enough to sustain fusion reactions.

Converting 0.7 percent of the 2×10^{32} grams of hydrogen into energy that is radiated at 3.8×10^{33} ergs/sec permits the Sun to shine for 3×10^{17} seconds, or 10 billion years at the present rate. Of the total radiation emitted by the Sun every second, about 1 part in 120 million is received by its attendant planets and their satellites. The energy output of the Sun has its peak at a wavelength of 0.47 micrometre (0.000019 inch; a micrometre is 10^{-6} metre). It radiates about 8 kilowatts per square cm (kW/cm^2) of its surface.

The process of energy generation results from the enormous pressure and density at the centre of the Sun, which makes it possible for nuclei to overcome electrostatic repulsion. (Nuclei are positive and thus repel each other.) Once in some billions of years a given proton (^{1}H, in which the superscript represents the mass of the isotope) is close enough to another to undergo a process called inverse beta-decay, in which one proton becomes a neutron and combines with the second to form a deuteron (^{2}D). While this is a rare event, hydrogen atoms are so numerous that it is the main solar energy source. Subsequent encounters proceed much faster: the deuteron encounters one of the ubiquitous protons to produce helium-3 (^{3}He), and these in turn form helium-4 (^{4}He). The net result is that four hydrogen atoms are fused into one helium atom. The energy is carried off by gamma-ray photons and neutrinos. Because the nuclei must have enough energy to overcome the electrostatic barrier, the rate of energy production varies as the fourth power of the temperature.

For every two hydrogen atoms converted, one neutrino of average energy 0.26 MeV carrying 1.3 percent of the total energy released is produced. This produces a flux of 8×10^{10} neutrinos per square cm per second at Earth. These neutrinos have an energy (less than 0.42 MeV) that is too low to be detected by present experiments, so there was considerable effort to develop experiments that can detect them. Subsequent processes produce higher-energy neutrinos that were detected in an experiment designed by the American scientist Raymond Davis (for which he won the Nobel Prize in Physics in 2002) and carried out in the 1970s deep in the Homestake gold mine in Lead, S.D., U.S. The number of these higher-energy neutrinos observed was far smaller than would be expected from the known energy-generation rate, but experiments established that these neutrinos did in fact come from the Sun. One possible reason for the small number detected was that the presumed rates of the subordinate process are not correct. Another more intriguing possibility was that the neutrinos produced in the core of the Sun interact with the vast solar mass and change to a different kind of neutrino that cannot be observed. The existence of such a process would have great significance for nuclear theory, for it requires a small mass for the neutrino. In 2002 results from the Sudbury Neutrino Observatory, nearly 2,100 metres (6,800 feet) underground in the Creighton nickel mine near Sudbury, Ont., Can., showed that the solar neutrinos did change their type and thus that the neutrino had a small mass.

In addition to being carried away as neutrinos, which simply disappear into the cosmos, the energy produced in the core of the Sun takes two other forms as well. Some is released as the kinetic energy of product particles, which heats the gases in the core, while some travels outward as gamma-ray photons until they are absorbed and reradiated by the local atoms. Because the nuclei at the core are completely ionized, or stripped of their electrons, the photons are simply scattered there into a different path. The density is so high that the photons travel only a few millimetres before they are scattered.

Farther out the nuclei have electrons attached, so they can absorb and reemit the photons, but the effect is the same: the photons take a so-called random walk outward until they escape from the Sun. The distance covered in a random walk is the average distance traveled between collisions (known as the mean free path) multiplied by the square root of the number of steps, in which a step is an interval between successive collisions. As the average mean free path in the Sun is about 10 cm (4 inches), the photon must take 5×10^{19} steps to travel 7×10^{10} cm. Even at the speed of light this process takes 10 million years, and so the light seen today was generated long ago. The final step from the Sun's surface to Earth, however, takes only eight minutes.

As photons are absorbed by the outer portion of the Sun, the temperature gradient increases and convection occurs. Great currents of hot plasma, or ionized gas, carry heat upward. These mass motions of conducting plasma in the convective zone, which constitutes approximately the outer 30 percent of the Sun, may be responsible for the sunspot cycle. The ionization of hydrogen plays an important role in the transport of energy through the Sun. Atoms are ionized at the bottom of the convective zone and are carried upward to cooler regions, where they recombine and liberate the energy of ionization. Just below the surface, radiation transport again becomes efficient, but the effects of convection are clearly visible in the photosphere.

EVOLUTION

The geologic record of Earth and the Moon reveals that the Sun has been shining at least four billion years. Considerable hydrogen has been converted to helium in the core, where the burning is most rapid. The helium remains there, where it absorbs radiation more readily than hydrogen. This raises the central temperature and increases the brightness. Model calculations conclude that the Sun becomes 10 percent brighter every billion years; hence it must now be at least 40 percent brighter than at the time of planet formation. This would produce an increase in Earth's temperature, but no such effect appears in the fossil record. However, there were probably compensating thermostatic effects in the atmosphere of Earth, such as the greenhouse effect and cloudiness. The increase in solar brightness can be expected to continue as the hydrogen in the core is depleted and the region of nuclear burning moves outward. At least as important for the future of Earth is the fact that tidal friction will slow down Earth's rotation until, in four billion years, its rotation will match that of the Moon, turning once in 30 of our present days.

The evolution of the Sun should continue on the same path as that taken by most stars. As the core hydrogen is used up, the nuclear burning will take place in a growing shell surrounding the exhausted core. The star will continue to grow brighter, and when the burning approaches the surface, the Sun will enter the red giant phase, producing an enormous shell that may extend as far as Venus or even Earth. Fortunately, unlike more massive stars that have evolved this far, the Sun will require billions of years to reach this state.

HELIOSEISMOLOGY

The structure of a star is uniquely determined by its mass and chemical composition. Unique models are constructed by varying the assumed composition with the known mass until the observed radius, luminosity, and surface temperature are matched. The process also requires assumptions about the convective zone. Such models can now be tested by the new science known as helioseismology.

Helioseismology is analogous to geoseismology; frequencies and wavelengths of various waves at the Sun's surface are measured to map the internal structure. On Earth the waves are observed only after earthquakes, while on the Sun they are continuously excited, probably by the currents in the convective zone. While a wide range of frequencies are observed, the intensity of the oscillation patterns, or modes, peaks strongly at a mode having a period of five minutes. The surface amplitudes range from a few centimetres per second to several metres per second. The modes where the entire Sun expands and contracts or where sound waves travel deeply through the Sun, only touching the surface in a few nodes (i.e., points of no vibration), make it possible to map the deep Sun. Modes with many nodes are, by contrast, limited to the outer regions. Every mode has a definite frequency determined by the structure of the Sun. From a compilation of thousands of mode frequencies, one can develop an independent solar model, which reproduces the observed oscillations quite well. The frequencies of the modes vary slightly with the sunspot cycle.

As the Sun rotates, one half is moving toward us, and the other away. This produces a splitting in the frequencies of the modes (owing to the Doppler shift from the two halves of the Sun). Because the different modes reach different depths in the Sun, the rotation at different depths can be mapped. The interior below the convective zone rotates as a solid body. At the surface rotation is fastest at the equator and slowest at the poles. This differential rotation is easily visible as sunspots rotate across the solar surface, and it has been known since the first telescopic studies. At the equator the sunspots rotate at a 25-day rate, and at high latitudes at a 28- or 29-day rate. The differential rotation, apparently generated by the convective zone, is thought to play an important role in the generation of the magnetic field of the Sun. Much is not understood, however, for many solar features show less differential rotation.

THE SOLAR ATMOSPHERE

Although there are no fires on the surface of the Sun, the photosphere seethes and roils, displaying the effects of the underlying convection. Photons flowing from below, trapped by the underlying layers, finally escape. This produces a dramatic drop in temperature and density. The temperature at the visible surface is about 5,800 K (5,500°C, 10,000°F) but drops to a minimum about 4,000 K (3,700°C, 6,700°F) at approximately 500 km (300 miles) above the photosphere. The density, about 10^{-7} g/cm^3 (5.78×10^{-7} oz/in^3), drops a factor of 2.7 every 150 km (90 miles). The solar atmosphere is actually a vacuum by most standards; the total density above any square centimetre is about 1 g (0.04 ounce), about 1,000 times less than the comparable mass in the atmosphere of Earth. One can see through the atmosphere of Earth but not through that of the Sun because the former is shallow, and the molecules absorb only radiation that lies outside of the visible spectrum. The hot photosphere of the Sun, by contrast, contains an ion called negative hydrogen, H$^-$, a hydrogen nucleus with two electrons attached. The H⁻ ion absorbs radiation voraciously through most of the spectrum.

The photosphere reveals two dominant features, a darkening toward the outermost regions, called limb darkening, and a fine rice-grain-like structure called granulation. The darkening occurs simply because the temperature is falling; when one looks at the edge of the Sun, one sees light from higher, cooler, and darker layers. The granules are convective cells that bring energy up from below. Each cell measures about 1,500 km (900 miles) across. Granules have a lifetime of about 25 minutes, during which hot gas rises within them at speeds of about 300 metres/sec (1,000 feet/sec). They then break up, either by fading out or by exploding into an expanding ring of granules. The granules occur all over the Sun. It is believed that the explosion pattern shapes the surrounding granules in a pattern called mesogranulation, although the existence of that pattern is in dispute. A larger, undisputed pattern called supergranulation is a network of outward velocity flows, each about 30,000 km (19,000 miles) across, which is probably tied to the big convective zone rather than to the relatively small granules. The flow concentrates the surface magnetic fields to the supergranulation-cell boundaries, creating a network of magnetic-field elements.

Associated with the granules are bright spots called faculae that arise at the interface between the surfaces of granules and the magnetic field at the granule boundaries. A sunspot always has an associated facula, though faculae may exist apart from such spots. Faculae are visible in ordinary white light near the Sun's limb (apparent edge), where the photospheric background is dimmer than near the centre of the disk. The extensions of faculae up into the chromosphere become visible over the entire disk in spectroheliograms taken at the wavelengths of hydrogen or ionized calcium vapour. When seen away from the limb, they are called chromospheric faculae or plages.

The photospheric magnetic fields extend up into the atmosphere, where the supergranular pattern dominates the conducting gas. While the temperature above the average surface areas continues to drop, it does not fall as rapidly as at the network edges, and a picture of the Sun at a wavelength absorbed somewhat above the surface shows the network edges to be bright. This occurs throughout the ultraviolet.

Joseph von Fraunhofer was the first to observe the solar spectrum, finding emission in all colours with many dark lines at certain wavelengths. He assigned letters to these lines, by which some are still known, such as the D-lines of sodium, the G-band, and the K-lines of ionized calcium. But it was the German physicist Gustav R. Kirchhoff who explained the meaning of the lines, explaining that the dark lines formed in cooler upper layers, absorbing the light emerging from below.

By comparing these lines with laboratory data, we can identify the elements responsible and their state of ionization and excitation.

The spectral lines seen are those expected to be common at 6,000 K (5,700°C, 10,300°F), where the thermal energy of each particle is about 0.5 volt. The most abundant elements, hydrogen and helium, are difficult to excite, while atoms such as iron, sodium, and calcium have many lines easily excited at this temperature. When Cecilia Payne, a British-born graduate student studying at Harvard College Observatory in Cambridge, Mass., U.S., recognized the great abundance of hydrogen and helium in 1925, she was persuaded by her elders to mark the result as spurious; only later was the truth recognized. The strongest lines in the visible spectrum are the H- and K- (Fraunhofer's letters) lines of ionized calcium. This happens because calcium is easily ionized, and these lines represent transitions in which energy is absorbed by ions in the ground, or lowest energy, state. In the relatively low density of the photosphere and higher up, where atoms are only illuminated from below, the electrons tend to fall to the ground state, since excitation is low. The sodium D-lines are weaker than Ca K because most of the sodium is ionized and does not absorb radiation.

The intensity of the lines is determined by both the abundance of the particular element and its state of ionization, as well as by the excitation of the atomic energy level involved in the line.

By working backward one can obtain the abundance of most of the elements in the Sun. This set of abundances occurs with great regularity throughout the universe; it is found in such diverse objects as quasars, meteorites, and new stars. The Sun is roughly 90 percent hydrogen by number of atoms and 9.9 percent helium. The remaining atoms consist of heavier elements, especially carbon, nitrogen, oxygen, magnesium, silicon, and iron, making up only 0.1 percent by number.

The Chromosphere

The chromosphere represents the dynamic transition between the cool temperature minimum of the outer photosphere and the diffuse million-degree corona above. It derives its name and pink colour from the red Hα line of hydrogen at 6562.8 angstroms (Å); 1 Å = 10^{-10} metre. Because this line is so strong, it is the best means for studying the chromosphere. For this reason special monochromators are widely used to study the Sun in a narrow wavelength band. Because density decreases with height more rapidly than magnetic field strength, the magnetic field dominates the chromospheric structure, which reflects the extension of the photospheric magnetic fields. The rules for this interplay are simple: Every point in the chromosphere where the magnetic field is strong and vertical is hot and hence bright, and every place where it is horizontal is dark. Supergranulation, which concentrates

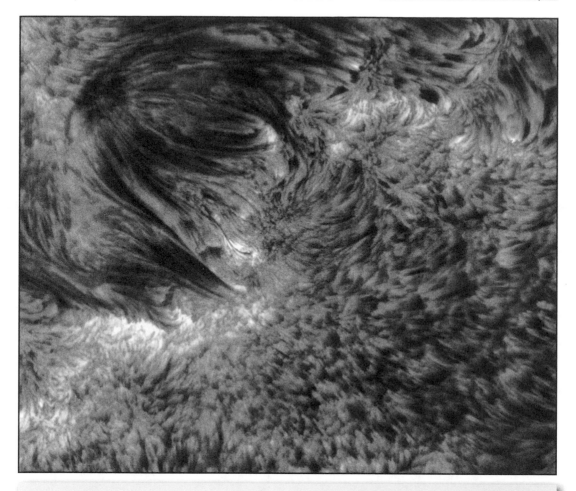

Active region toward the limb of the Sun, with spicules (right) *and some sunspots* (upper left). *Image captured on June 16, 2003, by the Swedish Solar Telescope, La Palma, Spain.* Lockheed Martin/Solar and Astrophysics Lab

the magnetic field on its edges, produces a chromospheric network of bright regions of enhanced magnetic fields.

The most prominent structures in the chromosphere, especially in the limb, are the clusters of jets, or streams, of plasma called spicules, which occur at the edges of the chromospheric network, where magnetic fields are stronger. Spicules extend up to 10,000 km (6,000 miles) above the surface of the Sun. They rise from the lower chromosphere at about 20 km/sec (12 miles/sec) to a height of several thousand kilometres, and then within 10–15 minutes they disperse or collapse. About 100,000 spicules are active on the Sun's surface at any given time. Although they are invisible in white light, early observers could see them in the hydrogen alpha (Hα) emission line with a spectrograph, comparing them to a "burning prairie."

Because it strongly emits the high-excitation lines of helium, the chromosphere was originally thought to be hot. But radio measurements, a particularly accurate means of measuring the temperature, show it to be only 8,000 K (7,700°C, 13,900°F), somewhat hotter than the photosphere. Detailed radio maps show that hotter regions coincide with stronger magnetic fields. Both hot and cold regions extend much higher than one might expect, tossed high above the surface by magnetic and convective action.

When astronomers observe the Sun from space at ultraviolet wavelengths, the chromosphere is found to emit lines formed at high temperatures, spanning the range from 10,000 to 1 million K (9,700 to 999,700°C, 17,500 to 1.8 million °F). The whole range of ionization of an atom can be found. For example, oxygen I (neutral) is found in the photosphere, oxygen II through VI (one to five electrons removed) in the chromosphere, and oxygen VII and VIII in the corona. This entire series occurs in a height range of about 5,000 km (3,000 miles). An image of the corona obtained at ultraviolet wavelengths has a much more diffuse appearance as compared with lower temperature regions, suggesting that the hot material in the magnetic elements spreads outward with height to occupy the entire coronal space. Interestingly, the emission of helium, which was the original clue that the temperature increased upward, is not patchy but uniform. This occurs because the helium atoms are excited by the more diffuse and uniform X-ray emission from the hot corona.

The structure of the chromosphere changes drastically with local magnetic conditions. At the network edges, clusters of spicules project from the clumps of magnetic field lines. Around sunspots, plages occur, where there are no spicules,

REVELATIONS IN THE DARK

When flash spectra (spectra of the atmosphere during an eclipse) were first obtained, astronomers found several surprising features. First, instead of absorption lines they saw emission lines (bright lines at certain wavelengths with nothing between them). This effect arises because the chromosphere is transparent between the spectrum lines, and only the dark sky is seen. Second, they discovered that the strongest lines were due to hydrogen, yet they still did not appreciate its high abundance. Finally, the next brightest lines had never been seen before. Because they came from the Sun, the unknown source element came to be called helium. Later helium was found on Earth.

but where the chromosphere is generally hotter and denser. In the areas of prominences the magnetic field lines are horizontal and spicules are absent.

THE CORONA

Another important set of unknown lines, revealed during an eclipse, come from the corona, and so its source element was called coronium. In 1940 the source of the lines had been identified as weak magnetic dipole transitions in various highly ionized atoms such as iron X (iron with nine electrons missing), iron XIV, and calcium XV, which can exist only if the coronal temperature is about 1 million K. These lines can only be emitted in a high vacuum. The strongest are from iron, which had alerted investigators to its high abundance, nearly equal to that of oxygen. Later errors in prior photospheric determinations had been discovered.

While the corona is one million times fainter than the photosphere in visible light (about the same as the full Moon at its base and much fainter at greater heights), its high temperature makes it a powerful source of extreme ultraviolet and X-ray emission. Loops of bright material connect distant magnetic fields. There are regions of little or no corona called coronal holes. The brightest regions are the active regions surrounding sunspots. Hydrogen and helium are entirely ionized, and the other atoms are highly ionized. The ultraviolet portion of the spectrum is filled with strong spectral lines of the highly charged ions. The density at the base of the corona is about 4×10^8 atoms per cubic cm, 10^{13} times more tenuous than the atmosphere of Earth at sea level. Because the temperature is high, the density drops slowly, by a factor of 2.7 every 50,000 km (31,000 miles).

Radio telescopes are particularly valuable for studying the corona because radio waves will propagate only when their frequency exceeds the so-called plasma frequency of the local medium. The plasma frequency varies according to the density of the medium, and so measurements of each wavelength tell us the temperature at the corresponding density. At higher frequencies (above 1,000 MHz) electron absorption is the main factor, and at those frequencies the temperature is measured at the corresponding absorbing density. All radio frequencies come to us from above the photosphere; this is the prime way of determining atmospheric temperatures. Similarly, all of the ultraviolet and X-ray emission of the Sun comes from the chromosphere and corona, and the presence of such layers can be detected in stars by measuring their spectra at these wavelengths.

Since the discovery of the nature of the corona, such low-density, super-hot plasmas have been identified throughout the universe: in the atmospheres of other stars, in supernova remnants, and in the outer reaches of galaxies. Low-density plasmas radiate so little that they can reach and maintain high temperatures.

By detecting excess helium absorption or X-ray emission in stars like the Sun, researchers have found that coronas are quite common. Many stars have coronas far more extensive than that of the Sun.

It is speculated that the high coronal temperature results from boundary effects connected with the steeply decreasing density at the solar surface and the convective currents beneath it. Stars without convective activity do not exhibit coronas. The magnetic fields facilitate a "crack-of-the-whip" effect, in which the energy of many particles is concentrated in progressively smaller numbers of ions. The result is the production of the high temperature of the corona. The key factor is the extremely low density, which hampers heat loss. The corona is a much more tenuous vacuum than anything produced on Earth.

SOLAR WIND

The conductivity of a hot ionized plasma is extremely high, and the coronal temperature decreases only as the $^2/_7$ power of the distance from the Sun. Thus, the temperature of the interplanetary medium is still more than 200,000 K (199,800°C, 360,000°F) near Earth. While the gravitational force of the Sun can hold the hot material near the surface, at a distance of $5R_{\odot}$ the gravitational force is 25 times less, but the temperature is only 40 percent less. Therefore, except where hindered by magnetic fields, a continuous outflow of particles known as the solar wind occurs, except where hindered by magnetic fields.

The solar wind flows along a spiral path dictated by magnetic fields carried out from the Sun into the interplanetary medium. The velocity is typically 400 km/sec (250 miles/sec), with wide variations. Where magnetic fields are strong, the coronal material cannot flow outward and becomes trapped; thus the high density and temperature above active regions is due partly to trapping and partly to heating processes, mostly solar flares. Where the magnetic field is open, the hot material escapes, and a coronal hole results. Analysis of solar wind data shows that coronal holes at the equator are associated with high-velocity streams in the solar wind, and recurrent geomagnetic storms are associated with the return of these holes. The coronal material is thought to originate from spicules.

The solar wind drags magnetic field lines out from the surface. Traveling at a speed of 500 km/sec (300 miles/sec), particles will reach the orbit of Saturn in one solar rotation—27 days—but in that time period the source on the Sun will have gone completely around. In other words, the magnetic field lines emanating from the Sun describe a spiral. It takes four days for the solar wind to arrive at Earth, having originated from a point that has rotated about 50° west (13° per day) from its original position facing Earth. The magnetic field lines, which do not break, maintain this path, and the plasma moves along them. The solar-wind flow has a continual effect on the upper atmosphere of Earth. The total mass, magnetic field, and angular momentum carried away by the solar wind is insignificant, even over the lifetime of the Sun. A higher level of activity in the past, however, might have played a role in the Sun's evolution, and stars larger than the Sun are known to lose considerable mass through such processes.

SOLAR ACTIVITY

Superposed on the Sun is an interesting 11-year cycle of magnetic activity, manifested primarily by what are known as sunspots. Related phenomena, such as prominences and flares, also occur as the result of solar activity. Frequently, Earth feels the effects of such conditions on the Sun. Both telecommunications and the weather are directly affected; solar activity is known to disrupt both radio signals and climate patterns.

SUNSPOTS

A wonderful rhythm in the ebb and flow of sunspot activity dominates the atmosphere of the Sun and influences life on Earth as well. Sunspots, the largest of which can be seen even without a telescope, are regions of extremely strong magnetic field found on the Sun's surface. A typical mature sunspot is seen in white light to have roughly the form of a daisy. It consists of a dark central core, the umbra, where the magnetic flux loop emerges vertically from below, surrounded by a less-dark ring of fibrils called the penumbra, where the magnetic field spreads outward horizontally. Sunspots generally block out the light and reduce emissions by a few tenths of a percent, but bright spots, called plages, that are associated with solar activity are more extensive and longer lived, so their brightness compensates for the darkness of the sunspots.

American astronomer George Ellery Hale observed the sunspot spectrum in the early 20th century with his new solar telescope and found it similar to that of cool red M-type stars observed with his new stellar telescope. Thus, he showed that the umbra appears dark because it is quite cool, only about 3,000 K (2,700°C, 4,900°F), as compared with the 5,800 K (5,500°C, 10,000°F) temperature of the surrounding photosphere. The spot pressure, consisting of magnetic and gas pressure, must balance the pressure of its surroundings; hence the spot must somehow cool until the inside gas pressure is considerably lower than that of the outside. Owing to the great magnetic energy present in sunspots, regions near the cool spots actually have the hottest and most intense activity. Sunspots are thought to be cooled by the suppression of their strong fields with the convective motions bringing heat from below. For this reason, there appears to be a lower limit on the size of the spots of approximately 500 km (300 miles). Smaller ones are rapidly heated by radiation from the surroundings and destroyed.

Although the magnetic field suppresses convection and random motions are much lower than in the surroundings, a wide variety of organized motions occur in spots, mostly in the penumbra, where the horizontal field lines permit detectable horizontal flows. One such motion is the Evershed effect, an outward flow at a rate of 1 km/sec (0.6 mile/sec) in the outer half of the penumbra that extends beyond the penumbra in the form of moving magnetic features. These features are elements of the magnetic field that flow outward across the area surrounding the spot. In the chromosphere above a sunspot, a reverse Evershed flow appears as material spirals into the spot; the inner half of the penumbra flows inward to the umbra.

Oscillations are observed in sunspots as well. When a section of the photosphere known as a light bridge crosses the umbra, rapid horizontal flow is seen. Although the umbral field is too strong to permit motion, rapid oscillations called umbral flashes appear in the chromosphere just above, with a 150-sec period. In the chromosphere above the penumbra, so-called running waves are observed to travel radially outward with a 300-sec period.

Magnetic poles, unlike positive protons or negative electrons, cannot exist singly in nature; an isolated magnetic pole could be formed only at enormous energies, and one has never been detected. Therefore, each magnetic pole seen on the Sun has a counterpart of opposite sign, although the two poles may be located far apart. Most frequently,

sunspots are likewise seen in pairs, or in paired groups of opposite polarity, which correspond to clusters of magnetic flux loops intersecting the surface. The flux loops emerge from below in pairs of opposite polarity connected by dark arches in the chromosphere above.

The members of a spot pair are identified by their position in the pair with respect to the rotation of the Sun; one is designated as the leading spot and the other as the following spot. In a given hemisphere (north or south), all spot pairs typically have the same polar configuration—e.g., all leading spots may have northern polarity, while all following spots have southern polarity. A new spot group generally has the proper polarity configuration for the hemisphere in which it forms; if not, it usually dies out quickly. Occasionally, regions of reversed polarity survive to grow into large, highly active spot groups. An ensemble of sunspots, the surrounding bright chromosphere, and the associated strong magnetic field regions constitute what is termed an active region. (Areas of strong magnetic fields that do not coalesce into sunspots form regions called plages, which are prominent in the red Hα line and at wavelengths of ionized calcium; they are also visible in continuous light near the limb. The plages are the extensions into the chromosphere of faculae and so are also called chromospheric faculae.)

The emergence of a new spot group emphasizes the three-dimensional structure of the magnetic loop. First we see a small brightening (called an emerging flux region, or EFR) in the photosphere and a greater one in the chromosphere. Within an hour, two tiny spots of opposite polarity are seen, usually with the proper magnetic polarities for that hemisphere. The spots are connected by dark arches (arch filaments) outlining the magnetic lines of force. As the loop rises, the spots spread apart and grow, but not symmetrically. The preceding spot moves westward at about 1 km/sec, while the follower is more or less stationary. A number of additional small spots, or pores, appear. The preceding pores then merge into a larger spot, while the following spot often dies out. If the spots separate farther, an EFR remains behind in the centre, and more flux emerges. But large growth usually depends on more EFRs, i.e., flux loops emerging near the main spots. In every case the north and south poles balance, since there are no magnetic monopoles.

Solar activity tends to occur over the entire surface of the Sun between +/-40° latitude in a systematic way, supporting the idea that the phenomenon is global. While there are sizable variations in the progress of the activity cycle, overall it is impressively regular, indicating a well-established order in the numbers and latitudinal positions of the spots. At the start of a cycle, the number of groups and their size increase rapidly until a maximum in number (known as sunspot maximum) occurs after about two or three years and a maximum in spot area about one year later. The average lifetime of a medium-sized spot group is about one solar rotation, but a small emerging group may only last a day. The largest spot groups and the greatest eruptions usually occur two or three years after the maximum of the sunspot number. At maximum there might be 10 groups and 300 spots across the Sun, but a huge spot group can have 200 spots in it. The progress of the cycle may be irregular; even near the maximum the number may temporarily drop to low values.

The sunspot cycle returns to a minimum after approximately 11 years. At sunspot minimum there are at most a few small spots on the Sun, usually at low latitudes, and there may be months with no spots at all. New-cycle spots begin to emerge at higher latitudes, between 25° and 40°, with polarity opposite the previous cycle. The new-cycle spots at high latitude and old-cycle spots at low latitude may be present on the Sun at once. The first new-cycle spots are small and last only a few days. Since the rotation period is 27 days (longer at higher latitudes), these spots usually do not return, and newer spots appear closer to the equator. For a given 11-year cycle, the magnetic polarity configuration of the spot groups is the same in a given hemisphere and is reversed in the opposite hemisphere. The magnetic polarity configuration in each hemisphere reverses in the next cycle. Thus, new spots at high latitudes in the northern hemisphere may have positive polarity leading and negative following, while the groups from the previous cycle, at low latitude, will have the opposite orientation. As the cycle proceeds, the old spots disappear, and new-cycle spots appear in larger numbers and sizes at successively lower latitudes. The latitude distribution of spots during a given cycle occurs in a butterfly-like pattern called the butterfly diagram. The most recent sunspot minimum was in 2009.

Since the magnetic polarity configuration of the sunspot groups reverses every 11 years, it returns to the same value every 22 years, and this length is considered to be the period of a complete magnetic cycle. At the beginning of each 11-year cycle, the overall solar field, as determined by the dominant field at the pole, has the same polarity as the following spots of the previous cycle. As active regions are broken apart, the magnetic flux is separated into regions of positive and negative sign. After many spots have emerged and died out in the same general area, large unipolar regions of one polarity or the other appear and move toward the Sun's corresponding pole. During each minimum the poles are dominated by the flux of the following polarity in that hemisphere, and that is the field seen from Earth. But if all magnetic fields are balanced, how can the magnetic fields be separated into large unipolar regions that govern the polar field? No answer has been found to this question. Owing to the differential

rotation of the Sun, the fields approaching the poles rotate more slowly than the sunspots, which at this point in the cycle have congregated in the rapidly rotating equatorial region. Eventually the weak fields reach the pole and reverse the dominant field there. This reverses the polarity to be taken by the leading spots of the new spot groups, thereby continuing the 22-year cycle.

While the sunspot cycle has been quite regular for some centuries, there have been sizable variations. In the period 1955–70 there were far more spots in the northern hemisphere, while in the 1990 cycle they dominated in the southern hemisphere. The two cycles that peaked in 1946 and 1957 were the largest in history. The English astronomer E. W. Maunder found evidence for a period of low activity, pointing out that very few spots were seen between 1645 and 1715. Although sunspots had been first detected about 1600, there are few records of spot sightings during this period, which is called the Maunder minimum. Experienced observers reported the occurrence of a new spot group as a great event, mentioning that they had seen none for years. After 1715 the spots returned. This period was associated with the coldest period of the long cold spell in Europe that extended from about 1500 to 1850 and is known as the Little Ice Age. Although cause and effect are not proved, the effect was so dramatic that the connection seems likely. There is some evidence for other such low-activity periods at roughly 500-year intervals. When solar activity is high, the strong magnetic fields carried outward by the solar wind block out the high-energy galactic cosmic rays approaching Earth and less carbon-14 is produced. Measurement of carbon-14 in dated tree rings confirms the low activity at this time. Still, the 11-year cycle was not detected until the 1840s, so observations prior to that time were somewhat irregular.

The origin of the sunspot cycle is not known. Because there is no reason that a star in radiative equilibrium should produce such fields, it is reasoned that relative motions in the Sun twist and enhance magnetic flux loops. The motions in the convective zone may contribute their energy to magnetic fields, but they are too chaotic to produce the regular effects observed. The differential rotation, however, is regular, and it could wind existing field lines in a regular way; hence, most models of the solar dynamo are based on the differential rotation in some respect. The reason for the differential rotation also remains unknown.

Besides sunspots, there exist many tiny spotless dipoles called ephemeral active regions, which last less than a day on average and are found all over the Sun rather than just in the spot latitudes. The number of active regions emerging on the entire Sun is about two per day, while ephemeral regions occur at a rate of about 600 per day. Therefore, even though the ephemeral regions are quite small, at any one time they may constitute most of the magnetic flux erupting on the Sun. However, because they are magnetically neutral and quite small, they probably do not play a role in the cycle evolution and the global field pattern.

PROMINENCES

Prominences are among the most beautiful of solar phenomena. They are the analogues of clouds in Earth's atmosphere, but they are supported by magnetic fields, rather than by thermal currents as clouds are. Because the plasma of ions and electrons that makes up the solar atmosphere cannot cross magnetic field lines in regions of horizontal magnetic fields, material is supported against gravity. This occurs at the boundaries between one magnetic polarity and its opposite, where the connecting field lines reverse direction. Thus, prominences are reliable indicators of sharp field transitions. (The fields are either up or down; tilted fields are unusual.) As with the chromosphere, prominences are transparent in white light and, except during total eclipses, must be viewed in Hα. At eclipse the red Hα line lends a beautiful pink to the prominences visible at totality. The density of prominences is much lower than that of the photosphere; there are few collisions to generate radiation. Prominences absorb radiation from below and emit it in all directions, a process called pure scattering. The visible light emitted toward Earth at the limb has been removed from the upward beam, so the prominences appear dark against the disk. But the sky is darker still, so they appear bright against the sky. The temperature of prominences is 5,000–50,000 K (4,700–49,700°C, 8,500–89,500°F). In the past, when radiative processes were not well understood, prominences seen dark against the disk were called filaments.

There are two basic types of prominences: (1) quiescent, or long-lived, and (2) transient. The former are associated with large-scale magnetic fields, marking the boundaries of unipolar magnetic regions or sunspot groups. Because the large unipolar plates are long-lived, the quiescent prominences are as well. These prominences may have varied forms—hedgerows, suspended clouds, or funnels—but they always take the form of two-dimensional suspended sheets. Stable filaments often become unstable and erupt, but they may also just fade away. Few quiescent prominences live more than a few days, but new ones may form on the magnetic boundary.

The equilibrium of the longer lived prominences is indeed curious. While one might expect them to eventually fall down, they always erupt upwards. This is because all unattached magnetic fields have a tremendous buoyancy and attempt to leave the Sun. When they do escape, they produce not only a splendid sight but also a transient shock wave in the corona called a coronal mass ejection, which can cause important geomagnetic effects.

Transient prominences are an integral part of solar activity. Sprays are the disorganized mass of material ejected by a flare. Surges are collimated streams of ejecta connected with small flares. In both cases some of the material returns to the surface. Loop prominences are the aftermath of flares. In the flare process a barrage of electrons heats the surface to millions of degrees and a hot (more than 10 million K), dense coronal cloud forms. This emits very strongly, cooling the material, which then, since there is no magnetic support, descends to the surface in elegant loops, following the magnetic lines of force.

The spectrum of prominences seen against the sky reflects their history. Quiescent prominences have no source of energy except some conduction from the corona, which is a small effect because heat cannot cross the field lines. The spectrum is similar to the chromosphere, except in the chromosphere, spicule motions produce broad lines, while the prominence lines are quite narrow until they erupt, indicating little internal motion. Surges and sprays also usually display low excitation because they are often cool material seized and ejected by magnetic forces. Loop prominences, on the other hand, are cooling from a very hot post-flare coronal condensation and have just become visible. Thus, they show high-excitation lines of ionized helium and strong ultraviolet emission, as befits a gas at 30,000 to 100,000 K (29,700 to 99,700°C, 53,500 to 179,500°F).

FLARES

The most spectacular phenomenon related to sunspot activity is the solar flare, which is an abrupt release of magnetic energy from the sunspot region. Despite the great energy involved, most flares are almost invisible in ordinary light because the energy release takes place in the transparent atmosphere, and only the photosphere, which relatively little energy reaches, can be seen in visible light. Flares are best seen in the Hα line, where the brightness may be 10 times that of the surrounding chromosphere, or 3 times that of the surrounding continuum. In Hα a big flare will cover a few thousandths of the Sun's disk, but in white light only a few small bright spots appear. The energy released in a great flare can reach 10^{33} ergs, which is equal to the output of the entire Sun in 0.25 sec. Most of this energy is initially released in high-energy electrons and protons, and the optical emission is a secondary effect caused by the particles impacting the chromosphere.

There is a wide range of flare size, from giant events that shower Earth with particles to brightenings that are barely detectable. Flares are usually classified by their associated flux of X-rays having wavelengths between one and eight angstroms: Cn, Mn, or Xn for flux greater than 10^{-6}, 10^{-5}, and 10^{-4} watts per square metre (W/m²), respectively, where the integer n gives the flux for each power of 10. Thus, M3 corresponds to a flux of 3×10^{-5} W/m² at Earth. This index is not linear in flare energy since it measures only the peak, not the total, emission. The energy released in the three or four biggest flares each year is equivalent to the sum of the energies produced in all the small flares. A flare can be likened to a giant natural synchrotron accelerating vast numbers of electrons and ions to energies above 10,000 electron volts (keV) and protons to more than 1 MeV. Almost all the flare energy initially goes into these high-energy particles, which subsequently heat the atmosphere or travel into interplanetary space. The electrons produce X-ray bursts and radio bursts and also heat the surface. The protons produce gamma-ray lines by collisionally exciting or splitting surface nuclei. Both electrons and protons propagate to Earth; the clouds of protons bombard Earth in big flares. Most of the energy heats the surface and produces a hot (40 million K) and dense cloud of coronal gas, which is the source of the X-rays. As this cloud cools, the elegant loop prominences appear and rain down to the surface.

The kinds of particles produced by flares vary somewhat with the place of acceleration. There are not enough particles between the Sun and Earth for ionizing collisions to occur, so they preserve their original state of ionization. Particles accelerated in the corona by shock waves show a typical coronal ionization of 2 million K. Particles accelerated in the flare body show a much higher ionization and remarkably high concentrations of He³, a rare He isotope with only one neutron.

Because flares generally occur in strong magnetic fields, it was natural to look for magnetic changes associated with them. The Russian astronomer A. B. Severny was the first to apply the newly developed Babcock magnetograph to this task. He found that the optical flares occur along neutral lines—i.e., boundaries between regions of opposite magnetic polarity. Actually this property is dictated by the fact that flares occur above the surface, that the energy flows down along lines of force, and that all magnetic lines of force have two ends, leading from north to south poles.

Because flare-monitoring telescopes were generally poor, it was not until 1960 that the German astronomer Horst Künzel recognized that a special kind of spot, called a δ spot, was responsible for most flares. While most sunspots have a single magnetic polarity, a δ spot has two or more umbras of opposite polarity within the same penumbra. Squeezing these spots together leads to a steep magnetic gradient, which stores energy and produces flares. Originally it was very difficult to detect the magnetic changes because it is the transverse (horizontal) component of the field that changes, and the horizontal field, perpendicular to the line of sight, is most difficult to measure. Most magnetographs are built for occasional use, but since the flare cannot be predicted, continuous observation is required. Change in the horizontal field can be measured with an ordinary continuous magnetograph when the flare is at the edge of the Sun, so the transverse field points at Earth and is easily measured. Magnetic fields have a minimum energy state called a potential field, which is smooth and without steep gradients. When the field is twisted or sheared by material motion, additional energy is stored in electrical currents sustaining these fields, and the energy is cataclysmically released in flares. Impulsive flares are accompanied by outward explosion and ejection of material; the material may be carried away with the erupting magnetic field or may be ejected by the high pressure in the flare. The highest recorded speed is 1,500 km/sec (900 miles/sec), but 100–300 km/sec (60–200 miles/sec) is more typical. Great clouds of coronal material are blown out; these make up a substantial fraction of the solar wind.

Since the main energy release in flares is the acceleration of electrons, imaging this process shows where it takes place. While the data are sketchy, it appears that the initial energy release is above the magnetic neutral line. The electrons travel down field lines and produce bright ribbons on the surface, from which material boils up and produces the soft X-ray source, a cloud with a temperature up to 50 million K. The energetic protons bombard the surface and produce a number of important nuclear reactions, which radiate gamma-rays in both lines and a continuum. Among the most important lines are the positron-electron annihilation line at 0.5 MeV and the neutron-proton capture (forming a deuteron) at 2.2 MeV, as well as a number of nuclear excitation lines produced by protons incident on heavier nuclei. These lines are a powerful tool for flare analysis.

Most of the great flares occur in a small number of superactive large sunspot groups. The groups are characterized by a large cluster of spots of one magnetic polarity surrounded by the opposite polarity. Although the occurrence of flares can be predicted from the presence of such spots, researchers cannot predict when these mighty regions will emerge from below the surface, nor do they know what produces them. Those that we see form on the disk usually develop complexity by successive eruptions of different flux loops. This is no accident, however; the flux loop is already complex below the surface.

SOLAR-TERRESTRIAL EFFECTS

Besides providing light and heat, the Sun affects Earth through its ultraviolet radiation, the steady stream of the solar wind, and the particle storms of great flares. The near-ultraviolet radiation from the Sun produces the ozone layer, which in turn shields the planet from such radiation. The soft (long-wavelength) X-rays from the solar corona produce those layers of the ionosphere that make short-wave radio communication possible. When solar activity increases, the soft X-ray emission from the corona (slowly varying) and flares (impulsive) increases, producing a better reflecting layer but eventually increasing ionospheric density until radio waves are absorbed and short-wave communications are hampered. The harder (shorter wavelength) X-ray pulses from flares ionize the lowest ionospheric layer (D-layer), producing radio fade-outs. Earth's rotating magnetic field is strong enough to block the solar wind, forming the magnetosphere, around which the solar particles and fields flow. On the side opposite to the Sun, the field lines stretch out in a structure called the magnetotail. When shocks arrive in the solar wind, a short, sharp increase in the field of Earth is produced. When the interplanetary field switches to a direction opposite Earth's field, or when big clouds of particles enter it, the magnetic fields in the magnetotail reconnect and energy is released, producing the aurora borealis (northern lights). Each time a big coronal hole faces Earth, the solar wind is fast, and a geomagnetic disturbance occurs. This produces a 27-day pattern of storms that is especially prominent at sunspot minimum. Big flares and other eruptions produce coronal mass ejections, clouds of energetic particles that form a ring current around the magnetosphere, which produces sharp fluctuations in Earth's field, called geomagnetic storms. These phenomena disturb radio communication and create voltage surges in long-distance transmission lines and other long conductors.

Perhaps the most intriguing of all terrestrial effects are the possible effects of the Sun on the climate of Earth. The Maunder minimum seems well established, but there are few other clear effects. Yet most scientists believe an important tie exists, masked by a number of other variations.

Because charged particles follow magnetic fields, corpuscular radiation is not observed from all big flares but only from those favourably situated in the Sun's western hemisphere. The solar rotation makes the lines of force from the western side of the Sun (as seen from Earth) lead back to Earth, guiding the flare particles there. These particles are mostly protons because hydrogen is the dominant constituent of the Sun. Many of the particles are trapped in a great shock front that blows out from the Sun at 1,000 km/sec (600 miles/sec). The flux of low-energy particles in big flares is so intense that it endangers the lives of astronauts outside the terrestrial magnetic field.

The magnetic effects of solar flares also cause an occasional decrease, the Forbush effect, in the intensity of cosmic rays as observed on Earth. The effect was discovered in 1937 by the American physicist Scott E. Forbush. Its cause became clearer in 1960, when, while the unmanned U.S. space probe Pioneer 5 was in flight some 5 million km (3 million miles) from Earth, a solar flare occurred, followed by an observation on Earth of the Forbush effect. Data from the probe indicated that the cause of the Forbush effect is a thin, hot plasma (of highly ionized gas) emitted by the Sun and carrying with it a tongue or lobe of the Sun's magnetic field as far as Earth; this magnetic field tends to deflect away from Earth the electrically charged particles that make up primary cosmic rays.

HISTORY OF SOLAR OBSERVATIONS

The existence of features on the Sun was known from the records of sunspots observed by ancient astronomers with the naked eye. However, no systematic studies were made of such features until the telescope was invented in the early 17th century. The Italian scientist Galileo and the German mathematician Christoph Scheiner were among the first to make telescopic observations of sunspots. Scheiner's drawings in the *Rosa Ursina* are of almost modern quality, and there was little improvement in solar imaging until 1905. In the 1670s the British astronomer John Flamsteed and the French astronomer Gian Domenico Cassini calculated the distance to the Sun; using data from observations of the transits of Venus in 1761 and 1769, scientists were able to determine the distance between the Sun and Earth more precisely—their estimations were quite close to modern values. Newton set forth the role of the Sun as the centre of attraction of the known planetary system.

While the quality of observations was good, consistent observation was lacking.

The sunspot cycle, a huge effect, was not discovered until 1843 by Heinrich Schwabe. The German amateur astronomer was looking for a planet inside the orbit of Mercury and made careful daily drawings to track its passage across the face of the Sun. Instead he found that the number of sunspots varied with a regular period. The Swiss astronomer Rudolf Wolf confirmed Schwabe's discovery by searching through previous reports of sunspots and established the period as 11 years. Wolf also introduced what is termed the Zurich relative sunspot number, a value equal to the sum of the spots plus 10 times the number of groups, which is still used today.

Much of the work at this time was carried out by wealthy amateurs such as Richard Christopher Carrington of Britain, who built a private observatory and discovered the differential rotation and the equatorward drift of activity during a sunspot cycle. He also was the first (with another Englishman, Richard Hodgson) to observe a solar flare. Photographic monitoring began in 1860, and soon spectroscopy was applied to the Sun, so the elements present and their physical state could begin to be investigated. In the early part of the 19th century, Fraunhofer mapped the solar spectrum. At the end of the 19th century, spectroscopy carried out during eclipses revealed the character of the atmosphere, but the million-degree coronal temperature was not established until 1940 by the German astrophysicist Walter Grotrian.

In 1891, while he was a senior at the Massachusetts Institute of Technology in Cambridge, Mass., George Ellery Hale invented the spectroheliograph, which can be used to take pictures of the Sun in any single wavelength. After using the instrument on the great Yerkes refractor in Williams Bay, Wis., U.S. (which he built), Hale developed the Mount Wilson Observatory in California and built the first solar tower telescopes there. Prior to the construction of the Mount Wilson facility, all solar observatories were located in cloudy places, and long-term studies were not possible. Hale discovered the magnetic fields of sunspots by observing the splitting of their spectral lines into a number of components; this splitting, known as the Zeeman effect, occurs in the presence of a strong magnetic field. By continuously studying the spots for two cycles, he discovered, with the American astronomer Seth Barnes Nicholson, the law of sunspot polarities. Later, in 1953, the American father-and-son team of astronomers Harold and Horace Babcock, working with the same instruments, developed the magnetograph, with which the polar field was detected. In the 1930s the French astronomer Bernard Lyot introduced the coronagraph, which made possible spectral observations of the corona when the Sun is not in eclipse, and the birefringent filter, which permitted two-dimensional monochromatic images. With the Lyot filter, cinematography of the solar activity of magnetic and velocity fields became a reality. In the 1960s the American astronomer Robert Leighton modified Hale's spectroheliograph so that it could measure both velocities and magnetic fields and with it discovered solar oscillations.

After 1950, new observatories were established in areas that were less cloudy. By 1960 astronomers realized that these sites not only had to be clear but that they also had to have stable air. By locating observatories near lakes and by employing electronic imaging and vacuum telescopes, astronomers were able to make new, higher-resolution observations. In 1969 the movement began with the Aerospace Corporation Observatory (now the San Fernando Observatory) and the Big Bear Solar Observatory, both in California. Free of ground effects, these observatories achieved a new level of stable images and were soon followed by lake-sited solar observatories in India and China.

An entirely new dimension of solar studies was initiated by the space age. With one or two exceptions, all of the important spectral lines from the chromosphere and corona are in the ultraviolet, and since the photosphere is relatively weak in the ultraviolet, it is easy to disentangle the images of the upper layer from the powerful visible radiation of the photosphere. Moreover, satellites sampling the solar particles have the ability to monitor directly solar waves and particles that do not reach the ground. However, the task is not easy. Ultraviolet optics demanded special coatings and films (now charge-coupled devices) for observing. Special solar trackers were required to keep the image steady, and good telemetry was needed for the large data flow. For the corona, special coronagraphs were developed, with a series of occulting disks in front of an ultraclean lens. For X-rays, a high rate of photon detections per unit time was required to avoid early problems with pulse pile-up. The development of instruments to study the Sun also benefited the creation of satellites that explored beyond the solar system.

The U.S. Orbiting Solar Observatory series of satellites (OSO 1–8, launched from 1962 to 1975) made the first observations of X-rays and gamma-rays from solar flares. They also were the first to observe gamma-rays emitted from nuclear reactions in flares and to use an externally occulted coronagraph to view coronal mass ejections. A huge advance in resolution came with Skylab, a manned U.S. space station that used leftover hardware from the Apollo project. Skylab produced the first high-resolution images in the ultraviolet lines as well as the first X-ray images of the corona. The Skylab images displayed the coronal holes for the first time, and the timing of their disk passage showed their role as a source of high-speed solar wind streams and geomagnetic disturbances.

The next important spacecraft was the U.S. Solar Maximum Mission (SMM), launched in 1980. New technological developments permitted greatly improved data, particularly on the solar-cycle dependence of the solar constant. Hard X-ray data could be obtained without saturation. In 1981 SMM's attitude control system malfunctioned, and the SMM mission was suspended until 1984 when it was repaired by the space shuttle *Challenger*.

Japan launched two very successful satellites, Hinotori and Yohkoh, in 1981 and 1991, respectively. Hinotori obtained the first measurements of a super-thermal (30 million–40 million K) cloud produced by solar flares, which is the source of the soft X-ray burst accompanying all solar flares. Yohkoh produced continuous images of the corona in soft X-rays, detected and located hard X-ray bursts, and produced important soft X-ray spectra.

There are several satellites actively observing the Sun. The U.S. satellites Solar and Heliospheric Observatory (SOHO) and Transition Region and Coronal Explorer (TRACE), launched in 1995 and 1998, respectively, have produced many important results. SOHO can observe the Sun continuously, and, among its many discoveries, it has found that sunspots are shallow and that the solar wind flows outward by waves in vibrating magnetic field lines. TRACE is a powerful tool for exploring the chromosphere-corona interface and has found that much of the heating in the corona takes place at its base. The European Space Agency spacecraft Ulysses, launched in 1990, is in a polar orbit around the Sun and has discovered that the solar wind speed does not increase continuously toward the poles but rather levels off at high latitudes at 750 km/sec (450 miles/sec).

CHAPTER 3

MERCURY

Mercury is the innermost planet of the solar system and the eighth in size and mass. Its closeness to the Sun and its smallness make it the most elusive of the planets visible to the unaided eye. Because its rising or setting is always within about two hours of the Sun's, it is never observable when the sky is fully dark. Mercury is designated by the symbol ☿.

The difficulty in seeing it notwithstanding, Mercury was known at least by Sumerian times, some 5,000 years ago. In classical Greece it was called Apollo when it appeared as a morning star just before sunrise and Hermes, the Greek equivalent of the Roman god Mercury, when it appeared as an evening star just after sunset. Hermes was the swift messenger of the gods, and the planet's name is thus likely a reference to its rapid motions relative to other objects in the sky. Even in more recent eras, many sky observers passed their entire lifetimes without ever seeing Mercury. It is reputed that Nicolaus Copernicus, whose heliocentric model of the heavens in the 16th century explained why Mercury and Venus always appear in close proximity to the Sun, expressed a deathbed regret that he had never set eyes on the planet Mercury himself.

Until the last part of the 20th century, Mercury was one of the least understood planets, and even now the shortage of information about it leaves many basic questions

Mercury as seen by the Messenger probe, Jan. 14, 2008. This image shows half of the hemi-sphere missed by Mariner 10 in 1974–75 and was snapped by Messenger's wide angle camera when it was about 27,000 km (17,000 miles) from the planet. NASA/Johns Hopkins University Applied Physics Laboratory/Carnegie Institution of Washington

unsettled. Indeed, the length of its day was not determined until the 1960s, and, even after the flybys of the Mariner 10 and Messenger (*Mercury Surface, Space Environment, Geochemistry, and Ranging*) probes, the appearance of much of its surface is still unknown. At first glance the hemisphere of the planet that has been imaged looks similar to the cratered terrain of the Moon, an impression

Two mosaic views of Mercury, each showing about half of the hemisphere of the planet that was illuminated when Mariner 10 made its first flyby in March 1974. In both views, the landscape is dominated by large impact basins and craters with extensive intercrater plains. NASA/JPL

reinforced by the roughly comparable size of the two bodies. Mercury is far denser, however, having a metallic core that takes up about 42 percent of its volume (compared with 4 percent for the Moon and 16 percent for Earth). Moreover, its surface shows significant differences from lunar terrain, including a lack of the massive dark-coloured lava flows known as maria on the Moon and the presence of buckles and scarps that suggest Mercury actually shrank during some period in its history.

Mercury's nearness to the Sun has given scientists bound to Earth many observational hurdles, which are now being overcome by spacecraft missions—such as that of Messenger, which was

PLANETARY DATA FOR MERCURY

mean distance from Sun	57,910,000 km (0.4 AU)
eccentricity of orbit	0.2056
inclination of orbit to ecliptic	7.004°
Mercurian year (sidereal period of revolution)	87.9694 Earth days
maximum visual magnitude	-1.9
mean synodic period*	116 Earth days
mean orbital velocity	47.9 km/sec
radius (equatorial and polar)	2,439.7 km
surface area	74,800,000 km^2
mass	3.30×10^{23} kg
mean density	5.43 g/cm^3
mean surface gravity	370 cm/sec^2
escape velocity	4.3 km/sec
rotation period (Mercurian sidereal day)	58.6462 Earth days
Mercurian mean solar day	175.9 Earth days
inclination of equator to orbit	less than 3°; probably nearly zero
magnetic field strength	0.003 gauss
mean surface temperature	440 K (332 °F, 167 °C)
surface temperature extremes	700 K (800 °F, 430 °C) to 90 K (-300 °F, -180 °C)
typical surface pressure	about 10^{-15} bar
number of known moons	none

*Time required for the planet to return to the same position in the sky relative to the Sun as seen from Earth.

launched in 2004, flew past the planet twice in 2008, and is scheduled to fly past it again in 2009 before settling into orbit in 2011. The same characteristic has also been exploited to confirm predictions made by relativity theory about the way gravity affects space and time.

BASIC ASTRONOMICAL DATA

Mercury is an extreme planet in several respects. Because of its nearness to the Sun—its average orbital distance is 58 million km (36 million miles)—it has the shortest year (a revolution period of 88 days) and receives the most intense solar radiation of all the planets. With a radius of about 2,440 km (1,516 miles), Mercury is the smallest major planet, smaller even than Jupiter's largest moon, Ganymede, or Saturn's largest moon, Titan. In addition, Mercury is unusually dense. Although its mean density is roughly that of Earth's, it has less mass and so is less compressed by its own gravity; when corrected for self-compression, Mercury's density is the highest of any planet. Nearly two-thirds of Mercury's mass is contained in its largely iron core, which extends from the planet's centre to a radius of about 1,800 km (1,100 miles), or three-quarters of the way to its surface. The planet's rocky outer shell—its surface crust and underlying mantle—is only some 600 km (400 miles) thick.

Observational Challenges

As seen from Earth's surface, Mercury hides in dusk and twilight, never getting more than about 28° in angular distance from the Sun. It takes about 116 days for successive elongations—i.e., for Mercury to return to the same point relative to the Sun—in the morning or evening sky; this is called Mercury's synodic period. Its nearness to the horizon also means that Mercury is always seen through more of Earth's turbulent atmosphere, which blurs the view. Even above the atmosphere, orbiting observatories such as the Hubble Space Telescope are restricted by the high sensitivity of their instruments from pointing as close to the Sun as would be required for observing Mercury. Because Mercury's orbit lies within Earth's, it occasionally

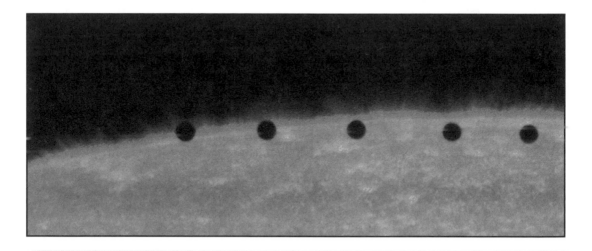

Transit of Mercury across the face of the Sun, a composite of five separate images in ultraviolet light taken by the Transition Region and Coronal Explorer (TRACE) satellite in Earth orbit, November 15, 1999. The time interval between successive images is about seven minutes. NASA/TRACE/SMEX

passes directly between Earth and the Sun. This event, in which the planet can be observed telescopically or by spacecraft instruments as a small black dot crossing the bright solar disk, is called a transit, and it occurs about a dozen times in a century.

Mercury also presents difficulties to study by space probe. Because the planet is located deep in the Sun's gravity field, a great deal of energy is needed to shape the trajectory of a spacecraft to get it from Earth's orbit to Mercury's in such a way that it can go into orbit around the planet or land on it. The first spacecraft to visit Mercury, Mariner 10, was in orbit around the Sun when it made three brief flybys of the planet in 1974–75. In developing subsequent missions to Mercury, such as the U.S. Messenger spacecraft launched in 2004, spaceflight engineers calculated complex routes, making use of gravity assists from repeated flybys of Venus and Mercury over the course of several years. In the Messenger mission design, after conducting observations from moderate distances during planetary flybys in 2008 and 2009, the spacecraft will enter into an elongated orbit around Mercury for close-up investigations in 2011. In addition, the extreme heat, not only from the Sun but also reradiated from Mercury itself, has challenged spacecraft designers to keep instruments cool enough to operate.

ORBITAL AND ROTATIONAL EFFECTS

Mercury's orbit is the most inclined of the planets, tilting about 7° from the ecliptic, the plane defined by the orbit of Earth around the Sun; it is also the most eccentric, or elongated planetary orbit. As a result of the elongated orbit, the Sun appears more than twice as bright in Mercury's sky when the planet is closest to the Sun (at perihelion), at 46 million km (29 million miles), than when it is farthest from the Sun (at aphelion), at nearly 70 million km (43 million miles). The planet's rotation period of 58.6 Earth days with respect to the stars—i.e., the length of its sidereal day—causes the Sun to drift slowly westward in Mercury's sky. Because Mercury is also orbiting the Sun, its rotation and revolution periods combine such that the Sun takes three Mercurian sidereal days, or 176 Earth days, to make a full circuit—the length of its solar day.

As described by Kepler's laws of planetary motion, Mercury travels around the Sun so swiftly near perihelion that the Sun appears to reverse course in Mercury's sky, briefly moving eastward before resuming its westerly advance. The two locations on Mercury's equator where this oscillation takes place at noon are called hot poles. As the overhead Sun lingers there, heating them preferentially, surface temperatures can exceed 700 K (430 °C, or 800 °F). The two equatorial locations 90° from the hot poles, called warm poles, never get nearly as hot. From the perspective of the warm poles, the Sun is already low on the horizon and about to set when it grows the brightest and performs its brief course reversal. Near the north and south rotational poles of Mercury, ground temperatures are even colder, below

200 K (–70 °C, or –100 °F), when lit by grazing sunlight. Surface temperatures drop to about 90 K (–180 °C, or –300 °F) during Mercury's long nights before sunrise.

Mercury's temperature range is the most extreme of the solar system's four inner, terrestrial planets, but the planet's nightside would be even colder if Mercury kept one face perpetually toward the Sun and the other in perpetual darkness. Until Earth-based radar observations proved otherwise in the 1960s, astronomers had long believed that to be the case, which would follow if Mercury's rotation were synchronous—that is, if its rotation period were the same as its 88-day revolution period. Telescopic observers, limited to viewing Mercury periodically under conditions dictated by Mercury's angular distance from the Sun, had been misled into concluding that their seeing the same barely distinguishable features on Mercury's surface on each viewing occasion indicated a synchronous rotation. The radar studies revealed that the planet's 58.6-day rotation period is not only different from its orbital period but also exactly two-thirds of it.

Mercury's orbital eccentricity and the strong solar tides—deformations raised in the body of the planet by the Sun's gravitational attraction—apparently explain why the planet rotates three times for every two times that it orbits the Sun. Mercury presumably had spun faster when it was forming, but it was slowed by tidal forces. Instead of slowing to a state of synchronous rotation, as has happened to many planetary satellites, including

Earth's Moon, Mercury became trapped at the 58.6-day rotation rate. At this rate the Sun tugs repeatedly and especially strongly on the tidally induced bulges in Mercury's crust at the hot poles. The chances of trapping the spin at the 58.6-day period were greatly enhanced by tidal friction between the solid mantle and molten core of the young planet.

Mercury in Tests of Relativity

Mercury's orbital motion has played an important role in the development and testing of theories of the nature of gravity because it is perturbed by the gravitational pull of the Sun and the other planets. The effect appears as a gyration, or precession, of Mercury's orbit around the Sun. This small motion, about 9.5′ (0.16°) of arc per century, has been known for two centuries, and, in fact, all but about 7 percent of it—corresponding to 43″ (0.012°) of arc—could be explained by the theory of gravity proposed by Isaac Newton. The discrepancy was too large to ignore, however, and explanations were offered, usually invoking as-yet-undiscovered planets within Mercury's orbit. In 1915 Albert Einstein showed that the treatment of gravity in his general theory of relativity could explain the small discrepancy. Thus, the precession of Mercury's orbit became an important observational verification of Einstein's theory.

Mercury was subsequently employed in additional tests of relativity, which made use of the fact that radar signals that are reflected from its surface when it is on the opposite side of the Sun from Earth (at superior conjunction) must pass close to the Sun. The general theory of relativity predicts that such electromagnetic signals, moving in the warped space caused by the Sun's immense gravity, will follow a slightly different path and take a slightly different time to traverse that space than if the Sun were absent. By comparing reflected radar signals with the specific predictions of the general theory, scientists achieved a second important confirmation of relativity.

MARINER 10 AND MESSENGER

Most of what scientists know about Mercury was learned during the three flybys by Mariner 10. Because the spacecraft was placed in an orbit around the Sun equal to one Mercurian solar day, it made each of its three passes when exactly the same half of the planet was in sunlight. Slightly less than the illuminated half, or about 45 percent of Mercury's surface, was eventually imaged. Mariner 10 also collected data on particles and magnetic fields during its flybys, which included two close nightside encounters and one distant dayside pass. Mercury was discovered to have a surprisingly Earthlike (though much weaker) magnetic field. Scientists had not anticipated a planetary magnetic field for such a small, slowly rotating body because the dynamo theories that described the phenomenon required thoroughly molten cores and rather rapid planetary spins. Even more

rapidly spinning bodies such as the Moon and Mars lack magnetic fields. In addition, Mariner 10's spectral measurements showed that Mercury has an extremely tenuous atmosphere.

The first significant telescopic data about Mercury after the Mariner mission resulted in the discovery in the mid-1980s of sodium in the atmosphere. Subsequently, better Earth-based techniques enabled the variations of several of Mercury's atmospheric components to be studied from place to place and over time. Also, ongoing improvement in the power and sensitivity of ground-based radar resulted in intriguing maps of the hemisphere unseen by Mariner 10 and, in particular, the discovery of condensed material, probably water ice, in permanently shadowed craters near the poles.

In 2008 the Messenger probe made its first flyby of Mercury and obtained photos of more than a third of the hemisphere that was unseen by Mariner 10. The probe passed within 200 km (120 miles) of the planet's surface and saw many previously unknown geologic features. In 2011 Messenger is slated to enter Mercury's orbit and study it for one year.

THE ATMOSPHERE

A planet as small and as hot as Mercury has no possibility of retaining a significant atmosphere, if it ever had one. To be sure, Mercury's surface pressure is less than one-trillionth that of Earth. Nevertheless, the traces of atmospheric components that have been detected have provided clues about interesting planetary processes. Mariner 10 found small amounts of atomic helium and even smaller amounts of atomic hydrogen near Mercury's surface. These atoms are mostly derived from the solar wind—the flow of charged particles from the Sun that expands outward through the solar system—and remain near Mercury's surface for very short times, perhaps only hours, before escaping the planet. Mariner also detected atomic oxygen, which, along with sodium, potassium, and calcium, discovered subsequently in telescopic observations, is probably derived from Mercury's surface soils or impacting meteoroids and ejected into the atmosphere either by the impacts or by bombardment of solar wind particles. The atmospheric gases tend to accumulate on Mercury's nightside but are dissipated by the brilliant morning sunlight.

Many atoms in Mercury's surface rocks and in its tenuous atmosphere become ionized when struck by energetic particles in the solar wind and in Mercury's magnetosphere. Unlike Mariner 10, the Messenger spacecraft has instruments that can measure ions. During Messenger's first flyby of Mercury in 2008, many ions were identified, including those of oxygen, sodium, magnesium, potassium, calcium, and sulfur. In addition, another instrument mapped Mercury's long cometlike tail, which is prominently visible in the spectral emission lines of sodium.

Although the measured abundances of sodium and potassium are extremely low—from hundreds to a few tens of thousands of atoms per cubic centimetre near the surface—telescopic spectral instruments are very sensitive to these two elements, and astronomers can watch thicker patches of these gases move across Mercury's disk and through its neighbourhood in space. Presumably many other gases that are harder to detect are present in similar minuscule quantities. Where these gases come from and go was primarily of theoretical, rather than practical, importance until the early 1990s. At that time Earth-based radar made the remarkable discovery of patches of highly radar-reflective materials at the poles, apparently only in permanently shadowed regions of deep, near-polar craters. Scientists believe that the reflecting material might be water ice.

The idea that the planet nearest the Sun might harbour significant deposits of water ice originally seemed bizarre. Yet, Mercury must have accumulated water over its history—for example, from impacting comets. Water ice on Mercury's broiling surface will immediately turn to vapour (sublime), and the individual water molecules will hop, in random directions, along ballistic trajectories. The odds are very poor that a water molecule will strike another atom in Mercury's atmosphere, although there is some chance that it will be dissociated by the bright sunlight. Calculations suggest that after many hops, perhaps 1 out of 10 water molecules eventually lands in a deep polar depression. Because Mercury's rotational axis is essentially perpendicular to the plane of its orbit, sunlight is always nearly horizontal at the poles. Under such conditions the bottoms of deep depressions would remain in permanent shadow and provide cold traps that could hold water molecules for millions or billions of years. Gradually a polar ice deposit would build up. The susceptibility of the ice to subliming away slowly—e.g., from the slight warmth of sunlight reflected from distant mountains or crater rims—could be reduced if it gradually became cloaked by an insulating debris layer, or regolith, made of dust and rock fragments ejected from distant impacts. Radar data suggest that the reflecting layer indeed is covered with as much as 0.5 metre (1.6 feet) of such debris.

It is far from certain that the volatile material near Mercury's poles is water ice. Additional radar studies found small patches of high reflectivity at latitudes as low as 71°, where water ice would be far less likely to form and survive. Moreover, the same reasoning about the possibility of water ice near Mercury's poles also has been applied to the Moon, where the accumulation process should have been even more robust. In its lunar orbital mission in 1998–99, the Lunar Prospector spacecraft found evidence for, at most, minimal water ice near the lunar poles. Perhaps another easily evaporated substance, but one less volatile than water, has been "cold-trapped" on Mercury. One candidate, atomic sulfur, is fairly abundant in the cosmos and, for other reasons, may be especially abundant on and within Mercury.

THE MAGNETIC FIELD AND MAGNETOSPHERE

As closely as Mariner 10's measurements could determine, Mercury's magnetic field, though only 1 percent as strong as Earth's, resembles Earth's field in being roughly dipolar and oriented along the planet's axis of rotation. While the existence of the field might conceivably have some other explanation—such as, for example, remanent magnetism, the retained imprint of an ancient magnetic field frozen into the rocks during crustal cooling—most researchers became convinced that it is produced, like Earth's field, by a magnetohydrodynamic dynamo mechanism (involving motions within an electrically conducting fluid) in the outer portions of Mercury's iron core. Measurements by Messenger's magnetometer, made during the spacecraft's first flyby in January 2008, confirm that Mercury's magnetic field is basically dipolar. They fail to reveal any crustal contributions that might be expected from remanent magnetism, so it seems clear that Mercury's dynamo is currently operating.

Mercury's magnetic field holds off the solar wind with a teardrop-shaped bubble, or magnetosphere, whose rounded end extends outward toward the Sun about one planetary radius from the surface. This is only about 5 percent of the sunward extent of Earth's magnetosphere. The planet's atmosphere is so thin that no equivalent to Earth's ionosphere exists at Mercury. Indeed, calculations suggest that on occasion the solar wind is strong enough to push the sunward boundary (magneto-pause) of the magnetosphere beneath Mercury's surface. Under these conditions solar wind ions would impinge directly on those portions of Mercury's surface immediately beneath the Sun. Even infrequent occurrences of such an event could dramatically alter the atomic composition of surface constituents. Preliminary measurements by Messenger suggest that Mercury's magnetosphere may have an unusual configuration, a kind of double magnetopause, perhaps due to the abundance of heavy ions, primarily sodium, that come from Mercury's surface and atmosphere.

Mercury's magnetospheric processes are of interest to geophysicists and space scientists, who hope one day to test their conception of Earth's magnetosphere through examination of an Earthlike field with a very different scale and in a different solar wind environment. For example, Mariner 10 instruments recorded rapidly varying energetic particles in the planet's magnetotail, the elongated portion of the magnetosphere downstream from the planet's nightside. This activity was much like the geomagnetic substorms

on Earth that are associated with auroral displays. The origin of such events on Earth may be more directly understood from comprehensive global data that will be gathered by Messenger once it enters orbit around Mercury in 2011.

CHARACTER OF THE SURFACE

The portions of Mercury imaged by Mariner 10 and Messenger look superficially like the Moon. Mercury is heavily pockmarked with impact craters of all sizes. The smallest craters visible in the highest-resolution Mariner photos are a

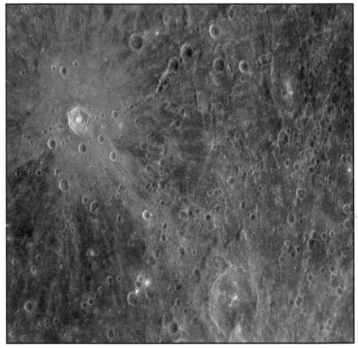

Meteorite crater surrounded by rays of ejected material on Mercury, in a photograph taken by the Messenger probe, Jan. 14, 2008. A chain of craters crosses the centre of the rayed crater. NASA/ Johns Hopkins University Applied Physics Laboratory/Carnegie Institution of Washington

few hundred metres in diameter. Interspersed among the larger craters are relatively flat, less-cratered regions termed intercrater plains. These are similar to but much more pervasive than the light-coloured plains that occupy intercrater areas on the heavily cratered highlands of the Moon. There are also some sparsely cratered regions called smooth plains, many of which surround the most prominent impact structure on Mercury, the immense impact basin known as Caloris, only half of which was in sunlight during the Mariner 10 encounters but which was fully revealed by Messenger during its first flyby of Mercury in January 2008.

The most common topographic features on Mercury are the craters that cover much of its surface. Although lunarlike in general appearance, Mercurian craters show interesting differences when studied in detail. Mercury's surface gravity is more than twice that of the Moon, partly because of the great density of the planet's huge iron core. The higher gravity tends to keep material ejected from a crater from traveling as far—only 65 percent of the distance that would be reached on the Moon. This may be one factor that contributes to the prominence on Mercury of secondary craters, which are those made by impact of the ejected material, as distinct from primary craters formed directly by asteroid or comet impacts. The higher gravity also means that the complex forms and structures characteristic of larger craters—central peaks, slumped crater walls, and flattened floors—occur in

The double-ringed crater Vivaldi (right) on Mercury as seen by the Messenger probe on Jan. 14, 2008. Vivaldi is about 200 km (120 miles) across. The older depression covered by Vivaldi was not visible in images taken by Mariner 10. NASA/Johns Hopkins University Applied Physics Laboratory/ Carnegie Institution of Washington

smaller craters on Mercury (minimum diameters of about 10 km [6 miles]) than on the Moon (about 19 km [12 miles]). Craters smaller than these minimums have simple bowl shapes.

Mercury's craters also show differences from those on Mars, although the two planets have comparable surface gravities. Fresh craters tend to be deeper on Mercury than craters of the same size on Mars. This may be because of a lower content of volatile materials in the

Mercurian crust or higher impact velocities on Mercury, since the velocity of an object in solar orbit increases with its nearness to the Sun.

Craters on Mercury larger than about 100 km (60 miles) in diameter begin to show features indicative of a transition to the "bull's-eye" form that is the hallmark of the largest impact basins. These latter structures, called multiring basins and measuring 300 km (200 miles) or more across, are products of the most energetic impacts. Several dozen multiring basins were tentatively recognized on the imaged portion of Mercury; new Messenger images and laser altimetry will greatly contribute to the understanding of these remnant scars from early asteroidal bombardment of Mercury.

On the other side of the planet exactly 180° opposite Caloris, is a region of weirdly contorted terrain. It is interpreted to have been formed at the same time as the Caloris impact by the focusing of seismic waves from that event to the antipodal area on Mercury's surface. Termed hilly and lineated terrain, it is an extensive area of elevations and depressions. The crudely polygonal hills are 5–10 km (3–6 miles) wide and up to 1.5 km (1 mile) high. Preexisting crater rims have been disrupted into hills and fractures by the seismic process that created the terrain. Some of these craters have smooth floors that have not been disrupted, which suggests a later infilling of material. Once Messenger has mapped the entire globe of Mercury, a thorough search can be made for similarly disrupted terrain antipodal to other large basins on Mercury.

PLAINS

Plains—relatively flat or smoothly undulating surfaces—are ubiquitous on Mercury and the other terrestrial planets. They represent a canvas on which other landforms develop. The covering or destruction of a rough topography and the creation of a smoother surface is called resurfacing, and plains are evidence of this process.

There are at least three ways that planets are resurfaced, and all three may have had a role in creating Mercury's plains. One way, raising the temperature, reduces the strength of the crust and its

CALORIS BASIN AND SURROUNDING REGION

The ramparts of the Caloris impact basin span a diameter of about 1,550 km (960 miles). (Estimates of its size from the part of Caloris seen by Mariner 10 were considerably smaller.) Its interior is occupied by smooth plains that are extensively ridged and fractured in a prominent radial and concentric pattern. The largest ridges are a few hundred kilometres long, about 3 km (2 miles) wide, and less than 300 metres (1,000 feet) high. More than 200 fractures that are comparable to the ridges in size radiate from the centre of Caloris. Many are depressions bounded by faults (grabens). Where grabens cross ridges, they usually cut through them, implying that the grabens formed later than the ridges.

Two types of terrain surround Caloris, the basin rim and the basin ejecta terrains. The rim consists of a ring of irregular mountain blocks approaching 3 km (2 miles) in height, the highest mountains yet seen on Mercury, bounded on the interior by a relatively steep slope, or escarpment. A second, much smaller escarpment ring stands about 100–150 km (60–90 miles) beyond the first. Smooth plains occupy the depressions between mountain blocks. Beyond the outer escarpment is a zone of linear, radial ridges and valleys that are partially filled by plains, some with numerous knobs and hills only a few hundred metres across. The origin of these plains, which form a broad annulus surrounding the basin, has been controversial. Some plains on the Moon were formed primarily by interaction of basin ejecta with the preexisting surface at the time a basin formed; this may also have been the case on Mercury. But the Messenger results suggest a prominent role for volcanism in forming many of these plains. Not only are they sparsely cratered, compared with the interior plains of Caloris—indicating a protracted period of plains formation in the annulus—but they show other traits more clearly associated with volcanism than could be seen on Mariner 10 images. Decisive evidence of volcanism was provided by Messenger images showing actual volcanic vents, many of which are distributed along the outer edge of Caloris.

Caloris is one of the youngest of the large multiring basins, at least on the observed portion of Mercury. It probably was formed at the same time as the last giant basins on the Moon, about 3.9 billion years ago. Messenger images revealed another, much smaller basin with a prominent interior ring that may have formed much more recently, which was named Raditladi.

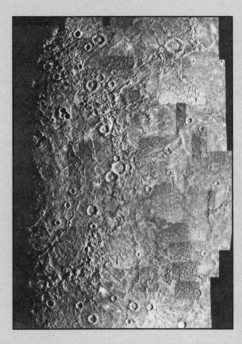

Mercury's Caloris impact basin, as seen in a mosaic of images captured by Mariner 10 during its three flybys. Only the eastern half of the structure is visible; it appears as partial concentric rings stretching from top to bottom (left portion of photo) within relatively smooth plains. The western half of Caloris was on the nightside of the planet during the Mariner encounters. NASA/JPL

ability to retain high relief; over millions of years the mountains sink and the crater floors rise. A second way involves the flow of material toward lower elevations under the influence of gravity; the material eventually collects in depressions and fills to higher levels as more volume is added. Flows of lava from the interior behave in this manner. A third way is for fragments of material to be deposited on a surface from above, first mantling and eventually obliterating the rough topography. Blanketing by impact crater ejecta

A double-ringed crater on Mercury filled with plains material, in an image taken by the Messenger probe on Jan. 14, 2008. NASA/Johns Hopkins University Applied Physics Laboratory/Carnegie Institution of Washington

and by volcanic ash are examples of this mechanism.

Other comparatively youthful plains on Mercury, which were especially prominent in regions illuminated by a low Sun during Messenger's first flyby, show prominent features of volcanism. For example, several older craters appear to have been "filled to the brim" by lava flows, very much like lava-filled craters on the Moon and Mars. However, the widespread intercrater plains on Mercury are more difficult to evaluate. Since they are older, any obvious volcanoes or other volcanic features may have been eroded or otherwise obliterated, making a definitive determination more difficult. Understanding these older plains is important, since they seem to be implicated in erasing a larger fraction of craters 10–30 km (6–20 miles) in diameter on Mercury as compared with the Moon.

SCARPS

The most important landforms on Mercury for gaining insight into the planet's otherwise largely unseen interior workings have been its hundreds of lobate scarps. These cliffs vary from tens to over a thousand kilometres in length and from about 100 metres (330 feet) to 3 km (2 miles) in altitude. Viewed from above, they have curved or scalloped edges, hence the term *lobate*. It is clear that they were formed from fracturing, or faulting, when one portion of the surface was thrust up and overrode the adjacent terrain. On Earth such thrust faults are limited in extent and result from local horizontal compressive (squeezing) forces in the crust. On Mercury, however, these features range across all of the surface that has been imaged so far, which implies that Mercury's crust must have contracted globally in the past. From the numbers and geometries of the lobate scarps, it appears that the planet shrank in diameter by at least 3 km (2 miles).

A scarp on Mercury, as seen by the Messenger probe on Jan. 14, 2008. The scarp (upper left) curves downward, ending in the large impact crater at the bottom. The region shown is about 200 km (120 miles) across. NASA/Johns Hopkins University Applied Physics Laboratory/ Carnegie Institution of Washington

Moreover, the shrinkage must have continued until comparatively recently in Mercury's geologic history—that is, since the time Caloris formed—because some lobate scarps have altered the shapes of some fresh-appearing (hence comparatively young) impact craters. The slowing of the planet's initial high rotation rate by tidal forces would have produced compression in Mercury's equatorial latitudes. The globally distributed lobate scarps, however, suggest another explanation: later cooling of the planet's mantle, perhaps combined with freezing of part of its once totally molten core, caused the interior to shrink and the cold surface crust to buckle. In fact, the contraction of Mercury estimated from cooling of its mantle should have produced even more compressional features on its surface than have been seen, which suggests that the planet has not finished shrinking.

SURFACE COMPOSITION

Scientists have attempted to deduce the makeup of Mercury's surface from studies of the sunlight reflected from different regions. One of the differences noted between Mercury and the Moon, beyond the fact that Mercury is on average somewhat darker than the Moon, is that the range of surface brightnesses is narrower on Mercury. For example, the Moon's maria—the smooth plains visible as large dark patches to the unaided eye—are much darker than its cratered highlands, whereas Mercury's plains are at most only slightly darker than its cratered terrains. Colour differences across Mercury are also less pronounced than on the Moon, although Messenger images taken through a set of colour filters have revealed some small patches, many associated with volcanic vents, that are quite colourful. These attributes of Mercury, as

Part of the surface of Mercury, in a composite image formed from data collected by Mariner 10 during its first flyby in March 1974. Kuiper is the prominent impact crater in the lower right of the image. NASA/JPL/Northwestern University

well as the relatively featureless visible and near-infrared spectrum of its reflected sunlight, suggest that the planet's surface is lacking in iron- and titanium-rich silicate minerals, which are darker in colour, compared with the lunar maria. In particular, Mercury's rocks may be low in oxidized iron (FeO). This leads to speculation that the planet was formed in conditions much more reducing—i.e., those in which oxygen was scarce—than other terrestrial planets.

Determination of the composition of Mercury's surface from such remote-sensing data involving reflected sunlight and the spectrum of Mercury's emitted thermal radiation is fraught with difficulties. For instance, strong radiation from the nearby Sun modifies the optical properties of mineral grains on Mercury's surface, rendering straightforward interpretations difficult. However, Messenger is equipped with several instruments, which were not aboard Mariner 10, that can measure chemical and mineral compositions directly. These instruments need to observe Mercury for long periods of time while the spacecraft remains near Mercury, so there can be no definitive results from Messenger's three early and brief flybys of the planet.

MERCURY'S FORMATION

Scientists once thought that Mercury's richness in iron compared with the other terrestrial planets' could be explained by its accretion from objects made up of materials derived from the extremely hot inner region of the solar nebula, where only substances with high freezing temperatures could solidify. The more volatile elements and compounds would not have condensed so close to the Sun. Modern theories of the formation of the solar system, however, discount the possibility that an orderly process of accretion led to progressive detailed differences in planetary chemistry with distance from the Sun. Rather, the components of the bodies that accreted into Mercury likely were derived from a wide part of the inner solar system. Indeed, Mercury itself may have formed anywhere from the asteroid belt inward. Subsequent gravitational interactions among the many growing protoplanets could have moved Mercury around.

Some planetary scientists have suggested that during Mercury's early epochs, after it had already differentiated (chemically separated) into a less-dense crust and mantle of silicate rocks and a denser iron-rich core, a giant collision stripped away much of the planet's outer layers, leaving a body dominated by its core. This event would have been similar to the collision of a Mars-sized object with Earth that is thought to have formed the Moon.

Nevertheless, such violent, disorderly planetary beginnings would not necessarily have placed the inherently densest planet closest to the Sun. Other processes may have been primarily responsible for Mercury's high density. Perhaps the materials that eventually formed Mercury experienced a preferential sorting of heavier metallic particles from lighter silicate ones because of aerodynamic drag by the gaseous solar nebula. Perhaps, because of the planet's nearness to the hot early Sun, its silicates were preferentially vaporized and lost. Each of these scenarios predicts different bulk chemistries for Mercury. In addition, infalling asteroids, meteoroids, and comets and implantation of solar wind particles have been augmenting or modifying the surface and near-surface materials on Mercury for billions of years. Because these materials are the ones most readily analyzed by telescopes and spacecraft, the task of extrapolating backward in time to an understanding of ancient Mercury, and the processes that subsequently shaped it, is formidable.

LATER DEVELOPMENT

Planetary scientists continue to puzzle over the ages of the major geologic and geophysical events that took place on Mercury after its formation. On the one hand, it is tempting to model the planet's history after that of the Moon, whose chronology has been accurately dated from the rocks returned by the U.S. Apollo manned landings and Soviet Luna robotic missions. By analogy, Mercury would have had a similar history, but one in which the planet cooled off and became geologically inactive shortly after the Caloris impact rather than experiencing persistent volcanism for hundreds of

millions of years, as did the Moon. On the presumption that Mercury's craters were produced by the same populations of remnant planetary building blocks (planetesimals), asteroids, and comets that struck the Moon, most of the craters would have formed before and during an especially intense period of bombardment in the inner solar system, which on the Moon is well documented to have ended about 3.8 billion years ago. Caloris presumably would have formed about that time, representing the final chapter in Mercury's geologic history, apart from occasional cratering.

On the other hand, there are many indications that Mercury is very much geologically alive even today. Its dipolar field seems to require a core that is still at least partially molten in order to sustain the magnetohydrodynamic dynamo. Indeed, recent radar measurements of Mercury's spin state have been interpreted as proving that at least the outer core is still molten. In addition, as suggested above, Mercury's scarps show evidence that the planet may not have completed its cooling and shrinking.

There are several approaches to resolving this apparent contradiction between a planet that died geologically before the Moon did and one that is still alive. One hypothesis is that most of Mercury's craters are younger than those on the Moon, having been formed by impacts from so-called vulcanoids—the name bestowed on a hypothetical remnant population of asteroid-sized objects orbiting the Sun inside Mercury's orbit—that would have cratered Mercury over the planet's age. In this case Caloris, the lobate scarps, and other features would be much younger than 3.8 billion years, and Mercury could be viewed as a planet whose surface has only recently become inactive and whose warm interior is still cooling down. No vulcanoids have yet been discovered, however, despite a number of searches for them. Moreover, objects orbiting the Sun so closely and having such high relative velocities could well have been broken up in catastrophic collisions with each other long ago.

A more likely solution to Mercury's thermal conundrum is that the outer shell of Mercury's iron core remains molten because of contamination, for instance, with a small proportion of sulfur, which would lower the melting point of the metal, and of radioactive potassium, which would augment production of heat. Also, the planet's interior may have cooled more slowly than previously calculated as a result of restricted heat transfer. Perhaps the contraction of the planet's crust, so evident about the time of formation of Caloris, pinched off the volcanic vents that had yielded such prolific volcanism earlier in Mercury's history. In this scenario, despite present-day Mercury's lingering internal warmth and churnings, surface activity ceased long ago, with the possible exception of a few thrust faults as the planet continues slowly to contract.

CHAPTER 4

VENUS

No planet approaches closer to Earth than Venus, the second planet from the Sun. At its nearest it is the closest large body to Earth other than the Moon. Because Venus's orbit is nearer the Sun than Earth's, the planet is always roughly in the same direction in the sky as the Sun and can be seen only in the hours near sunrise or sunset. When it is visible, it is the most brilliant planet in the sky. Venus is designated by the symbol ♀. Venus is the sixth largest planet in the solar system in size and mass.

Venus was one of the five planets—along with Mercury, Mars, Jupiter, and Saturn—known in ancient times, and its motions were observed and studied for centuries prior to the invention of advanced astronomical instruments. Its appearances were recorded by the Babylonians, who equated it with the goddess Ishtar, about 3000 BCE, and it also is mentioned prominently in the astronomical records of other ancient civilizations, including those of China, Central America, Egypt, and Greece. Like the planet Mercury, Venus was known in ancient Greece by two different names—Phosphorus when it appeared as a morning star and Hesperus when it appeared as an evening star. Its modern name comes from the Roman goddess of love and beauty (the Greek equivalent being Aphrodite), perhaps because of the planet's luminous jewel-like appearance.

Venus has been called Earth's twin because of the similarities in their masses, sizes, and densities and their similar relative locations in the solar system. Because they presumably formed in the solar nebula from the same kind of rocky planetary building blocks, they also likely have similar overall chemical compositions. Early telescopic observations of the planet revealed a perpetual veil of clouds, suggestive of a substantial atmosphere and leading to popular speculation that Venus was a warm, wet world, perhaps similar to Earth during its prehistoric age of swampy carboniferous forests and abundant life. Scientists now know, however, that Venus and Earth have evolved surface conditions that could hardly be more different. Venus is extremely hot, dry, and in other ways so forbidding that it is improbable that life as it is understood on Earth could have developed there. One of scientists' major goals in studying Venus is to understand how its harsh conditions came about, which may hold important lessons about the causes of environmental change on Earth.

Venus photographed in ultraviolet light by the Pioneer Venus Orbiter (Pioneer 12) spacecraft, Feb. 26, 1979. Although Venus's cloud cover is nearly featureless in visible light, ultraviolet imaging reveals distinctive structure and pattern, including global-scale V-shaped bands that open toward the west (left). NASA/JPL

BASIC ASTRONOMICAL DATA

Viewed through a telescope, Venus presents a brilliant yellow-white, essentially featureless face to the observer. Its obscured appearance results from the surface of the planet being hidden from sight by a continuous and permanent

Global image of the topography of Venus below its obscuring clouds, based on radar data from the Magellan spacecraft with supplemental data from Venera and Pioneer Venus missions and Earth-based radar studies. NASA/JPL/California Institute of Technology

cover of clouds. Features in the clouds are difficult to see in visible light. When observed at ultraviolet wavelengths, the clouds exhibit distinctive dark markings, with complex swirling patterns near the equator and global-scale bright and dark bands that are V-shaped and open toward the west. Because of the all-enveloping clouds, little was known about Venus's surface, atmosphere, and evolution before the early 1960s, when the first radar observations were undertaken and spacecraft made the first flybys of the planet.

Venus orbits the Sun at a mean distance of 108 million km (67 million miles), which is about 0.7 times Earth's distance from the Sun. It has the least eccentric orbit of any planet, with a deviation from a perfect circle of only about 1 part in 150. Consequently, its distances at perihelion and aphelion (i.e., when it is nearest and farthest from the Sun, respectively) vary little from the mean distance. The period of its orbit—that is, the length of the Venusian year—is 224.7 Earth days. As Venus and Earth revolve around the Sun, the distance between them varies from a minimum of about 42 million km (26 million miles) to a maximum of about 257 million km (160 million miles). Because Venus's orbit lies within Earth's, the planet exhibits phases like those of the Moon when viewed from Earth. In fact, the discovery of these phases by the Italian scientist Galileo in 1610 was one of the most important in the history of astronomy. In Galileo's day the prevailing model of the universe was based on the assertion by the Greek astronomer Ptolemy almost 15 centuries earlier that all celestial objects revolve around Earth. Observation of the phases of Venus was inconsistent with this view but was consistent with the Polish astronomer Nicolaus Copernicus's idea that the solar system is centred on the Sun. Galileo's observation of the phases of Venus provided the first direct observational evidence for Copernican theory.

The rotation of Venus on its axis is unusual in both its direction and its speed. The Sun and most of the planets in the solar system rotate in a counter-clockwise direction when viewed from above their north poles; this direction is called direct, or prograde. Venus, however, rotates in the opposite, or retrograde, direction. Were it not for the planet's clouds, an observer on Venus's surface would see the Sun rise in the west and set in the east. Venus spins very slowly, taking about 243 Earth days to complete one rotation with respect to the stars—the length of its sidereal day. Venus's spin and orbital periods are very nearly synchronized with Earth's orbit such that, when the two planets are at their closest, Venus presents almost the same face toward Earth. The reasons for this are complex and have to do with the gravitational interactions of Venus, Earth, and the Sun, as well as the effects of Venus's massive rotating atmosphere. Because Venus's spin axis is tilted only about 3° toward the plane of its orbit, the planet does not have appreciable seasons. Astronomers as yet have no satisfactory explanation for Venus's peculiar rotational characteristics. The idea cited most often is that, when Venus was forming from the accretion of planetary building blocks, or planetesimals, one of the largest of these bodies collided with the proto-Venus in such a way

PLANETARY DATA FOR VENUS	
mean distance from Sun	108,200,000 km (0.72 AU)
eccentricity of orbit	0.007
inclination of orbit to ecliptic	3.4°
Venusian year (sidereal period of revolution)	224.7 Earth days
maximum visual magnitude	-4.6
mean synodic period*	584 Earth days
mean orbital velocity	35 km/s
radius (equatorial and polar)	6,051.8 km
surface area	4.6×10^8 km^2
mass	4.87×10^{24} kg
mean density	5.25 g/cm^3
mean surface gravity	860 cm/s^2
escape velocity	10.4 km/s
rotation period (Venusian sidereal day)	243 Earth days (retrograde)
Venusian mean solar day	116.8 Earth days
inclination of equator to orbit	177°
atmospheric composition	carbon dioxide, 96%; molecular nitrogen, 3.5%; water, 0.02%; trace quantities of carbon monoxide, molecular oxygen, sulfur dioxide, hydrogen chloride, and other gases
mean surface temperature	737 K (867 °F, 464 °C)
surface pressure at mean radius	95 bars
mean visible cloud temperature	about 230 K (-46 °F, -43 °C)
number of known moons	none

*Time required for the planet to return to the same position in the sky relative to the Sun as seen from Earth.

as to tip it over and possibly slow its spin as well.

Venus's mean radius is 6,051.8 km (3,760.4 miles), or about 95 percent of Earth's at the equator, while its mass is 4.87 × 10²⁴ kg, or 81.5 percent that of Earth. The similarities to Earth in size and mass produce a similarity in density—5.25 g/cm³ (3.04 oz/in³) for Venus, compared with 5.52 for Earth. They also result in a comparable surface gravity; humans standing on Venus would possess nearly 90 percent of their weight on Earth. Venus is more nearly spherical than most planets. A planet's rotation generally causes a bulging at the equator and a slight flattening at the poles, but Venus's very slow spin allows it to maintain its highly spherical shape.

THE ATMOSPHERE

Venus has the most massive atmosphere of the planets in the inner solar system. Its gaseous envelope is composed of more than 96 percent carbon dioxide and 3.5 percent molecular nitrogen. Trace amounts of other gases are present, including carbon monoxide, sulfur dioxide, water vapour, argon, and helium. The atmospheric pressure at the planet's surface varies with surface elevation; at the elevation of the planet's mean radius it is about 95 bars, or 95 times the atmospheric pressure at Earth's surface. This is the same pressure found at a depth of about 1 km (0.6 mile) in Earth's oceans.

Venus's upper atmosphere extends from the fringes of space down to about 100 km (60 miles) above the surface. There the temperature varies considerably, reaching a maximum of about 300–310 K (27–37 °C, or 80–98 °F) in the daytime and dropping to a minimum of 100–130 K (-173 to -143 °C, or -280 to -226 °F) at night. In the middle atmosphere the temperature increases smoothly with decreasing altitude, from about 173 K (-100 °C, or -148 °F) at 100 km above the surface to roughly 263 K (-10 °C, or 14 °F) at the top of the continuous cloud deck, which lies at an altitude of more than 60 km (37 miles). Below the cloud tops the temperature continues to increase sharply through the lower atmosphere, or troposphere, reaching 737 K (464 °C, or 867 °F) at the surface at the planet's mean radius. This temperature is higher than the melting point of lead or zinc.

The clouds that enshroud Venus are enormously thick. The main cloud deck rises from about 48 km (30 miles) in altitude to 68 km (42 miles). In addition, thin hazes exist above and below the main clouds, extending as low as 32 km (20 miles) and as high as 90 km (56 miles) above the surface. The upper haze is somewhat thicker near the poles than in other regions.

The main cloud deck is formed of three layers. All of them are quite tenuous—an observer in even the densest cloud regions would be able to see objects at distances of several kilometres. The opacity of the clouds varies rapidly with space and time, which suggests a high level of meteorologic activity. Radio waves characteristic of lightning have been observed in Venus's clouds. The clouds are bright and yellowish when viewed from above, reflecting roughly 85 percent of the sunlight striking them. The material responsible for the yellowish colour has not been confidently identified.

The microscopic particles that make up the Venusian clouds consist of liquid droplets and perhaps also solid crystals. The dominant material is highly concentrated sulfuric acid. Other materials that may exist there include solid sulfur, nitrosylsulfuric acid, and phosphoric acid. Cloud particles range in size from less than 0.5 micrometres (0.00002 inch) in the hazes to a few micrometres in the densest layers.

The reasons that some cloud-top regions appear dark when viewed in ultraviolet light are not fully known. Materials that may be present in minute quantities above the cloud tops and that may be responsible for absorbing ultraviolet light in some regions include sulfur dioxide, solid sulfur, chlorine, and iron (III) chloride.

The circulation of Venus's atmosphere is quite remarkable and is unique among the planets. Although the planet rotates only three times in two Earth years, the cloud features in the atmosphere circle Venus completely in about four days. The wind at the cloud tops blows from east to west at a velocity of about 100 metres/sec (360 km/hour [220 miles/hour]). This enormous velocity decreases markedly with decreasing height such that winds at the planet's surface are quite sluggish—typically no more

than 1 metre/sec (less than 4 km/hour [2.5 miles/hour]). Much of the detailed nature of the westward flow above the cloud tops can be attributed to tidal motions induced by solar heating. Nevertheless, the fundamental cause of this "superrotation" of Venus's dense atmosphere is unknown, and it remains one of the more intriguing mysteries in planetary science.

Most information about wind directions at the planet's surface comes from observations of wind-blown materials. Despite low surface-wind velocities, the great density of Venus's atmosphere enables these winds to move loose fine-grained materials, producing surface features that have been seen in radar images. Some features resemble sand dunes, while others are "wind streaks" produced by preferential deposition or erosion downwind from topographic features. The directions assumed by the wind-related features suggest that in both hemispheres the surface winds blow predominantly toward the equator. This pattern is consistent with the idea that simple hemispheric-scale circulation systems called Hadley cells exist in the Venusian atmosphere. According to this model, atmospheric gases rise upward as they are heated by solar energy at the planet's equator, flow at high altitude toward the poles, sink to the surface as they cool at higher latitudes, and flow toward the equator along the planet's surface until they warm and rise again. Some deviations from the equatorward flow

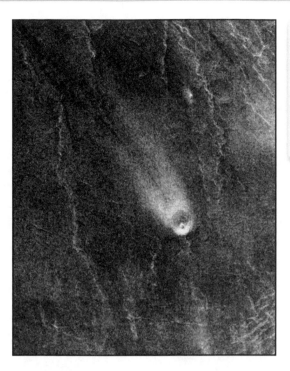

pattern are observed on regional scales. They may be caused by the influence of topography on wind circulation.

A major consequence of Venus's massive atmosphere is that it produces an enormous greenhouse effect, which intensely heats the planet's surface. Because of its bright continuous cloud cover, Venus actually absorbs less of the Sun's light than does Earth. Nevertheless, the sunlight that does penetrate the clouds is absorbed both in the lower atmosphere and at the surface. The surface and the gases of the lower atmosphere, which are heated by the absorbed light, reradiate this energy at infrared wavelengths. On Earth most reradiated infrared radiation escapes back into space, which allows Earth to maintain a reasonably cool surface temperature. On Venus, in contrast, the dense carbon dioxide atmosphere and the thick cloud layers trap much of the infrared radiation. The trapped radiation heats the lower atmosphere further, ultimately raising the surface temperature by hundreds of degrees. Study of the Venusian greenhouse effect has led to an improved understanding of the more subtle but very important influence of greenhouse gases in Earth's atmosphere and a greater appreciation of the effects of energy use and of other human activities on Earth's energy balance.

Above the main body of the Venusian atmosphere lies the ionosphere. As its name implies, the ionosphere is composed of ions, or charged particles, produced both by absorption of ultraviolet solar radiation and by the impact of the solar wind—the flow of charged particles streaming outward from the Sun—on the upper atmosphere. The primary ions in the Venusian ionosphere are forms of oxygen (O^+ and O_2^+) and carbon dioxide (CO_2^+).

INTERACTION WITH THE SOLAR WIND

Unlike most planets, including Earth, Venus does not exhibit an intrinsic magnetic field. Sensitive measurements by orbiting spacecraft have shown that any dipole field originating from within Venus must be no more than 1/8,000 that of Earth's. The lack of a magnetic field may be related in part to the planet's slow rotation because, according to the dynamo theory that explains the origin of planetary magnetic fields, rotation helps to drive the fluid motions within the planet's interior that produce the field. It is also possible that Venus may lack a magnetic field because its core is fluid but does not circulate or simply because the core is solid and hence is incapable of supporting a dynamo.

As the solar wind bombards a planet at supersonic speeds, it generally forms a bow shock on the planet's sunward side—that is, a standing wave of plasma that slows down, heats, and deflects the flow around the planet. For some planets the bow shock lies at a considerable distance from the surface, held off by the planet's magnetic field. For example, because of Jupiter's enormous magnetic field, the bow shock exists about 3 million km (1,900,000 miles) from the planet; for Earth the distance is about 65,000 km (40,000 miles). Because Venus lacks a detectable field, however, its bow shock lies just a few thousand kilometres above the surface, held off only by the planet's ionosphere. This closeness of the bow shock to the surface leads to particularly intense interactions between the solar wind and Venus's atmosphere. In fact, the top of the ionosphere, known as the ionopause, lies at a much lower altitude on the dayside of Venus than on the nightside owing to the pressure exerted by the solar wind. The density of the ionosphere is also far greater on the dayside of the planet than on the nightside.

Venus's interaction with the solar wind results in a gradual, continuous loss to space of hydrogen and oxygen from the planet's upper ionosphere. This process is equivalent to a gradual loss of water from the planet. Over the course of Venus's history, the total amount of water lost via this mechanism could have been as much as a few percent of a world ocean the size of Earth's.

CHARACTER OF THE SURFACE

The high atmospheric pressure, the low wind velocities, and, in particular, the extremely high temperatures create a surface environment on Venus that is markedly different from any other in the solar system. A series of landings by robotic Soviet spacecraft in the 1970s and early '80s provided detailed data on surface composition and appearance. Views of the Venusian landscape, typified in colour images obtained by the Soviet Union's Venera 13 lander in 1982, show rocky plains that stretch toward the horizon. Despite the heavy cloud cover, the surface is well illuminated by the yellow-orange light that filters through the clouds.

The most striking characteristic of the surface at the Venera 13 site and most other Venera landing sites is the flat, slabby, layered nature of the rocks. Both volcanic and sedimentary rocks on Earth can develop such an appearance under appropriate conditions, but the reason that the Venusian rocks have done so is not known with certainty. Also present among the rocks is a darker, fine-grained soil. The grain size of the soil is unknown, but some of it was fine enough to be lifted briefly into the atmosphere by the touchdown of the Venera lander, which suggests that some grains are no more than a few tens of micrometres in diameter. Scattered throughout the soil and atop the rocks are pebble-size particles that could be either small rocks or clods of soil.

The general surface appearance at the Venera landing sites is probably common on Venus, but it is likely not representative of all locations on the planet. Radar data from the U.S. Magellan spacecraft, which studied Venus from orbit in the early 1990s, provided global information about the roughness of the Venusian surface at scales of metres to tens of metres. Although much of the planet is indeed covered by lowland plains that appear smooth to radar, some terrains were found to be very much rougher. These include areas covered by ejecta (the material expelled from impact craters and extending around them), steep slopes associated with tectonic activity, and some lava flows. How such terrains would appear from a lander's perspective is not known, but large boulders and other sorts of angular blocks presumably would be more common than at the Venera sites.

Surface Composition

A number of the Soviet landers carried instruments to analyze the chemical composition of the surface materials of Venus. Because only the relative proportions of a few elements were measured, no definitive information exists concerning the rock types or minerals present. Two techniques were used to measure the abundances of various elements. Gamma-ray spectrometers, which were carried on the Soviet Venera 8, 9, and 10 missions and the landers of the Soviet Vega 1 and 2 missions, measured the concentrations of naturally radioactive isotopes of the elements uranium, potassium, and thorium. X-ray fluorescence instruments, carried on Veneras 13 and 14 and Vega 2, measured the concentrations of a number of major elements.

The Venera 8 site gave indications that the rock composition may be similar to that of granite or other igneous rocks that compose Earth's continents. This inference, however, was based only on rather uncertain measurements of the concentrations of a few radioactive elements. Measurements of radioactive elements at the Venera 9 and 10 and Vega 1 and 2 landing sites suggested that the compositions there resemble those of basalt rocks found on Earth's ocean floors and in some volcanic regions such as

Hawaii and Iceland. The Venera 13 and 14 and Vega 2 X-ray instruments measured concentrations of silicon, aluminum, magnesium, iron, calcium, potassium, titanium, manganese, and sulfur. Although some differences in composition were seen among the three sites, on the whole the elemental compositions measured by all three landers were similar to those of basalts on Earth.

A surprising result of orbital radar observations of Venus is that the highest elevations on the planet exhibit anomalously high radar reflectivity. The best interpretation seems to be that the highest elevations are coated with a thin layer of some semiconducting material. Its composition is unknown, but it could be an iron-containing mineral such as pyrite or magnetite, which formed at cooler, higher elevations from low concentrations of atmospheric iron (II) chloride vapour in the atmosphere.

SURFACE FEATURES

Earth-based observatories and Venus-orbiting spacecraft have provided global-scale information on the nature of the planet's surface. All have used radar systems to penetrate the thick Venusian clouds.

The entire surface of the planet is dry and rocky. Because there is no sea level in the literal sense, elevation is commonly expressed as a planetary radius—i.e., as the distance from the centre of the planet to the surface at a given location. Another method, in which elevation is expressed as the distance above or below the planet's mean radius, is also used. Most of the planet consists of gently rolling plains. In some areas the elevations change by only a few hundred metres over distances of hundreds of kilometres. Globally, more than 80 percent of the surface deviates less than 1 km (0.6 mile) from the mean radius. At several locations on the plains are broad, gently sloping topographic depressions, or lowlands, that may reach several thousand kilometres across; they include Atalanta Planitia, Guinevere Planitia, and Lavinia Planitia.

Two striking features are the continent-sized highland areas, or terrae—Ishtar Terra in the northern hemisphere and Aphrodite Terra along the equator. In addition to the two main terrae are several smaller elevated regions,

(Top) *Global topographic map of Venus derived from laser altimetry data gathered by the Magellan spacecraft. Selected major topographic features and spacecraft landing sites are labeled. The most prominent features are the two continent-sized highland areas—Ishtar Terra in the northern hemisphere and Aphrodite Terra along the equator.* Encyclopædia Britannica, Inc. (Bottom) *A close-up view of western Ishtar Terra reveals gently rolling plains, the dominant feature of Venus's surface. The highlands of Ishtar Terra are centred on the lava-covered plateau Lakshmi Planum* (upper right). Courtesy of NASA/JPL/Caltech

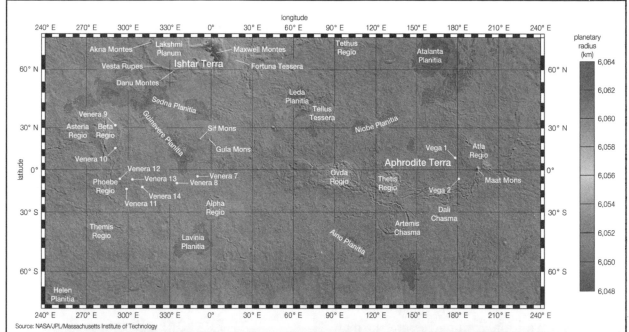

longitude

planetary
radius
(km)

6,064
6,062
6,060
6,058
6,056
6,054
6,052
6,050
6,048

Akna Montes   Lakshmi   Maxwell Montes   Tethus   Atalanta
                Planum   Regio   Planitia
Vesta Rupes   Ishtar Terra   Fortuna Tessera
Danu Montes
                                Leda
                Sedna Planitia   Planitia
Venera 9   Tellus
Asteria Beta   Tessera
Regio   Regio   Sif Mons   Niobe Planitia
Venera 10   Gula Mons   Vega 1   Atla
                                                            Regio
                                Aphrodite Terra
Venera 12   Venera 7   Maat Mons
Phoebe   Venera 13 Venera 8   Ovda   Vega 2
Regio   Regio   Thetis
         Venera 14   Regio
Venera 11   Dali
              Alpha   Chasma
              Regio   Artemis
Themis   Chasma
Regio
         Lavinia   Aino Planitia
         Planitia
Helen
Planitia

Source: NASA/JPL/Massachusetts Institute of Technology

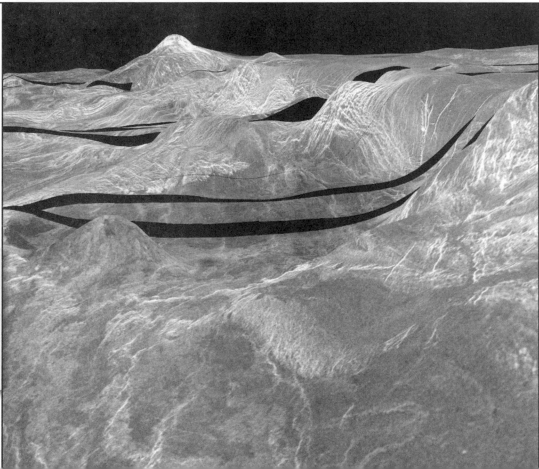

including Alpha Regio, Beta Regio, and Phoebe Regio.

Ishtar is the smaller of the two main terrae and is roughly the size of Australia. It extends from about latitude 45°N to 75° N and from about longitude 300°E to 75° E. Ishtar possesses the most spectacular topography on Venus, comprising several distinct physiographic provinces. The dominant feature of western Ishtar is Lakshmi Planum, a high, flat, lava-covered plateau. Lakshmi is bounded on most sides by mountain ranges and has been likened to the Plateau of Tibet.

The eastern portion of Ishtar is geologically complex, consisting largely of tessera terrain. Fortuna Tessera, the main feature of eastern Ishtar, appears extraordinarily rugged and highly deformed in radar images, displaying many different trends of parallel ridges and troughs that cut across one another at a wide range of angles. The geologic processes that formed Ishtar are not well understood, but they probably included thickening of the Venusian crust in response to motions in the planet's mantle.

Aphrodite Terra is twice the size of Ishtar Terra and is comparable in area to South America. It extends from about longitude 60° E to 150° E. The topography of Aphrodite, more complex than that of Ishtar, is characterized by a number of distinct mountain ranges and several deep, narrow troughs. Its western extremity consists of two large curving ridges that partially surround a broad circular region of low-lying rugged terrain. Most of Aphrodite is formed by two broad upland regions, Ovda Regio in the central part and Thetis Regio farther east. Ovda spans about 4,000 km (2,500 miles) from north to south, Thetis about 3,000 km (1,900 miles). Both are composed primarily of tessera terrain. At its eastern extremity Aphrodite Terra merges into a complex of rift valleys and other tectonic features. The geologic processes that formed Aphrodite remain to be established, but they probably included thickening of the Venusian crust in response to motions in the planet's mantle.

Features Due to Tectonic Activity

Many of the surface features on Venus can be attributed to tectonic activity—that is, to deformational motions within the crust. These include mountain belts, plains deformation belts, rifts, coronae, and tesserae.

Belts and Rifts

Found in the terrae, Venus's mountain belts are in some ways similar to ones on Earth such as the Himalayas of Asia and the Andes of South America. Among the best examples are those that encircle Lakshmi Planum, which include Freyja, Akna, and Danu Montes.

The tallest mountain range on Venus is Maxwell Montes, which is particularly

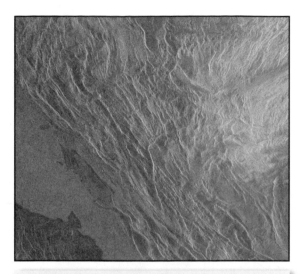

Akna Montes, a mountain belt on Venus bordering Lakshmi Planum in Ishtar Terra, in a radar image obtained by the Magellan spacecraft. North is up. NASA/Goddard Space Flight Center

broad and comparable in size to the Himalayas, rising to about 11 km (7 miles) above the planet's mean radius. First observed as a bright feature in Earth-based radar observations of the planet made in the 1960s, the region initially was dubbed Maxwell after the British physicist James Clerk Maxwell, whose formulation of the laws that relate electricity and magnetism is the basis of radar. Subsequent Earth-based and spacecraft radar observations revealed its mountainous nature.

A major feature of Maxwell Montes is Cleopatra, a circular depression near its eastern margin that has a diameter of slightly more than 100 km (60 miles) and a depth of more than 2.5 km (1.6 miles). Suspected after its discovery of being a volcanic caldera, Cleopatra was later generally recognized to be an impact crater.

In radar images Maxwell Montes is one of the brightest features on Venus. This high radar reflectivity, responsible for the region's early discovery, is due in part to its very rugged nature. It apparently is also due to the highest elevations on Venus being coated with some as-yet-unidentified material, perhaps an iron-containing mineral such as pyrite or magnetite, that is unusually reflective at radar wavelengths.

Venus's mountain belts typically consist of parallel ridges and troughs with spacings of 5–10 km (3–6 miles). They probably developed when broad bands of the lithosphere were compressed from the sides and became thickened, folding and thrusting surface materials upward. Their formation in some respects thus resembles the building of many mountain ranges on Earth. On the other hand, because of the lack of liquid water or ice on Venus, their appearance differs in major ways from their counterparts on Earth. Without the flow of rivers or glaciers to wear them down, Venusian mountain belts have acquired steep slopes as a result of folding and faulting. In some places the slopes have become so steep that they have collapsed under their own weight. The erosional forms common in mountainous regions on Earth are absent.

Although plains deformation belts are similar in some ways to mountain belts, they display less pronounced relief and are found primarily in low-lying areas of the planet, such as Lavinia Planitia and Atalanta Planitia. Like mountain belts, they show strong evidence for parallel folding and faulting and may form primarily by compression, deformation, and uplift of the lithosphere. Within a given lowland, it is common for deformation belts to lie roughly parallel to one another, spaced typically several hundred kilometres apart.

Rifts are among the most spectacular tectonic features on Venus. The best-developed rifts are found atop broad, raised areas such as Beta Regio, sometimes radiating outward from their centres like the spokes of a giant wheel. Beta and several other similar regions on Venus appear to be places where large areas of the lithosphere have been forced upward from below, splitting the surface to form great rift valleys. The rifts are composed of innumerable faults, and their floors typically lie 1–2 km (0.6–1.2 miles) below the surrounding terrain. In many ways the rifts on Venus are similar to great rifts elsewhere, such as the East African Rift on Earth or Valles Marineris on Mars; volcanic eruptions, for example, appear to have been associated with all these features. The Venusian rifts differ from Earth and Martian ones, however, in that little erosion has taken place within them owing to the lack of water.

Coronae and Tesserae

Coronae (Latin: "garlands" or "crowns") are landforms that apparently owe their origin to the effects of hot, buoyant blobs of material, known from terrestrial geology as diapirs, that originate deep beneath the surface of Venus. Coronae evolve through several stages. As diapirs first rise through the planet's interior and approach the surface, they can lift the rocks above them, fracturing the surface in a radial pattern. This results in a distinctive starburst of faults and fractures, often lying atop a broad, gently sloping topographic rise. (Such features are sometimes called novae, a name given to them when their evolutionary relationship to coronae was less certain.)

Once a diapir has neared the surface and cooled, it loses its buoyancy. The initially raised crust then can sag under its own weight, developing concentric faults as it does so. The result is a circular-to-oval pattern of faults, fractures, and ridges. Volcanism can occur through all stages of corona formation. During the late stages it tends to obscure the radial faulting that is characteristic of the early stages.

Coronae are typically a few hundred kilometres in diameter. Although they may have a raised outer rim, many coronae sag noticeably in their interiors and also outside their rims. Hundreds of coronae are found on Venus, observed at all stages of development. The radially fractured domes of the early stages are

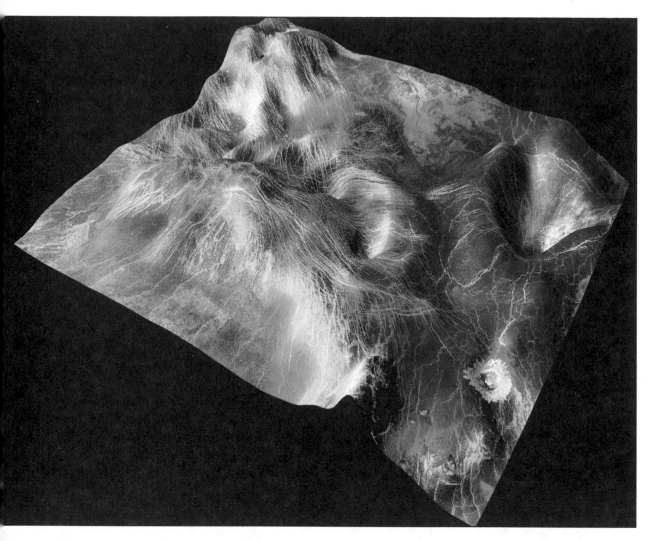

Oblique view of coronae in the Sedna Planitia lowlands of Venus, generated by computer from data collected by the Magellan spacecraft's radar imaging system. The topographic rise left of centre is a corona in an early evolutionary stage characterized by raised crust that is fractured in a radial pattern. The depression at the far right represents a corona in a later stage, in which the raised crust has sagged at the centre, with concentric fractures added to the radial ones. The image is highly exaggerated in its vertical direction—the more mature corona, for example, is about 100 km (62 miles) across but actually only about 1 km deep.
NASA/JPL/Caltech

comparatively uncommon, while the concentric scars characteristic of mature coronae are among the most numerous large tectonic features on the planet.

Tesserae (Latin: "mosaic tiles") are the most geologically complex regions seen on Venus. Gravity data suggest that the thickness of the crust is fairly uniform over much of the planet, with typical values of perhaps 20–50 km (12–30 miles). Possible exceptions are the tessera highlands, where the crust may

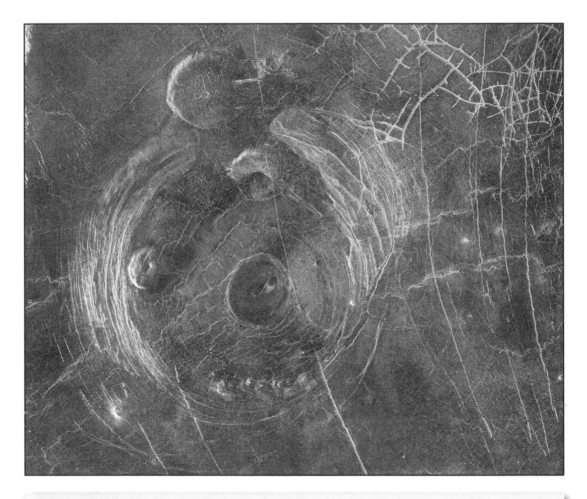

Aine Corona and other volcanic features in a region on Venus to the south of Aphrodite Terra, shown in an image obtained from radar data gathered by the Magellan spacecraft. Aine Corona is the central large circular structure bounded by numerous arc-shaped concentric faults. It measures about 200 km (125 miles) across. Also visible are two flat-topped pancake domes, one to the north of the corona and a second inside its western border, and a complex fracture pattern in the upper right of the image. NASA/JPL

be significantly thicker. Several large elevated regions, such as Alpha Regio, are composed largely of tessera terrain. Such terrain appears extraordinarily rugged and highly deformed in radar images, and in some instances it displays several different trends of parallel ridges and troughs that cut across one another at a wide range of angles. The deformation in tessera terrain can be so complex that sometimes it is difficult to determine what kinds of

stresses in the lithosphere were responsible for forming it. In fact, probably no single process can explain all tessera formation.

Tesserae typically appear very bright in radar images, which suggests an extremely rough and blocky surface at scales of metres. Some tesserae may be old terrain that has been subjected to more episodes of mountain building and faulting than have the materials around it, each one superimposed on its predecessor to produce the complex pattern observed.

VOLCANIC FEATURES

Along with intense tectonic activity, Venus has undergone much volcanism. The largest volcanic outpourings are the huge lava fields that cover most of the rolling plains. These are similar in many respects to fields of overlapping lava flows seen on other planets, including Earth, but they are far more extensive. Individual flows are for the most part long and thin, which indicates that the erupting lavas were very fluid and hence were able to flow long distances over gentle slopes. Lavas on Earth and the

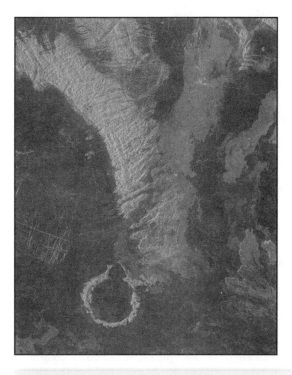

Highlands of tessera terrain rising from the plains region known as Leda Planitia in Venus's northern hemisphere, in an image produced from radar data collected by the Magellan spacecraft. Having an extraordinarily rugged appearance in radar images, the terrain displays several different patterns of ridges and troughs crisscrossing in various directions. Tesserae are the most geologically complex terrains known on Venus and may be the result of numerous consecutive episodes of mountain building. NASA/JPL

Moon that flow this readily typically consist of basalts, and so it is probable that basalts are common on the plains of Venus as well.

Of the many types of lava-flow features seen on the Venusian plains, none are more remarkable than the long, sinuous *canali*. These meandering channels usually have remarkably constant widths, which can be as much as 3 km (2 miles). They commonly extend as far as 500 km (300 miles) across the surface; one is 6,800 km (4,200 miles) long. *Canali* probably were carved by very low-viscosity lavas that erupted at sustained high rates of discharge. In a few instances segments of *canali* appear to proceed uphill, which suggests that crustal deformation took place after the channels were carved and reversed the gentle downward surface slopes to upward ones. Other channel-like volcanic features on Venus include sinuous rilles that may be collapsed lava tubes and large, complex compound valleys that apparently result from particularly massive outpourings of lava.

In many locations on Venus, volcanic eruptions have built edifices similar to the great volcanoes of Hawaii on Earth or those associated with the Tharsis region on Mars. Sif Mons is an example of such a volcano. Located at the western end of the elevated region Eistla Regio, south of Ishtar Terra, it is about 2 km (1.2 miles) high and has a base 300 km (200 miles) in diameter. There are more than 100 others distributed widely over the planet. Known as shield volcanoes, they reach heights of several kilometres above the surrounding plains and can be hundreds of kilometres across at their base. Made up of many individual lava flows piled on

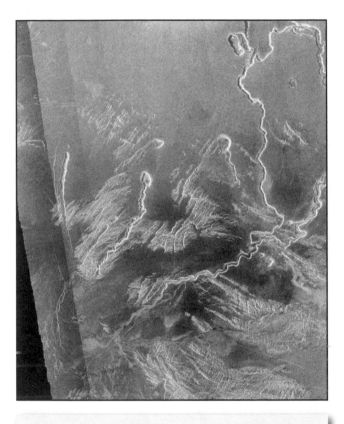

Canali, or lava channels, in Venus's Lo Shen Valles *region, north of the equatorial elevated terrain Ovda Regio, shown in a radar image from the Magellan spacecraft. Collapsed source areas for some of the meandering lava flows are visible in the image.* NASA/Goddard Space Flight Center

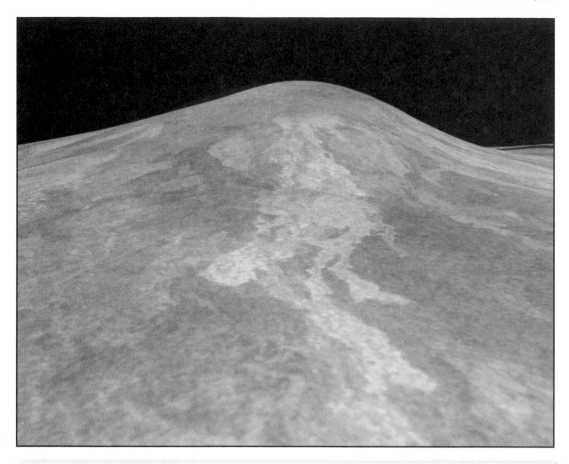

Sif Mons, in a low-angle computer-generated view based on radar data from the Magellan spacecraft. In this radar image, lava flows having rougher surfaces appear brighter than smoother flows and are therefore presumably more recent. NASA/JPL

one another in a radial pattern, they develop when a source of lava below the surface remains fixed and active at one location long enough to allow the volcanic materials it extrudes to accumulate above it in large quantities. Like those found on the rolling plains, the flows constituting the shield volcanoes are generally very long and thin and are probably composed of basalt.

When a subsurface source of lava is drained of its contents, the ground above it may collapse, forming a depression called a caldera. Many volcanic calderas are observed on Venus, both atop shield volcanoes and on the widespread lava plains. They are often roughly circular in shape and overall are similar to calderas observed on Earth and Mars. The summit region of Sif Mons, for example, exhibits a caldera-like feature 40–50 km (25–30 miles) in diameter.

Along with the extensive lava plains and the massive shield volcanoes are many smaller volcanic landforms. Enormous numbers of small volcanic cones are distributed throughout the plains. Particularly unusual in appearance are so-called pancake domes, which are typically a few tens of kilometres in diameter and about 1 km (0.6 mile) high and are remarkably circular in shape. Flat-topped and steep-sided, they appear to have formed when a mass of thick lava was extruded from a central vent and spread outward for a short distance in all directions before solidifying. The lavas that formed such domes clearly were

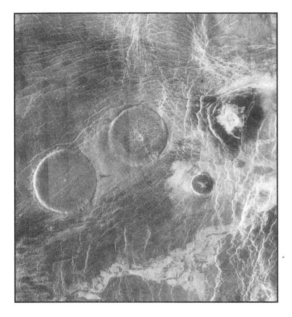

Volcanic pancake domes in the elevated region Eistla Regio on Venus, in a radar image produced from Magellan spacecraft data. The two larger domes, each about 65 km (40 miles) across, have broad flat tops less than 1 km (0.6 miles) high. They apparently were formed from unusually thick lava that oozed to the surface and spread in all directions. NASA

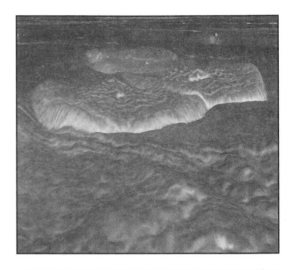

Merged pancake domes on the eastern edge of the Alpha Regio highland area of Venus, in an oblique view generated by computer from radar data gathered by the Magellan spacecraft. The volcanic features, each about 25 km (15 miles) in diameter and about 750 metres (0.5 mile) high, are thought to have been formed from the extrusion of extremely viscous lava onto the surface. The vertical scale of the image is exaggerated to bring out topological detail. NASA/JPL/Caltech

much more viscous than most lavas on Venus. Their composition is unknown, but—given the knowledge of lavas on Earth—they are likely to be much richer in silica than the basalts thought to predominate elsewhere on the planet.

Volcanic edifices are not uniformly distributed on Venus. Although they are common everywhere, they are particularly concentrated in the Beta-Atla-Themis region, between longitudes 180° and 300° E. This concentration may be the consequence of a broad active upwelling of the Venusian mantle in this area, which has led to enhanced heat flow and formation of magma reservoirs.

IMPACT CRATERS

The Venusian surface has been altered by objects from outside the planet as well as by forces from within. Impact craters dot the landscape, created by meteorites that passed through the atmosphere and struck the surface. Nearly all solid bodies in the solar system bear the scars of meteoritic impacts, with small craters typically being more common than large ones. This general tendency is encountered on Venus as well—craters a few hundred kilometres across are present but rare, while craters tens of kilometres in diameter and smaller are common.

Venus has an interesting limitation, however, in that craters smaller than about 1.5–2 km (1–1.2 miles) in diameter are not found. Their absence is attributable to the planet's dense atmosphere,

which causes intense frictional heating and strong aerodynamic forces as meteorites plunge through it at high velocities. The larger meteorites reach the surface intact, but the smaller ones are slowed and fragmented in the atmosphere. In fact, craters several kilometres in size— i.e., near the minimum size observed—tend not to be circular. Instead they have complex shapes, often with several irregular pits rather than a single central depression, which suggests that the impacting body broke up into a number of fragments that struck the surface individually. Radar images also show diffuse dark and bright "smudges" that may have resulted from the explosions of small meteorites above the surface.

The large craters that are seen on Venus are different in a number of respects from those observed on other planets. Most impact craters, on Venus and elsewhere, show ejecta around them. Venusian ejecta is unusual, however, in that its outer border commonly shows a lobed or flower-petal pattern, which suggests that much of it poured outward in a ground-hugging flow rather than arcing high above the ground ballistically and falling back to the surface. This behaviour was probably produced by dense atmospheric gases that became entrained in the flow and resulted in a turbulent cloud of gas and ejecta. Another peculiarity of large Venusian craters is the sinuous flows that have emerged from the ejecta, spreading outward from it just as lava flows would. These flows are apparently

A trio of impact craters in Lavinia Planitia, a lowland plain in the southern hemisphere of Venus, shown in a computer-generated image created from Magellan spacecraft radar data. Named (clockwise, from foreground) Saskia, Danilova, and Aglaonice, they range between about 40 and 60 km (25 and 40 miles) across and are of average size for the planet. The craters' surrounding ejecta blankets stand out as bright (and hence comparatively rough) terrain in the radar image. NASA/JPL

composed of rock that was melted by the high pressures and temperatures reached during the impact. The prevalence of these flow features on Venus must be due in large part to the planet's high surface temperature—rocks are closer to their melting temperature when craters form, which allows more melt to be produced than on other planets. For the same reason, the molten rock will remain fluid longer, which allows it to flow for significant distances.

Perhaps the strangest property of Venusian craters is one associated with some of the youngest. In addition to the normal ejecta, these craters are partially surrounded by huge parabola-shaped regions of dark material, a feature not found elsewhere in the solar system. In every case, the parabola opens to the west, and the crater is nestled within it, toward its eastern extremity. In radar images the dark materials tend to be smooth at small scales. It is likely that these parabolas are composed of deposits of fine-grained ejecta that was thrown upward during the impact event. Apparently the material rose above the Venusian atmosphere, fell back, and was picked up by the high-speed westward-blowing winds that encircle the planet. It was then carried far downwind from the impact site, eventually descending to the surface to form a parabola-shaped pattern.

For planets and moons that have impact craters, crater populations are an important source of information about the ages of the surfaces on which they lie. The concept is simple in principle—on a given body older surfaces have more craters than do younger ones. Determining an absolute age in years is difficult, however, and requires knowledge about the rate of crater formation, which usually

Adivar Crater on Venus, in a radar image from the Magellan spacecraft. About 30 km (20 miles) in diameter, the impact scar is surrounded by ejected material in the flower-petal pattern characteristic of Venus's larger craters. Unusual, however, is the much larger region affected by the impact, which includes materials, bright in radar images, distributed mostly to the west (left) of the crater and a surrounding radar-dark westward-opening parabolic border. NASA/JPL

must be inferred indirectly. The absolute ages of materials on the surface of Venus are not known, but the overall density of craters on Venus is lower than on many other bodies in the solar system. Estimates vary, but the average age of materials on Venus is almost certainly less than one billion years and may in fact be substantially less.

The spatial distribution of craters on Venus is essentially random. If craters were clustered in distinct regions, scientists could infer that a wide range of surface ages was represented over the planet. With a near-random global crater distribution, however, they are led instead to the conclusion that essentially the entire planet has been geologically resurfaced in the last billion years or less and that much of the resurfacing took place in a comparatively brief time.

INTERIOR STRUCTURE AND GEOLOGIC EVOLUTION

Much less is known about the interior of Venus than about its surface and atmosphere. Nevertheless, because the planet is much like Earth in overall size and density and because it presumably accreted from similar materials, scientists expect that it evolved at least a crudely similar internal state. Therefore, it probably has a core of metal, a mantle of dense rock, and a crust of less-dense rock. The core, like that of Earth, is probably composed primarily of iron and nickel, although Venus's somewhat lower density may indicate that its core also

contains some other, less dense material such as sulfur. Because no intrinsic magnetic field has been detected for Venus, there is no direct evidence for a metallic core, as there is for Earth. Calculations of Venus's internal structure suggest that the outer boundary of the core lies a little more than 3,000 km (1,860 miles) from the centre of the planet.

Above the core and below the crust lies Venus's mantle, making up the bulk of the planet's volume. Despite the high surface temperatures, temperatures within the mantle are likely similar to those in Earth's mantle. Even though a planetary mantle is composed of solid rock, the material there can slowly creep or flow, just as glacial ice does, allowing sweeping convective motions to take place. Convection is a great equalizer of the temperatures of planetary interiors. Similar to heat production within Earth, heat within Venus is thought to be generated by the decay of natural radioactive materials. This heat is transported to the surface by convection. If temperatures deep within Venus were substantially higher than those within Earth, the viscosity of the rocks in the mantle would drop sharply, speeding convection and removing the heat more rapidly. Therefore, the deep interiors of Venus and Earth are not expected to differ dramatically in temperature.

Convective motions in a planet's mantle can cause materials near the surface to experience stress, and motions in the Venusian mantle may be largely responsible for the tectonic deformation observed in radar images. On Venus the gravity field is found to correlate more strongly with topography over broad regional scales than it is on Earth—i.e., large regions where the topography is higher than the mean elevation on Venus also tend to be regions where the measured gravity is higher than average. This implies that much of the increased mass associated with the elevated topography is not offset by a compensating deficit of mass in the underlying crust that supports it (so-called low-density roots), as it is on Earth. Instead, some of the broad-scale relief on Venus may owe its origin directly to present-day convective motions in the mantle. Raised topography, such as Beta Regio, could lie above regions of mantle upwelling, whereas lowered topography, such as Lavinia Planitia, could lie above regions of mantle downwelling.

Despite the many overall similarities between Venus and Earth, the geologic evolution of the two planets has been strikingly different. Evidence suggests that the process of plate tectonics does not now operate on Venus. Although deformation of the lithosphere does indeed seem to be driven by mantle motions, lithospheric plates do not move mainly horizontally relative to each other, as they do on Earth. Instead, motions are mostly vertical, with the lithosphere warping up and down in response to the underlying convective motions. Volcanism, coronae, and rifts tend to be concentrated in regions of upwelling, while plains deformation belts are concentrated in regions

of downwelling. The formation of rugged uplands such as Aphrodite and Ishtar is not as well understood, but the mechanism probably involves some kind of local crustal thickening in response to mantle motions.

The lack of plate tectonics on Venus may be due in part to the planet's high surface temperature, which makes the upper rigid layer of the planet—the lithosphere—more buoyant and hence more resistant to subduction than Earth's lithosphere, other factors being equal. Interestingly, there is evidence that the Venusian lithosphere may be thicker than Earth's and that it has thickened with time. A gradual, long-term thickening of Venus's lithosphere in fact could be related to the curious conclusion drawn from Venus's cratering record—that most of the planet underwent a brief but intense period of geologic resurfacing less than a billion years ago. One possible explanation is that Venus may experience episodic global overturns of its mantle, in which an initially thin lithosphere slowly thickens until it founders on a near-global scale, triggering a brief, massive geologic resurfacing event. How many times this may have occurred during the planet's history and when it may happen again are unknown.

OBSERVATIONS FROM EARTH

Since Galileo's discovery of Venus's phases, the planet has been studied in detail, using Earth-based telescopes, radar, and other instruments. Over the centuries telescopic observers, including Gian Domenico Cassini of France and William Herschel of England, have reported a variety of faint markings on its disk. Some of these markings may have corresponded to the cloud features observed in modern times in ultraviolet light, while others may have been illusory. Important early telescopic observations of Venus were conducted in the 1700s during the planet's solar transits. In a solar transit an object passes directly between the Sun and Earth and is silhouetted briefly against the Sun's disk. Transits of Venus are rare events, occurring in pairs eight years apart with more than a century between pairs. They were extremely important events to 18th-century astronomy, since they provided the most accurate method known at that time for determining the distance between Earth and the Sun. (This distance, known as the astronomical unit, is one of the fundamental units of astronomy.) Observations of the 1761 transit were only partially successful but did result in the first suggestion, by the Russian scientist Mikhail V. Lomonosov, that Venus has an atmosphere.

The second transit of the pair, in 1769, was observed with somewhat greater success. Transits must be viewed from many points on Earth to yield accurate distances, and the transits of 1761 and, particularly, 1769 prompted the launching of many scientific expeditions to remote parts of the globe. Among these was the first of the three voyages of exploration by the British naval officer James Cook, who, with scientists from the Royal

Society, observed the 1769 transit from Tahiti. The transit observations of the 1700s not only gave an improved value for the astronomical unit but also provided the impetus for many unrelated but important discoveries concerning Earth's geography.

By the time the subsequent pair of transits occurred, in 1874 and 1882, the nascent field of celestial photography had advanced enough to allow scientists to record on glass plates what they saw through their telescopes. No transits took place in the 20th century; the first of the next pair was widely observed and imaged in 2004.

In the modern era Venus has also been observed at wavelengths outside the visible spectrum. The cloud features were discovered with certainty in 1927–28 in ultraviolet photographs. The first studies of the infrared spectrum of Venus, in 1932, showed that its atmosphere is composed primarily of carbon dioxide. Subsequent infrared observations revealed further details about the composition of both the atmosphere and the clouds. Observations in the microwave portion of the spectrum, beginning in earnest in the late 1950s and early '60s, provided the first evidence of the extremely high surface temperatures on the planet and prompted the study of the greenhouse effect as a means of producing these temperatures.

After finding that Venus is completely enshrouded by clouds, astronomers turned to other techniques to study its surface. Foremost among these has been radar. If equipped with an appropriate transmitter, a large radio telescope can be used as a radar system to bounce a radio signal off a planet and detect its return. Because radio wavelengths penetrate the thick Venusian atmosphere, the technique is an effective means of probing the planet's surface.

Earth-based radar observations have been conducted primarily from Arecibo Observatory in the mountains of Puerto Rico, the Goldstone tracking station complex in the desert of southern California, and Haystack Observatory in Massachusetts. The first successful radar observations of Venus took place at Goldstone and Haystack in 1961 and revealed the planet's slow rotation. Subsequent observations determined the rotation properties more precisely and began to unveil some of the major features on the planet's surface. The first features to be observed were dubbed Alpha Regio, Beta Regio, and Maxwell Montes.

By the mid-1980s Earth-based radar technology had advanced such that images from Arecibo were revealing surface features as small as a few kilometres in size. Nevertheless, because Venus always presents nearly the same face toward Earth when the planets are at their closest, much of the surface went virtually unobserved from Earth.

SPACECRAFT EXPLORATION

The greatest advances in the study of Venus were achieved through the use of robotic spacecraft. The first spacecraft to reach the vicinity of another planet and return data was the U.S. Mariner 2 in its flyby of Venus in 1962. Since then, Venus has been the target of more than 20 spacecraft missions.

Successful early Venus missions undertaken by the United States involved Mariner 2, Mariner 5 (1967), and Mariner 10 (1974). Each spacecraft made a single

Descent capsule of the Soviet Venera 4 spacecraft prior to its launch to Venus on June 12, 1967. Tass/Sovfoto

close flyby, providing successively improved scientific data in accord with concurrent advances in spacecraft and instrument technology. After visiting Venus, Mariner 10 went on to a successful series of flybys of Mercury. In 1978 the United States launched the Pioneer Venus mission, comprising two complementary spacecraft. The Orbiter went into orbit around the planet, while the Multiprobe released four entry probes—one large probe and three smaller ones—that were targeted to widely separated points in the Venusian atmosphere to collect data on atmospheric structure and composition. The Orbiter carried 17 scientific instruments, most of them focused on study of the planet's atmosphere, ionosphere, and interaction with the solar wind. Its radar altimeter provided the first high-quality map of Venus's surface topography. Pioneer Venus Orbiter was one of the longest-lived planetary spacecraft, returning data for more than 14 years.

Venus was also a major target of the Soviet Union's planetary exploration program during the 1960s, '70s, and '80s, which achieved several spectacular successes. After an early sequence of failed missions, in 1967 Soviet scientists launched Venera 4, comprising a flyby spacecraft as well as a probe that entered the planet's atmosphere. Equipped with a parachute and several instruments for measuring atmospheric temperature, pressure, and density, it reached its destination on October 18, becoming the first

human-made object to travel through the atmosphere of another planet and return data to Earth.

Highlights of subsequent missions included the first successful soft landing on another planet (Venera 7 in 1970), the first images returned from the surface of another planet (Venera 9 and 10 landers in 1975), and the first spacecraft placed in orbit around Venus (Venera 9 and 10 orbiters).

In terms of the advances they provided in the global understanding of Venus, the most important Soviet missions were Veneras 15 and 16 in 1983. The twin orbiters carried the first radar systems flown to another planet that were capable of producing high-quality images of the surface. They produced a map of the northern quarter of Venus with a resolution of 1–2 km (0.6–1.2 miles), and many types of geologic features now known to exist on the planet were either discovered or first observed in detail in the Venera 15 and 16 data. Late the following year the Soviet Union launched two more spacecraft to Venus, Vegas 1 and 2. These delivered Venera-style landers and dropped off two balloons in the Venusian atmosphere, each of which survived for about two days and transmitted data from their float altitudes in the middle cloud layer. The Vega spacecraft themselves continued past Venus to conduct successful flybys of Halley's Comet in 1986.

The most ambitious mission yet to Venus, the U.S. Magellan spacecraft, was launched in 1989 and the next year

Magellan spacecraft and attached Inertial Upper Stage (IUS) rocket being released into a temporary Earth orbit from the payload bay of the space shuttle orbiter Atlantis *on May 4, 1989. Shortly afterward, the IUS propelled the spacecraft on a Sun-looping trajectory toward Venus, where it arrived on Aug. 10, 1990.* NASA/JPL

entered orbit around the planet, where it conducted observations until late 1994. Magellan carried a radar system capable of producing images with a resolution better than 100 metres (330 feet). Because the orbit was nearly polar, the spacecraft was able to view essentially all latitudes on the planet. On each orbit the radar system obtained an image strip about 20 km (12 miles) wide and typically more than 16,000 km (almost 10,000 miles) long, extending nearly from pole to pole. The image strips were assembled into mosaics, and high-quality radar images of about 98 percent of the planet were ultimately produced. Magellan also carried a radar altimeter system that measured the planet's surface topography as well as some properties of its surface materials. After the main radar objectives of the mission were completed, the spacecraft's orbit was modified slightly so that it passed repeatedly through the upper fringes of the Venusian atmosphere. The resulting drag on the spacecraft gradually removed energy from its orbit, turning an initially elliptical orbit into a low, circular one. This procedure, known as aerobraking, has since been used on other planetary missions to conserve large amounts of fuel by reducing the use of thrusters for orbital reshaping. From its new circular orbit, the Magellan spacecraft was able to make the first detailed map of Venus's gravitational field.

In 1990, on its way to Jupiter, the U.S. Galileo spacecraft flew by Venus. Among its more notable observations were images at near-infrared wavelengths that viewed deep into the atmosphere and showed the highly variable opacity of the main cloud deck.

The U.S. Cassini-Huygens spacecraft flew by Venus twice, in 1998 and 1999, on the way to its primary target, Saturn.

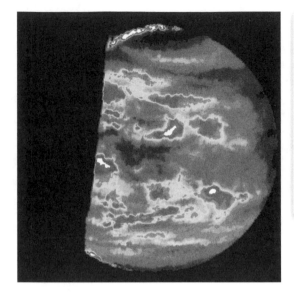

Deep-level clouds on the nightside of Venus, from an image made by the Galileo spacecraft during its gravity-assisted flyby of the planet in February 1990. In a view that penetrates 10–16 km (6–10 miles) below the cloud surface visible to the human eye, the image shows the relative transparency of the sulfuric acid cloud deck to the radiant heat emanating from the much warmer underlying lower atmosphere. NASA/JPL

During its brief passages near Venus, Cassini failed to corroborate signs of the existence of lightning in the planet's atmosphere that had been observed by previous spacecraft. This suggested to some scientists that lightning on Venus is either rare or different from the lightning that occurs on Earth.

The European Space Agency's Venus Express, which was launched in 2005, entered into orbit around Venus the following year, becoming the first European spacecraft to visit the planet. Venus Express carried a camera, a visible-light and infrared imaging spectrometer, and other instruments to study Venus's magnetic field, plasma environment, atmosphere, and surface for a planned mission of more than two Venusian years. Among its early accomplishments was the return of the first images of cloud structures over the planet's south pole.

CHAPTER 5

EARTH

Our planet, Earth, is the third from the Sun and the fifth largest in the solar system in terms of size and mass. Its single most outstanding feature is that its near-surface environments are the only places in the universe known to harbour life. It is designated by the symbol ⊕. Earth's name in English, the international language of astronomy, derives from Old English and Germanic words for *ground* and *earth*, and it is the only name for a planet of the solar system that does not come from Greco-Roman mythology.

Since the Copernican revolution of the 16th century, at which time the Polish astronomer Nicolaus Copernicus proposed a Sun-centred model of the universe, enlightened thinkers have regarded Earth as a planet like the others of the solar system. Concurrent sea voyages provided practical proof that Earth is a globe, just as Galileo's use of his newly invented telescope in the early 17th century soon showed various other planets to be globes as well. It was only after the dawn of the space age, however, when photographs from rockets and orbiting spacecraft first captured the dramatic curvature of Earth's horizon, that the conception of Earth as a roughly spherical planet rather than as a flat entity was verified by direct human observation. Humans first witnessed Earth as a complete orb floating in the inky blackness of space in December 1968 when Apollo 8 carried astronauts around the Moon. Robotic space probes on their way to destinations beyond Earth, such as the Galileo and the Near Earth

The planet Earth, as photographed from the Galileo spacecraft during its December 1990 flyby en route to Jupiter. The predominance of water on Earth is apparent, both as ocean and in the form of swirling clouds. The landmass at centre right is Australia, and the bright white patch at the bottom is the South Polar ice cap covering Antarctica. NASA/JPL

Asteroid Rendezvous (NEAR) spacecraft in the 1990s, also looked back with their cameras to provide other unique portraits of the planet.

Viewed from another planet in the solar system, Earth would appear bright and bluish in colour. Easiest to see through a large telescope would be its atmospheric features, chiefly the swirling white cloud patterns of midlatitude and tropical storms, ranged in roughly latitudinal belts around the planet. The polar regions also would appear a brilliant white, because of the clouds above and the snow and ice below. Beneath the changing patterns of clouds would appear the much darker blue-black oceans, interrupted by occasional tawny patches of desert lands. The green landscapes that harbour most human life would not be easily seen from space. Not only do they constitute a modest fraction of the land area, which itself is less than one-third of Earth's surface, but they are often obscured by clouds. Over the course of the seasons, some changes in the storm patterns and cloud belts on Earth would be observed. Also prominent would be the growth and recession of the winter snowcap across land areas of the Northern Hemisphere.

Scientists have applied the full battery of modern instrumentation to studying Earth in ways that have not yet been possible for the other planets; thus, much more is known about its structure and composition. This detailed knowledge, in turn, provides deeper insight into the mechanisms by which planets in general cool down, by which their magnetic fields are generated, and by which the separation of lighter elements from heavier ones as planets develop their internal structure releases additional energy for geologic processes and alters crustal compositions.

It is convenient to consider separate parts of Earth in terms of concentric, roughly spherical layers. Extending from the interior outward, these are the core, the mantle, the crust (including the rocky surface), the hydrosphere (predominantly the oceans, which fill in low places in the crust), the atmosphere (itself divided into spherical zones such as the troposphere, where weather occurs, and the stratosphere, where lies the ozone layer that shields Earth's surface and its organisms against the Sun's ultraviolet rays), and the magnetosphere (an enormous region in space where Earth's magnetic field dominates the behaviour of electrically charged particles coming from the Sun).

BASIC PLANETARY DATA

The mean distance of Earth from the Sun is about 150 million km (93 million miles). The planet orbits the Sun in a path that is presently more nearly a circle (less eccentric) than are the orbits of all but two of the other planets, Venus and Neptune. Earth makes one revolution, or one complete orbit of the Sun, in about 365.25 days. The direction of

THE ASTRONOMICAL UNIT

Astronomers studying the solar system use a unit of length, the astronomical unit (AU), that provides a convenient way to express and relate distances of objects in the solar system and to carry out various astronomical calculations. The astronomical unit is effectively equal to the average, or mean, distance between Earth and the Sun. Alternately, it can be considered the length of the semimajor axis—i.e., the length of half of the maximum diameter—of Earth's elliptical orbit around the Sun. An astronomical constant is defined in terms of a form of Kepler's third law of planetary motion and has a value of 149,597,870 km (92,955,808 miles). Thus, stating that the planet Jupiter is 5.2 AU (5.2 Earth distances) from the Sun and that Pluto is nearly 40 AU gives ready comparisons of the distances of all three bodies.

In principle, the easiest way to determine the value of the astronomical unit would be to measure the Earth-Sun distance directly by means of the parallax method. In this approach, two observers stationed at the ends of a long, accurately known baseline—ideally, a baseline as long as Earth's diameter—would simultaneously record the position of the Sun against the essentially motionless background of the distant stars. Comparison of the observations would reveal an apparent shift, or angular (parallax) displacement, of the Sun against the remote stars. A simple trigonometric relationship incorporating this angular value and the baseline length then could be used to find the Earth-Sun distance. In practice, however, the method cannot be applied, because the Sun's intense glare blots out the background stars needed for the parallax measurement.

By the 17th century, astronomers understood the geometry of the solar system and the motion of the planets well enough to develop a proportional model of objects in orbit around the Sun, a model that was independent of a particular scale. To establish the scale for all orbits and to determine the astronomical unit, all that was needed was an accurate measurement of the distance between any two objects at a given instant. In 1672 the Italian-born French astronomer Gian Domenico Cassini made a reasonably close estimate of the astronomical unit based on a determination of the parallax displacement of the planet Mars—and thus its distance to Earth. Later efforts made use of widely separated observations of the transit of Venus across the Sun's disk to measure the distance between Venus and Earth. In 1932, determination of the parallax displacement of the asteroid Eros as it made a close approach to Earth yielded what was at the time a very precise value for the astronomical unit. Since the mid-20th century, astronomers have further refined their knowledge of the dimensions of the solar system and the value of the astronomical unit through a combination of radar ranging of Mercury, Venus, and Mars; laser ranging of the Moon (making use of light reflectors left on the lunar surface by Apollo astronauts); and timing of signals returned from spacecraft as they orbit or make close passes of objects in the solar system.

revolution—counterclockwise as viewed down from the north—is in the same sense, or direction, as the rotation of the Sun; Earth's spin, or rotation about its axis, is also in the same sense, which is called direct or prograde. The rotation period, or length of a sidereal day—23 hours, 56 minutes, and 4 sec—is similar to that of Mars. The 23.5° tilt, or inclination, of Earth's axis to its orbital plane, also typical, results in greater heating and more hours of daylight in one hemisphere or the other over the course of a year and so is responsible for the cyclic change of seasons.

With an equatorial radius of 6,378 km (3,963 miles), Earth is the largest of the four inner, terrestrial (rocky) planets, but it is considerably smaller than the gas giants of the outer solar system. Earth has a single satellite, the Moon, which orbits the planet at a mean distance of about 384,400 km (238,900 miles). The Moon is one of the bigger natural satellites in the solar system; only the giant planets have moons comparable or larger in size. Some planetary astronomers consider the Earth-Moon system a double planet, with some similarity in that regard to the dwarf planet Pluto and its largest moon, Charon.

Earth's gravitational field is manifested as the attractive force acting on a free body at rest, causing it to accelerate in the general direction of the centre of the planet. Departures from the spherical shape and the effect of Earth's rotation cause gravity to vary with latitude over the terrestrial surface. The average gravitational acceleration at sea level is about 980 cm/sec^2 (32.2 feet/sec^2).

Earth's gravity keeps the Moon in its orbit around the planet and also generates tides in the solid body of the Moon. Such deformations are manifested in the form of slight bulges at the lunar surface, detectable only by sensitive instruments. In turn, the Moon's mass—relatively large for a natural satellite—exerts a gravitational force that causes tides on Earth. The Sun, much more distant but vastly more massive, also raises tides on Earth. The tides are most apparent during the daily rise and fall of the ocean water, although tidal deformations occur in the solid Earth and in the atmosphere as well. The movement of the water throughout the ocean basins as a result of the tides (as well as, to a lesser extent, the tidal distortion of the solid Earth) dissipates orbital kinetic energy as heat, producing a gradual slowing of Earth's rotation and a spiraling outward of the Moon's orbit. Currently this slowing lengthens the day by a few thousandths of a second per century, but the rate of slowing varies with time as plate tectonics and sea-level changes alter the areas covered by inland bays and shallow seas. (For additional orbital and physical data, see the table.)

Blankets of volatile gases and liquids near and above the surface of Earth are, along with solar energy, of prime importance to the sustenance of life on Earth. They are distributed and recycled

PLANETARY DATA FOR EARTH	
mean distance from Sun	149,600,000 km (1.0 AU)
eccentricity of orbit	0.0167
inclination of orbit to ecliptic	0.000°
Earth year (sidereal period of revolution)	365.256 days
mean orbital velocity	29.79 km/sec
equatorial radius	6,378.14 km
polar radius	6,356.78 km
surface area	510,066,000 km²
mass	5.976×10^{24} kg
mean density	5.52 g/cm³
mean surface gravity	980 cm/sec²
escape velocity	11.2 km/sec
rotation period (Earth sidereal day)	23.9345 hr (23 hr 56 min 4 sec) of mean solar time
Earth mean solar day	24.0657 hr (24 hr 3 min 57 sec) of mean sidereal time
inclination of Equator to orbit	23.45°
magnetic field strength at Equator	0.3 gauss (but weakening)
dipole moment	7.9×10^{25} gauss/cm³
tilt angle of magnetic axis	11.5°
atmospheric composition (by volume)	molecular nitrogen, 78%; molecular oxygen, 21%; argon, 0.93%; carbon dioxide, 0.037% (presently rising); water, about 1% (variable)
mean surface pressure	1 bar
mean surface temperature	288 K (59 °F, 15 °C)
number of known moons	1 (the Moon)

throughout the atmosphere and hydro-sphere of the planet.

THE ATMOSPHERE

Earth is surrounded by a relatively thin atmosphere (commonly called air) con-sisting of a mixture of gases, primarily molecular nitrogen (78 percent) and molecular oxygen (21 percent). Also pres-ent are much smaller amounts of gases such as argon (nearly 1 percent), water vapour (averaging 1 percent but highly variable in time and location), carbon dioxide (0.037 percent [370 parts per mil-lion] and presently rising), methane (0.00015 percent [1.5 parts per million]), and others, along with minute solid and liquid particles in suspension.

Because Earth has a weak gravitational field (by virtue of its size) and warm atmo-spheric temperatures (due to its proximity to the Sun) compared with the giant plan-ets, it lacks the most common gases in the universe that they possess: hydrogen and helium. Whereas both the Sun and Jupiter are composed predominantly of these two elements, they could not be retained long on early Earth and rapidly evaporated into interplanetary space. The high oxygen content of Earth's atmosphere is out of the ordinary. Oxygen is a highly reactive gas that, under most planetary conditions, would be combined with other chemicals in the atmosphere, surface, and crust. It is in fact supplied continuously by biological processes; without life, there would be vir-tually no free oxygen. The 1.5 parts per

million of methane in the atmosphere is also far out of chemical equilibrium with the atmosphere and crust: it, too, is of bio-logical origin, with the contribution by human activities far outweighing others.

The gases of the atmosphere extend from the surface of Earth to heights of thousands of kilometres, eventually merg-ing with the solar wind—a stream of charged particles that flows outward from the outermost regions of the Sun. The composition of the atmosphere is more or less constant with height to an altitude of about 100 km (60 miles), with particular exceptions being water vapour and ozone.

The atmosphere is commonly described in terms of distinct layers, or regions. Most of the atmosphere is con-centrated in the troposphere, which extends from the surface to an altitude of about 10–15 km (6–9 miles), depending on latitude and season. The behaviour of the gases in this layer is controlled by convection. This process involves the tur-bulent, overturning motions resulting from buoyancy of near-surface air that is warmed by the Sun. Convection main-tains a decreasing vertical temperature gradient—i.e., a temperature decline with altitude—of roughly 6 °C (10.8 °F) per km through the troposphere. At the top of the troposphere, which is called the tropo-pause, temperatures have fallen to about –80 °C (–112 °F). The troposphere is the region where nearly all water vapour exists and essentially all weather occurs.

The dry, tenuous stratosphere lies above the troposphere and extends to an altitude of about 50 km (30 miles). Convective motions are weak or absent in the stratosphere; motions instead tend to be horizontally oriented. The temperature in this layer increases with altitude. In the upper stratospheric regions, absorption of ultraviolet light from the Sun breaks down molecular oxygen (O_2); recombination of single oxygen atoms with O_2 molecules into ozone (O_3) creates the shielding ozone layer.

Above the relatively warm stratopause is the even more tenuous mesosphere, in which temperatures again decline with altitude to 80–90 km (50–56 miles) above the surface, where the mesopause is defined. The minimum temperature attained there is extremely variable with season. Temperatures then rise with increasing height through the overlying layer known as the thermosphere. Also above about 80–90 km there is an increasing fraction of charged, or ionized, particles, which from this altitude upward defines the ionosphere. Spectacular visible auroras are generated in this region, particularly along approximately circular zones around the poles, by the interaction of nitrogen and oxygen atoms in the atmosphere with episodic bursts of energetic particles originating from the Sun.

Earth's general atmospheric circulation is driven by the energy of sunlight, which is more abundant in equatorial latitudes. Movement of this heat toward the poles is strongly affected by Earth's rapid rotation and the associated Coriolis force at latitudes away from the equator (which adds an east-west component to the direction of the winds), resulting in multiple cells of circulating air in each hemisphere. Instabilities (perturbations in the atmospheric flow that grow with time) produce the characteristic high-pressure areas and low-pressure storms of the midlatitudes as well as the fast, eastward-moving jet streams of the upper troposphere that guide the paths of storms. The oceans are massive reservoirs of heat that act largely to smooth out variations in Earth's global temperatures, but their slowly changing currents and temperatures also influence weather and climate, as in the El Niño/Southern Oscillation weather phenomenon.

Earth's atmosphere is not a static feature of the environment. Rather its composition has evolved over geologic time in concert with life and is changing more rapidly today in response to human activities. Roughly halfway through the history of Earth, the atmosphere's unusually high abundance of free oxygen began to develop, through photosynthesis by blue-green algae (also known as cyanobacteria) and saturation of natural surface sinks of oxygen (e.g., relatively oxygen-poor minerals and hydrogen-rich gases exuded from volcanoes). Accumulation of oxygen made it possible for complex cells, which consume oxygen during metabolism and of which all plants and animals are composed, to develop.

Earth's climate at any location varies with the seasons, but there are also longer-term variations in global climate. Volcanic explosions, such as the 1991 eruption of Mount Pinatubo in the Philippines, can inject great quantities of dust particles into the stratosphere, which remain suspended for years, decreasing atmospheric transparency and resulting in measurable cooling worldwide. Much rarer, giant impacts of asteroids and comets can produce even more profound effects, including severe reductions in sunlight for months or years, such as many scientists believe led to the mass extinction of living species at the end of the Cretaceous period, 65 million years ago. The dominant climate variations observed in the recent geologic record are the ice ages, which are linked to variations in Earth's tilt and its orbital geometry with respect to the Sun.

The physics of hydrogen fusion leads astronomers to conclude that the Sun was 30 percent less luminous during the earliest history of Earth than it is today. Hence, all else being equal, the oceans should have been frozen. Observations of Earth's planetary neighbours, Mars and Venus, and estimates of the carbon locked in Earth's crust at present suggest that there was much more carbon dioxide in Earth's atmosphere during earlier periods. This would have enhanced warming of the surface via the greenhouse effect and so allowed the oceans to remain liquid.

Today there is 100,000 times more carbon dioxide buried in carbonate rocks in Earth's crust than in the atmosphere, in sharp contrast to Venus, whose atmospheric evolution followed a different course. On Earth, the formation of carbonate shells by marine life is the principal mechanism for transforming carbon dioxide to carbonates; abiotic processes involving liquid water also produce carbonates, albeit more slowly. On Venus, however, life never had the chance to arise and to generate carbonates. Because of the planet's location in the solar system, early Venus received 10–20 percent more sunlight than falls on Earth even today, despite the fainter young Sun at the time. Most planetary scientists believe that the elevated surface temperature that resulted kept water from condensing to a liquid. Instead, it remained in the atmosphere as water vapour, which, like carbon dioxide, is an efficient greenhouse gas. Together the two gases caused surface temperatures to rise even higher so that massive amounts of water escaped to the stratosphere, where it was dissociated by solar ultraviolet radiation. With conditions now too hot and dry to permit abiotic carbonate formation, most or all of the planet's inventory of carbon remained in the atmosphere as carbon dioxide. Models predict that Earth may suffer the same fate in a billion years, when the Sun exceeds its present brightness by 10 to 20 percent.

Between the late 1950s and the end of the 20th century, the amount of carbon dioxide in Earth's atmosphere increased by more than 15 percent because of the burning of fossil fuels (e.g., coal, oil, and natural gas) and the destruction of tropical rain forests, such as that of the Amazon River basin. Computer models predict that a net doubling of carbon dioxide by the middle of the 21st century could lead to a global warming of 1.5–4.5 °C (2.7–8.1 °F) averaged over the planet, which would have profound effects on sea level and agriculture. Although this conclusion has been criticized by some on the basis that the warming observed so far has not kept pace with the projection, analyses of ocean temperature data have suggested that much of the warming during the 20th century actually occurred in the oceans themselves—and will eventually appear in the atmosphere.

Another present concern regarding the atmosphere is the impact of human activities on the stratospheric ozone layer. Complex chemical reactions involving traces of man-made chlorofluorocarbons (CFCs) were found in the mid-1980s to be creating temporary holes in the ozone layer, particularly over Antarctica, during polar spring. Yet more disturbing was the discovery of a growing depletion of ozone over the highly populated temperate latitudes, since the short-wavelength ultraviolet radiation that the ozone layer effectively absorbs has been found to cause skin cancer. International agreements in place to halt the production of the most egregious ozone-destroying CFCs will eventually halt and reverse the depletion, but only by the middle of the 21st century, because of the long residence time of these chemicals in the stratosphere.

THE HYDROSPHERE

Earth's hydrosphere is a discontinuous layer of water at or near the planet's surface; it includes all liquid and frozen surface waters, groundwater held in soil and rock, and atmospheric water vapour. Unique within the solar system, the hydrosphere is essential to all life as it is presently understood. Almost 71 percent of Earth's surface is covered by saltwater oceans, with a volume of about 1.4 billion cubic km (336 million cubic miles) and an average temperature of about 4 °C (39.2 °F), not far above the freezing point of water.

The oceans contain about 97 percent of the planet's water volume. The remainder occurs as freshwater, three-quarters of which is locked up in the form of ice at polar latitudes. Most of the remaining freshwater is groundwater held in soils and rocks; less than 1 percent of it occurs in lakes and rivers. In terms of percentage, atmospheric water vapour is negligible, but the transport of water evaporated from the oceans onto land surfaces is an integral part of the hydrologic cycle that renews and sustains life.

The hydrologic cycle involves the transfer of water from the oceans through the atmosphere to the continents and back to the oceans over and beneath the land surface. The cycle includes processes such as precipitation, evaporation, transpiration, infiltration, percolation, and runoff. These processes operate throughout the entire hydrosphere, which extends from about 15 km (9 miles) into the atmosphere to roughly 5 km (3 miles) into the crust.

About one-third of the solar energy that reaches Earth's surface is expended on evaporating ocean water. The resulting atmospheric moisture and humidity condense into clouds, rain, snow, and dew. Moisture is a crucial factor in determining weather. It is the driving force behind storms and is responsible for separating electrical charge, which is the cause of lightning and thus of natural wildland fires, which have an important role in some ecosystems. Moisture wets the land, replenishes subterranean aquifers, chemically weathers the rocks, erodes the landscape, nourishes life, and fills the rivers, which carry dissolved chemicals and sediments back into the oceans.

Water also plays a vital role in the carbon dioxide cycle (a part of the more inclusive carbon cycle). Under the action of water and dissolved carbon dioxide, calcium is weathered from continental rocks and carried to the oceans, where it combines to form calcium carbonates (including shells of marine life). Eventually the carbonates are deposited on the seafloor and are lithified to form limestones. Some of these carbonate rocks are later dragged deep into Earth's interior by the global process of plate tectonics and melted, resulting in a rerelease of carbon dioxide (from volcanoes, for example) into the atmosphere. Cyclic processing of water, carbon dioxide, and oxygen through geologic and biological systems on Earth has been fundamental to maintaining the habitability of the planet with time and to shaping the erosion and weathering of the continents.

THE OUTER SHELL

Earth's outermost, rigid, rocky layer is called the crust. It is composed of low-density, easily melted rocks; the continental crust is predominantly granitic rock, while composition of the oceanic crust corresponds mainly to that of basalt and gabbro. Analyses of seismic waves, generated by earthquakes within Earth's interior, show that the crust extends about 50 km (30 miles) beneath the continents but only 5–10 km (3–6 miles) beneath the ocean floors

At the base of the crust, a sharp change in the observed behaviour of seismic waves marks the interface with the mantle. The mantle is composed of denser rocks, on which the rocks of the crust float. On geologic timescales, the mantle behaves as a very viscous fluid and responds to stress by flowing. Together the uppermost mantle and the crust act mechanically as a single rigid layer, called the lithosphere

The lithospheric outer shell of Earth is not one continuous piece but is broken, like a slightly cracked eggshell, into about a dozen major separate rigid blocks, or plates. There are two types of plates, oceanic and continental. An example of an oceanic plate is the Pacific Plate, which extends from the East Pacific Rise to the deep-sea trenches bordering the western part of the Pacific basin. A continental plate is exemplified by the North

American Plate, which includes North America as well as the oceanic crust between it and a portion of the Mid-Atlantic Ridge. The latter is an enormous submarine mountain chain that extends down the axis of the Atlantic basin, passing midway between Africa and North and South America.

The lithospheric plates are about 60 km (35 miles) thick beneath the oceans and 100–200 km (60–120 miles) beneath the continents. (It should be noted that these thicknesses are defined by the mechanical rigidity of the lithospheric material. They do not correspond to the thickness of the crust, which is defined at its base by the discontinuity in seismic wave behaviour, as cited above.) They ride on a weak, perhaps partially molten, layer of the upper mantle called the asthenosphere. Slow convection currents deep within the mantle generated by radioactive heating of the interior drive lateral movements of the plates (and the continents on top of them) at a rate of several centimetres per year. The plates interact along their margins, and these boundaries are classified into three general types on the basis of the relative motions of the adjacent plates: divergent, convergent, and transform (or strike-slip)

In areas of divergence, two plates move away from each other. Buoyant upwelling motions in the mantle force the plates apart at rift zones (such as along the middle of the Atlantic Ocean floor), where magmas from the underlying mantle rise to form new oceanic crustal rocks.

Lithospheric plates move toward each other along convergent boundaries. When a continental plate and an oceanic plate come together, the leading edge of the oceanic plate is forced beneath the continental plate and down into the asthenosphere—a process called subduction. Only the thinner, denser slabs of oceanic crust will subduct, however. When two thicker, more buoyant continents come together at convergent zones, they resist subduction and tend to buckle, producing great mountain ranges. The Himalayas, along with the adjacent Plateau of Tibet, were formed during such a continent-continent collision, when India was carried into the Eurasian Plate by relative motion of the Indian-Australian Plate.

At the third type of plate boundary, the transform variety, two plates slide parallel to one another in opposite directions. These areas are often associated with high seismicity, as stresses that build up in the sliding crustal slabs are released at intervals to generate earthquakes. The San Andreas Fault in California is an example of this type of boundary, which is also known as a fault or fracture zone.

Most of Earth's active tectonic processes, including nearly all earthquakes, occur near plate margins. Volcanoes form along zones of subduction, because the oceanic crust tends to be remelted as it descends into the hot mantle and then rises to the surface as lava. Chains of active, often explosive volcanoes are thus formed in such places as the western Pacific and the west coasts of the

Americas. Older mountain ranges, eroded by weathering and runoff, mark zones of earlier plate-margin activity. The oldest, most geologically stable parts of Earth are the central cores of some continents (such as Australia, parts of Africa, and northern North America). Called continental shields, they are regions where mountain building, faulting, and other tectonic processes are diminished compared with the activity that occurs at the boundaries between plates. Because of their stability, erosion has had the time to flatten the topography of continental shields. It is also on the shields that geologic evidence of crater scars from ancient impacts of asteroids and comets is better-preserved. Even there, however, tectonic processes and the action of water have erased many ancient features. In contrast, much of the oceanic crust is substantially younger (tens of millions of years old), and none dates back more than 200 million years.

This conceptual framework in which scientists now understand the evolution of Earth's lithosphere—termed plate tectonics—is almost universally accepted, although many details remain to be worked out. For example, scientists have yet to reach a general agreement as to when the original continental cores formed or how long ago modern plate-tectonic processes began to operate. Certainly the processes of internal convection, segregation of minerals by partial melting and recrystallization, and basaltic volcanism were operating more vigorously in the first billion years of

Earth's history, when the planet's interior was much hotter than it is today; nevertheless, how the surface landmasses were formed and were dispersed may have been different.

Once major continental shields grew, plate tectonics was characterized by the cyclic assembly and breakup of supercontinents created by the amalgamation of many smaller continental cores and island arcs. Scientists have identified two such cycles in the geologic record. A supercontinent began breaking up about 700 million years ago, in late Precambrian time, into several major continents, but by about 250 million years ago, near the beginning of the Triassic period, the continued drifting of these continents resulted in their fusion again into a single supercontinental landmass called Pangea. Some 70 million years later, Pangea began to fragment, gradually giving rise to today's continental configuration. The distribution is still asymmetric, with continents predominantly located in the Northern Hemisphere opposite the Pacific basin.

Startlingly, of the four terrestrial planets, only Earth shows evidence of long-term, pervasive plate tectonics. Both Venus and Mars exhibit geology dominated by basaltic volcanism on a largely immovable crust, with only faint hints of possibly limited episodes of horizontal plate motion. Mercury is intrinsically much denser than the other terrestrial planets, which implies a larger metallic core; its surface is mostly covered with impact craters, but it also shows a global pattern of scarps suggesting shrinkage of the planet, associated perhaps with interior cooling. Apparently essential to the kind of plate tectonics that occurs on Earth is large planetary size (hence, high heat flow and thin crust), which eliminates Mars, and pervasive crustal water to soften the rock, which Venus lost very early in its history. Although Earth is indeed geologically active and hence possesses a youthful surface, Venus's surface may have been completely renewed by global basaltic volcanism within the past billion years, and small portions of Mars's surface may have experienced very recent erosion from liquid water or landslides.

THE INTERIOR

More than 90 percent of Earth's mass is composed of iron, oxygen, silicon, and magnesium, elements that can form the crystalline minerals known as silicates. Nevertheless, in chemical and mineralogical composition, as in physical properties, Earth is far from homogeneous. Apart from the superficial lateral differences near the surface (i.e., in the compositions of the continental and oceanic crusts), Earth's principal differences vary with distance toward the centre. This is due to increasing temperatures and pressures and to the original segregation of materials, soon after Earth accreted from the solar nebula about 4.56 billion years ago, into a metal-rich core, a silicate-rich mantle, and the more highly refined crustal rocks. Earth is geochemically differentiated to a great extent. Crustal rocks contain several times as much of the rock-forming element aluminum as does the rest of the solid Earth and many dozens of times as much uranium. On the other hand, the crust, which accounts for a mere 0.4 percent of Earth's mass, contains less than 0.1 percent of its iron. Between 85 and 90 percent of Earth's iron is concentrated in the core.

The increasing pressure with depth causes phase changes in crustal rocks at depths between 5 and 50 km (3 and 30 miles), which marks the top of the upper mantle, as mentioned above. This transition area is called the Mohorovičić discontinuity, or Moho. Most basaltic magmas are generated in the upper mantle at depths of hundreds of kilometres. The upper mantle, which is rich in the olivine, pyroxene, and silicate perovskite minerals, shows significant lateral differences in composition. A large fraction of Earth's interior, from a depth of about 650 km (400 miles) down to 2,900 km (1,800 miles), consists of the lower mantle, which is composed chiefly of magnesium- and iron-bearing silicates, including the high-pressure equivalents of olivine and pyroxene.

The mantle is not static but rather churns slowly in convective motions, with hotter material rising up and cooler material sinking; through this process, Earth gradually loses its internal heat. In addition to being the driving force of horizontal plate motion, mantle convection is manifested in the occurrence of temporary superplumes—huge, rising jets of hot, partially molten rock—which may originate from a deep layer near the core-mantle interface. Much larger than ordinary thermal plumes, such as that associated with the Hawaiian island chain in the central Pacific, superplumes may have had profound effects on Earth's geologic history and even on its climate. One outburst of global volcanism about 65 million years ago, which created the vast flood basalt deposits known as the Deccan Traps on the Indian subcontinent, may have been associated with a superplume, though this model is far from universally accepted.

With a radius of almost 3,500 km (2,200 miles), Earth's core is about the size of the entire planet Mars. About one-third of Earth's mass is contained in the core, most of which is liquid iron alloyed with some lighter, cosmically abundant components (e.g., sulfur, oxygen, and, controversially, even hydrogen). Its liquid nature is revealed by the failure of shear-type seismic waves to penetrate the core. A small, central part of the core, however, below a depth of about 5,100 km (3,200 miles), is solid. Temperatures in the core are extremely hot, ranging from 4,000–5,000 K (roughly 3,700–4,700 °C, or 6,700–8,500 °F) at the outer part of the core to 5,000–7,000 K (4,700–6,700 °C, or 8,500–12,100 °F) in the centre, comparable to the surface of the Sun. Large uncertainties in temperature arise from questions as to which compounds form alloys with

iron in the core, and more recent data favour the lower end of the temperature estimates for the inner core.

The core's reservoir of heat may contribute as much as one-fifth of all the internal heat that ultimately flows to the surface of Earth. The basic structure of Earth—crust, mantle, and core—appears to be replicated on the other terrestrial planets, though with substantial variations in the relative size of each region

THE GEOMAGNETIC FIELD AND MAGNETOSPHERE

Helical fluid motions in Earth's electrically conducting liquid outer core have an electromagnetic dynamo effect, giving rise to the geomagnetic field. The planet's sizable, hot core, along with its rapid spin, probably accounts for the exceptional strength of the magnetic field of Earth compared with those of the other terrestrial planets.

Earth's main magnetic field permeates the planet and an enormous volume of space surrounding it. A great teardrop-shaped region of space called the magnetosphere is formed by the interaction of Earth's field with the solar wind. At a distance of about 65,000 km (40,000 miles) outward toward the Sun, the pressure of the solar wind is balanced by the geomagnetic field. This serves as an obstacle to the solar wind, and the flow of charged particles, or plasma, is deflected around Earth by the resulting bow shock. The magnetosphere so produced streams out into an elongated magnetotail that stretches several million kilometres downstream from Earth away from the Sun.

Plasma particles from the solar wind can leak through the magnetopause, the sunward boundary of the magnetosphere, and populate its interior; charged particles from Earth's ionosphere also enter the magnetosphere. The magnetotail can store for hours an enormous amount of energy—several billion megajoules, which is roughly equivalent to the yearly electricity production of many small countries. This occurs through a process called reconnection, in which the Sun's magnetic field, dragged into interplanetary space by the solar wind, becomes linked with the magnetic field in Earth's magnetosphere. The energy is released in dynamic structural reconfigurations of the magnetosphere, called geomagnetic substorms, which often result in the precipitation of energetic particles into the ionosphere, giving rise to fluorescing auroral displays.

Converging magnetic field lines fairly close to Earth can trap highly energetic particles so that they gyrate between the Northern and Southern Hemispheres and slowly drift longitudinally around the planet in two concentric doughnut-shaped zones known as the Van Allen radiation belts. Many of the charged particles trapped in these belts are produced when energetic cosmic rays strike Earth's upper atmosphere, producing neutrons that then decay into electrons, which are negatively charged, and protons, which are positively charged. Others come from the solar wind or Earth's atmosphere. The inner radiation belt was detected in 1958 by the American physicist James Van Allen and colleagues, using a Geiger-Müller counter aboard the first U.S. satellite, Explorer 1; the outer belt was distinguished by other U.S. and Soviet spacecraft launched the same year. Earth's magnetosphere has been extensively studied ever since, and space physicists have extended their studies of plasma processes to the vicinities of comets and other planets.

An important characteristic of Earth's magnetic field is polarity reversal. In this process the direction of the dipole component reverses—i.e., the north magnetic pole becomes the south magnetic pole and vice versa. From studying the direction of magnetization of many rocks, geologists know that such reversals occur, without a discernible pattern, at intervals that range from tens of thousands of years to millions of years, though they are still uncertain about the mechanisms responsible. It is likely that during the changeover, which is believed to take a few thousand years, a nondipolar field remains, at a small fraction of the strength of the normal field. In the temporary absence of the dipole component, the solar wind would approach much closer to Earth, allowing particles that are normally deflected by the field or are trapped in its outer portions to reach the surface. The increase in particle radiation could lead to increased rates of genetic damage and thus of mutations or sterility in plants and animals, leading to the disappearance of some species. Scientists have looked for evidence of such changes in the fossil record at times of past field reversals, but the results have been inconclusive.

DEVELOPMENT OF EARTH'S STRUCTURE AND COMPOSITION

ACCRETION OF THE EARLY EARTH

As the gas making up the solar nebula beyond the Sun cooled with time, mineral grains are thought to have condensed and aggregated to form the earliest meteoritic material. In addition, as is suggested by the finding of anomalous concentrations of isotopes in a few meteorites, solid material from outside the solar system, apparently existing prior to the formation of the Sun, was occasionally incorporated into these developing small bodies.

The concentrations of isotopes that decay radioactively and of isotopes that are produced by radioactive decay provide scientists the information required to determine when meteorites and the planets formed. For example, the concentrations of rubidium-87 and the strontium-87 into which it decays, or those of samarium-147 and its decay product neodymium-143, indicate that the oldest meteorites formed some 4.56 billion years ago. Other isotope studies demonstrate that Earth formed within, at most, a few tens of millions of years after the birth of the Sun.

The most abundant elements in the Sun, hydrogen and helium, are severely lacking in the inner, terrestrial planets. When the relative abundances of the less volatile elements are compared for the Sun, for a class of primitive, largely chemically unaltered meteorites called CI carbonaceous chondrites (considered by many researchers the most pristine samples of original solar system material), and for the estimated composition of Earth, their values are all in close agreement. This is the basis for the chondritic model, which holds that Earth (and presumably the other terrestrial planets) was essentially built up from bodies made of such meteoritic material. This idea is corroborated by isotopic studies of rocks derived from interior regions of Earth considered to be little changed throughout the planet's history. Thus, it appears that the composition of Earth is roughly what would be expected given the observed elemental abundances in the Sun and accounting for the loss of the more volatile elements.

Stony meteorites and iron meteorites (those composed largely of iron alloyed with nickel and sulfur) both fall on Earth today, and both types are thought to have been present during the formation of the planetesimals that would accrete to become Earth. In other words, Earth seems to have accreted only after most, if not all, solid matter had already condensed. Thus, a wide range of minerals was included in the grains, the larger fragments, and even the planetesimals that were accumulated by the growing planet. Apparently, such an aggregation of dense metallic fragments and less dense rocky fragments is not very stable. Calculations based on the measured strengths of rocks indicate that the metallic fragments probably sank downward as Earth grew. Although the planet was relatively cold at this stage—less than 500 K (230 °C, or 440 °F)—the rock was weak. This is an important point because it leads to the conclusion that Earth's metallic core began to form during accretion of the planet and probably before the planet had grown to one-fifth of its present volume.

EFFECTS OF PLANETESIMAL IMPACTS

During its accretion, Earth is thought to have been shock-heated by the impacts of meteorite-size bodies and larger planetesimals. For a meteorite collision, the heating is concentrated near the surface where the impact occurs, which allows the heat to radiate back into space. A planetesimal, however, can penetrate sufficiently deeply on impact to produce heating well beneath the surface. In addition, the debris formed on impact can blanket the planetary surface, which helps to retain heat inside the planet. Some scientists have suggested

that, in this way, Earth may have become hot enough to begin melting after growing to less than 15 percent of its final volume.

Among the planetesimals striking the forming Earth, at least one is considered to have been comparable in size to Mars. Although the details are not well understood, there is good evidence that the impact of such a large planetesimal created the Moon. Among the more persuasive indications is that the relative abundances of many trace elements in rocks from the Moon are close to the values obtained for Earth's mantle. Unless this is a fortuitous coincidence, it points to the Moon having been derived from the mantle. Computer simulations have shown that a glancing collision of a Mars-size planetary body could have been sufficient to excavate from Earth's interior the material that would form the Moon. Again, the evidence for such large collisions suggests that Earth was very effectively heated during accretion.

It is apparent, then, that many processes contributing to the early development of Earth occurred almost simultaneously, within tens to hundreds of million of years after the Sun was formed. Meteorites and Earth were formed within this time, and the Moon, which has been dated at more than four billion years in age, apparently was formed in the same time period. Simultaneously, Earth's core was accumulating and may have been completely formed during the planet's growth period. In addition to the possible accretional heating caused by planetesimal impacts, the sinking of metal to form the core released enough gravitational energy to heat the entire planet by 1,000 K (700 °C, or 1,300 °F) or more. Thus, once core formation began, Earth's interior became sufficiently hot to convect. Although it is not known whether or in what form plate tectonics was active at the surface, it seems quite possible that the underlying mantle convection began even before the planet had grown to its final dimensions. Only later in Earth's development did radioactivity become an important heat source as well.

PLANETARY DIFFERENTIATION

Once hot, Earth's interior could begin its chemical evolution. For example, outgassing of a fraction of volatile substances that had been trapped in small amounts within the accreting planet probably formed the earliest atmosphere. Outgassing of water to Earth's surface began before 4.3 billion years ago, a time based on analysis of ancient zircons that show the effects of alteration by liquid water. In Earth's deepest interior, chemical reactions between the mantle and the core became possible. Perhaps the most important event for Earth's surface, however, was the formation of the earliest crust by partial melting of the interior. This chemical separation by partial melting and outgassing of volatiles is termed differentiation. As the interior differentiated, less dense liquids rose from the melt toward the surface and crystallized to form crust.

Uncertainty exists over when and how the continental crust began to grow, because the record of the first 600 million years has not been found. The oldest known rocks date to only about 4 billion years. Because these are metamorphic rocks—i.e., because they were changed by heat and pressure from preexisting crustal rocks at the time of their dated age—it can be inferred that crust was present earlier in Earth's history. In fact, two tiny grains of zircon from Australia have been dated at 4.28 billion and 4.4 billion years, but their relation to the formation of continental crust is uncertain.

Although direct evidence is not available, indirect evidence derived from the compositions of rocks indicates that continental crust formed early. Isotopic analyses suggest that the average age of the present continental crust is about 2.5 billion years. Thus, in all probability, repeated partial melting of the upper mantle formed successively more refined, continent-like crustal rocks starting before 4 billion years ago. Over the first billion years, however, much of the continental crust that was formed appears to have been reincorporated into the mantle—the isotopic data infers that on average about one-third of the continental crust was recycled every billion years. As a result, only a few fragments of crust older than 3.5 billion years remain, virtually none older than 4 billion years.

The process of partial melting and formation of crust, especially continental crust, leads to a depletion of certain elements (e.g., silicon and aluminum) from the mantle. Undepleted and thus relatively primitive regions still exist, making up about one-third to one-half of the mantle, according to the isotopic models. The distribution of depleted and undepleted regions, however, is uncertain. Although much (perhaps all) of the upper mantle appears to be depleted, it is not known whether depleted rocks also exist in the lower mantle.

What is recognized is that Earth is still differentiating into chemically distinct layers or regions. This is most evident in the processes of plate tectonics that involve ongoing production of crust at divergent plate boundaries such as the midocean ridges. As this material is cycled back down into the mantle at subduction zones and then upward again, it continues to undergo chemical processing from basaltic to andesitic and eventually to granitic (continental) composition. Thus, chemical and thermal evolution of the interior, intimately connected through mantle convection, is still vigorously in progress some 4.56 billion years after the formation of the planet.

EARTH IMPACTS

Earth benefits from the life-giving light of the Sun. For millennia, mariners have sailed with the tides caused by the Moon. However, other interactions within the inner solar system neighbourhood are occasionally not so benign. There is an ever-present danger to Earth from collisions with small bodies whose orbits around the Sun carry them near Earth. These objects include the rocky asteroids and their larger fragments and the icy nuclei of comets.

Space in the vicinity of Earth contains a great number of solid objects in a range of sizes. The tiniest (millimetre-size and smaller) and by far most abundant ones, called micrometeoroids or interplanetary dust particles, hit Earth's atmosphere continually. They are also the least dangerous; they either burn up in the atmosphere or settle to the surface as dust. Of the somewhat larger objects—i.e., mostly asteroidal in origin—the great majority that reach the ground as meteorites are too small to endanger human life or property on a significant scale. Occasionally there are reports of roughly softball-size meteorite fragments damaging houses or cars. (The apparently only verified case of a meteorite hitting and injuring a human being occurred in 1954.) Reports of falls of meteorites with masses in the one-ton range are less frequent; when these objects strike the ground, they can excavate craters a few metres across.

It is only the biggest projectiles, those that collide with Earth very infrequently on average, that are acknowledged to pose a great potential danger to human beings and possibly to all life on the planet. Recognition that such a danger might exist dates back at least to the English astronomers Edmond Halley and

The impact of a near-Earth object 65 million years ago in what is today the Caribbean region, as depicted in an artist's conception. Many scientists believe that the collision of a large asteroid or comet nucleus with Earth triggered the mass extinction of the dinosaurs and many other species near the end of the Cretaceous period. NASA; illustration by Don Davis

Isaac Newton and their work on the Great Comet of 1680, whose orbit they showed crossed that of Earth. Modern interest was rekindled in 1980 when the experimental physicist Luis Alvarez of the University of California, Berkeley, and colleagues presented evidence that the impact of an asteroid or comet having a diameter of about 10 km (6 miles) was responsible for the mass extinction at the end of the Cretaceous period 65 million years ago, in which most species of dinosaurs and much of the marine life of the day perished.

Since that time scientists have identified the probable site of the impact, called the Chicxulub crater, off Mexico's Yucatán Peninsula, and have come to suspect that similar catastrophic impacts may have triggered other mass extinctions as well. In addition to causing tremendous immediate devastation and ensuing earthquakes, firestorms, and giant sea waves (tsunamis), collisions of such magnitude are believed to be capable of perturbing Earth's environment globally by throwing large quantities of fine debris high into the atmosphere. The consequences would include a decrease in the amount of sunlight reaching the surface and a prolonged depression of surface temperatures—a so-called impact winter—leading to loss of photosynthesizing plant life and worldwide starvation and disease.

In the early 1980s astronomers in the United States, followed by those in several other countries, began studies aimed at better defining the risk posed by cosmic impacts, developing programs to detect threatening objects, and determining if anything could be done to protect Earth from the most devastating impacts. One outgrowth of these efforts was the development of a scale for categorizing the potential impact hazard of objects newly discovered to be orbiting near Earth.

Objects That Pose a Threat

All objects that can someday cross Earth's orbit have the potential to collide with the planet. This includes not only objects that regularly approach Earth but also others whose paths may change over time in a way that would make them cross Earth's orbit. The objects that fall into this category are asteroids and comets in short-period orbits—together called near-Earth objects (NEOs)—and those long-period comets that make their closest approach to the Sun inside Earth's orbit. Short-period comets complete their orbits in less than 200 years and so likely have been observed before; they generally approach along the plane of the solar system, near which lie the orbits of most of the planets, including Earth. Like short-period comets, most known Earth-approaching asteroids have orbits tilted by less than 20° to the plane of the solar system and periods of less than about three years. Long-period comets have orbital periods greater than 200 years and usually much greater; they can approach from any direction.

The amount of damage caused by the impact of an object with Earth is determined primarily by two factors: the object's mass and its relative velocity. These determine the total kinetic energy released. A typical NEO would strike Earth with a velocity of about 20 km/sec (12 miles/sec) and a typical long-period comet with a greater velocity, 50 km/sec (30 miles/sec) or higher. For objects with diameters less than a few hundred metres, their physical properties are important in calculating how much

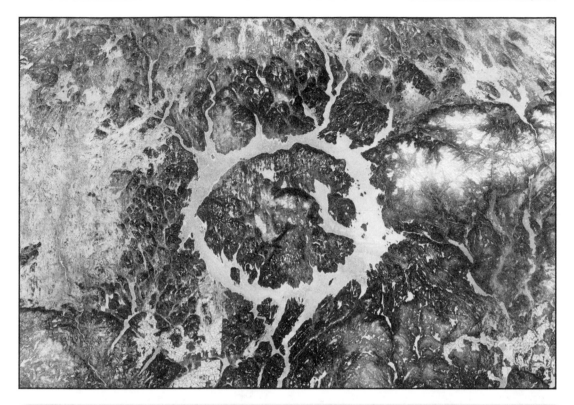

Crater in Quebec, Can., one of the largest fairly well-preserved impact craters on Earth, as seen from the International Space Station on April 28, 2002. A ring-shaped hydroelectric reservoir lake 70 km (40 miles) in diameter occupies the centre of the crater. The original outer rim, which measured 100 km across, has been worn down by erosional processes. The impact that formed the crater is estimated to have happened some 210 million years ago, near the end of the Triassic period, and may have played a role in the mass extinction of species that occurred about the same time. NASA/Johnson Space Center

destruction would result, but for larger bodies only the total energy of the impact is important. Hence, most damage assessments are based on the kinetic energy of an impact rather than the diameter or mass of the projectile. This energy is expressed in millions of tons (megatons) of TNT, the same units used to quantify the energy released by thermonuclear bombs.

The energy released by an impact falls between about 10 megatons and 1 billion megatons—i.e., between 700 and 70 billion times the energy of the 15-kiloton atomic bomb dropped on Hiroshima, Japan, in 1945. This very wide range

Meteor Crater (or Barringer Crater), Arizona, U.S., a pit 1.2 km (0.75 mile) in diameter excavated about 50,000 years ago by the explosive impact of an object with the composition of a nickel-iron asteroid and a diameter of perhaps 50 metres (160 feet), at the low end of the size range for destructive impacts. Estimates of the energy released by the impact range between 15 and 40 megatons. D.J. Roddy/U.S. Geological Survey Manicouagan

corresponds to NEOs with diameters from about 50 metres (160 feet) to 20 km (12 miles) or to long-period comets with diameters about half as large. (Objects smaller than about 50 metres would break up high in the atmosphere; the damage would be limited to less than a few hundred square kilometres around the impact point.) For an object at the lower end of this size range, an ocean impact could cause more damage than one on land because it would result in large tsunamis that would devastate coastal areas for many kilometres inland.

FREQUENCY OF IMPACTS

Because there are far fewer large NEOs and long-period comets in space than smaller ones, the chances of a collision decrease rapidly with increasing size. The impact-hazard community—primarily scientists with an interest in the issue— has defined a global catastrophe to be an impact that leads to the death of one-fourth or more of the world's population. An impact by a 1-km- (0.6-mile-) diameter NEO, the smallest believed capable of causing such a catastrophe, is estimated to occur about once per 100,000 years on average, based on the assumed population in space of such objects. On the other hand, an impact by a 100-metre (300-foot) NEO, the smallest believed capable of causing regional devastation, is estimated to occur about once every 1,000 years on average. The hazard posed by long-period comets is less certain because fairly few such objects are known, but it is thought to be perhaps as high as 25 percent of that for NEOs.

The major difference between the threat posed by the impact of an asteroid or comet and that posed by other natural disasters is the extent of the damage that could be done. In some parts of the world at high risk for floods or earthquakes, the chances of dying in such an event are 100 to 200 times greater than the risk of dying from a

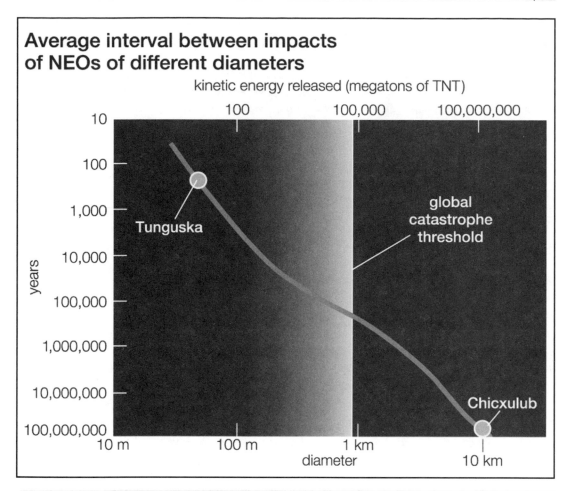

Average interval between impacts of NEOs of different diameters

kinetic energy released (megatons of TNT)

Tunguska

global catastrophe threshold

Chicxulub

Estimated average times between impacts on Earth for near-Earth objects (NEOs) over a range of sizes and equivalent amounts of released kinetic energy. Because there are far fewer large NEOs than smaller ones, the chance of an impact drops off rapidly with increasing size. Objects of the size thought to have resulted in the explosion over the Tunguska region of Siberia in 1908 and in the Chicxulub crater off Mexico's Yucatán Peninsula 65 million years ago are located on the curve for reference. Encyclopædia Britannica, Inc.

cosmic impact. What distinguishes the impact hazard, however, is that it is the only known natural disaster, with the possible exception of an exceedingly large volcanic eruption, that could result in the death of a significant fraction of Earth's population and, in the most extreme case, the extinction of the human species.

THE TUNGUSKA EVENT

On June 30, 1908, about 7:40 AM, an enormous explosion occurred at an altitude of 5–10 km (3–6 miles), flattening some 2,000 square km (500,000 acres) and charring more than 100 square km (25,000 acres) of pine forest near the Podkamennaya Tunguska River in central Siberia (60°55′ N, 101°57′ E), Russia. The energy of the explosion is estimated to have been equivalent to that of about 15 megatons of TNT, a thousand times more powerful than the atomic bomb dropped on Hiroshima, Japan, on Aug. 6, 1945.

It is believed that the cause was a small asteroid (large meteoroid) perhaps 50–100 metres (150–300 feet) in diameter and having a stony or carbonaceous composition—or, though less likely, a comet—that entered the atmosphere at a speed of 15–30 km/sec (30,000–60,000 miles/hour). Objects of this size are estimated to collide with Earth once every few hundred years on average. Because the object exploded in the atmosphere high above Earth's surface, it created a fireball and blast wave but no impact crater, and no fragments of the object have yet been found. The radiant energy from such an explosion would be enough to ignite forests, but the subsequent blast wave would quickly overtake the fires and extinguish them. Thus, the Tunguska blast charred the forest but did not produce a sustained fire.

The remote site of the explosion was first investigated from 1927 to 1930 in expeditions led by Russian scientist Leonid Alekseyevich Kulik. Around the epicentre (the location on the ground directly below the explosion) Kulik found felled, splintered trees lying radially for some 15–30 km (10–20 miles). Everything had been devastated and scorched, and very little was growing two decades after the event. The epicentre was easy to pinpoint because the felled trees all pointed away from it; at that spot investigators observed a marshy bog but no crater.

Eyewitnesses who had observed the event from a distance spoke of a fireball lighting the horizon, followed by trembling ground and hot winds strong enough to throw people down and shake buildings as in an earthquake. (At the time, seismographs in western Europe recorded seismic waves from the blast.) The blast had been initially visible from about 800 km (500 miles) away, and, because the object vaporized, gases were dispersed into the atmosphere, thus causing the abnormally bright nighttime skies in Siberia and Europe for some time after the event. Additional on-site investigations were performed by Soviet scientists in 1958 through 1961 and by an Italian-Russian expedition in 1999.

NEO SEARCH PROGRAMS

The outlook for detecting long-period comets that are specifically on a collision course with Earth is poor. Long-period comets, by definition, would likely be discovered on their way into the inner solar system only a few months—or, at best, a few years—before impact. (It is possible that an NEO destined for a collision with Earth also might not be discovered until the "last minute," but the probability of finding it many years before impact is much higher because

NEOs make frequent passages near Earth before colliding with it.) Although it might be feasible to detect long-period comets as early as about six months before impact, this knowledge would be useful only if a practical technology were already in place for preventing the collision. And if the comet is not on a collision course, then it is of little immediate concern, because it will not return for at least 200 years and perhaps not for millennia.

In principle, the outlook for identifying the larger NEOs is more promising. Using current technology, it is possible to find virtually all NEOs with diameters greater than 1 km (0.6 mile) and most of those half as large.

A number of loosely coordinated programs to search for NEOs have been instituted. Among them are several sponsored by the NASA in the United States and others in China, Japan, and Italy (as a joint Italian-German project). Their objective is to find objects capable of causing global catastrophe were they to hit Earth. In 1998 NASA stated its official program goal to be the "detection of 90 percent of the NEO population larger than 1 km within a decade." As of 2009, nearly 800 NEOs at least a kilometre in size were known.

These search programs use charge-coupled-diode (CCD) sensors, similar to those in digital cameras, on reflecting telescopes with primary mirrors in the 1-metre- (40-inch-) diameter range to obtain three or more images of the same region of the sky over a short period of time, generally some tens of minutes. The images are then compared with one another to find objects that have moved rapidly. The distance that the object has moved between images and its brightness provide clues to its distance and size. For example, fast-traveling, bright objects are almost certainly very close to Earth. A definitive orbit, however, is required before an accurate prediction can be made of the object's true distance and future path through space. This generally requires several days to acquire an "arc" of sufficient length to allow computation of an accurate orbit.

For every NEO a kilometre or larger in size, there are thousands more as small as about 100 metres (300 feet). An impact by a 100-metre object has the explosive power of about 100 megatons of TNT, roughly equivalent to the largest man-made nuclear explosions. Search programs in the 1990s discovered several NEOs in this smaller size range passing close enough to Earth to attract attention in the popular press. In fact, for each one detected, hundreds of unobserved objects passed just as close or closer. Dozens in this range were larger than 100 metres and thus large enough to cause a devastating tsunami or, if one were to hit land, to destroy an area the size of a small country. The chance of an impact by a 100-metre NEO is about 1 in 10 per century. For each actual impact, however, there will be numerous near misses. Many of these NEOs are certain to be detected as a by-product of searches for the larger objects capable of causing global catastrophes.

DETERMINING THE HAZARD POTENTIAL OF AN NEO

When an NEO is first discovered, its orbit and size are uncertain. If sufficient observations are made during its discovery apparition, a fairly good orbit can be computed. In practice, however, few orbits are reliably determined during the first apparition, and later observations of the object are required to learn how its position has changed in the interim. Observations to determine its size are rarely made (perhaps several in 100 are so observed), because they require specialized techniques such as radar or thermal infrared radiometry; rather, the size of an NEO is estimated from its brightness. Sizes estimated this way are uncertain by about a factor of 2—that is, an object reported as being 1 km (0.6 mile) in diameter could have a diameter between 0.5 and 2 km (0.3 and 1.2 miles).

In most cases, sufficient observation of an object will establish that the chances of its colliding with Earth are negligible. In some cases, however, there is no opportunity for additional observation. This happens, for example, when the object is small and discovered while passing very close to Earth; it quickly becomes too faint to observe further. Even a larger and more distant object can be lost because of poor weather (a factor taken into account in choosing observing sites for search programs). Without the observations needed to compute a reliable orbit, prediction of the object's future close approaches to Earth is highly uncertain.

When computations indicate that a NEO estimated to be larger than about 200 metres (650 feet) could strike Earth during the next century or two, the object is called a potentially hazardous asteroid (PHA). As of 2009 there were more than 1,000 identified PHAs. Observations of PHAs are continued until their orbits are refined to the point where their future positions can be reliably predicted.

While an object remains on the PHA list, its hazard potential is described by the Torino Impact Hazard Scale, an indicator named after the city of Turin (Italian: Torino), Italy, where it was presented at an international NEO conference in 1999. The purpose of the scale is to quantify the level of public concern warranted. The scale's values, which are integers between 0 and 10, are based on both an object's collision probability and its estimated kinetic energy. The value for a given object can change as probability and energy estimates are refined by additional observations.

On the Torino scale, a value of 0 indicates that the likelihood of a collision is zero or well below the chance that a random object of the same size will strike Earth within the next few decades. This designation also applies to any small object that, should it collide, is unlikely to reach Earth's surface intact. A value of 10 indicates that a collision is certain to occur and is capable of causing a global climatic catastrophe; such events occur on timescales of 100,000 years or longer (the mass extinction event at the end of the Cretaceous period falls here).

Intermediate values categorize impacts according to various levels of probability and destructiveness. A Torino scale value is always reported together with the predicted date of the close encounter to convey further the level of urgency that is warranted. Since the implementation of the Torino scale, there has been only one known NEO with a final value greater than 0. For asteroid 2007 VK184, there is a 1 in 3,030 chance that it will strike Earth on June 3, 2048; this asteroid ranks as a 1 on the Torino scale. Other objects often have received higher initial values, but these values have proved fictitious once the needed additional observations have been made and more accurate orbits have been calculated.

DEFENDING EARTH FROM A COLLIDING OBJECT

Even with the best of search programs, whether anything can be done about an object found to be on a collision course with Earth depends on many factors. The most important are the amount of lead time and the physical properties of the object—its size, shape, spin rate, density, strength, and other characteristics. Scientists believe that kinetic energy interception is adequate for the majority of objects, including those of intermediate size and most likely to cause destructive tsunamis. Such a strategy would involve the use of a nonexplosive projectile sent to strike the object in a particular location at high speed to change its orbit and possibly to fragment it.

For the remainder, more aggressive measures, likely involving the use of powerful thermonuclear devices, are thought to be necessary to achieve the same results. Because the physical properties of NEOs are so poorly known, however, it is possible that such measures could do more harm than good—e.g., by breaking a large object into numerous smaller, but still potentially destructive, pieces without deflecting them enough to miss Earth. Validating these options requires additional theory, laboratory experiments, and safe experiments involving actual NEOs in space. In the early years of the 21st century, few, if any, such efforts were being made.

CHAPTER 6

THE MOON

The Moon is Earth's sole natural satellite and nearest large celestial body. Known since prehistoric times, it is the brightest object in the sky after the Sun. It is designated by the symbol ☾. Its name in English, like that of Earth, is of Germanic and Old English derivation.

The Moon's desolate beauty has been a source of fascination and curiosity throughout history and has inspired a rich cultural and symbolic tradition. In past civilizations the Moon was regarded as a deity, its dominion dramatically manifested in its rhythmic control over the tides and the cycle of female fertility. Ancient lore and legend tell of the power of the Moon to instill spells with magic, to transform humans into beasts, and to send people's behaviour swaying perilously between sanity and lunacy (from the Latin *luna*, "Moon"). Poets and composers were invoking the Moon's romantic charms and its darker side, and writers of fiction were conducting their readers on speculative lunar journeys long before Apollo astronauts, in orbit above the Moon, sent back photographs of the reality that human eyes were witnessing for the first time.

Centuries of observation and scientific investigation have been centred on the nature and origin of the Moon. Early studies of the Moon's motion and position allowed the prediction of tides and led to the development of calendars. The Moon was the first new world on which humans set foot;

The familiar near side of Earth's Moon, photographed on December 7, 1992, by the Galileo spacecraft on its way to Jupiter. Two primary kinds of terrain are visible—the lighter areas, which constitute the heavily cratered and very old highlands, and the darker, roughly circular plains, traditionally called maria, which are relatively young lava-filled impact basins. NASA/JPL/Caltech

the information brought back from those expeditions, together with that collected by automated spacecraft and remote-sensing observations, has led to a knowledge of the Moon that surpasses that of any other cosmic body except Earth itself. Although many questions remain about its composition, structure, and history, it has become clear that the Moon holds keys to understanding the origin of Earth and the solar system. Moreover, given its nearness to Earth, its rich potential as a source of materials and energy, and its qualifications as a laboratory for planetary science and a place to learn how to live and work in space for extended times, the Moon remains a prime location for human-kind's first settlements beyond Earth orbit.

DISTINCTIVE FEATURES

The Moon is a spherical rocky body, prob-ably with a small metallic core, revolving around Earth in a slightly eccentric orbit at a mean distance of about 384,000 km (238,600 miles). Its equatorial radius is 1,738 km (1,080 miles), and its shape is slightly flattened in a such a way that it bulges a little in the direction of Earth. Its mass distribution is not uniform—the centre of mass is displaced about 2 km (1.2 miles) toward Earth relative to the centre of the lunar sphere, and it also has surface mass concentrations, called mas-cons for short, that cause the Moon's gravitational field to increase over local

areas. The Moon has no global magnetic field like that of Earth, but some of its surface rocks have remanent magnetism, which indicates one or more periods of magnetic activity in the past. The Moon presently has very slight seismic activity and little heat flow from the interior, indi-cations that most internal activity ceased long ago.

Scientists now believe that more than four billion years ago the Moon was subject to violent heating—probably from its formation—that resulted in its differentiation, or chemical separation, into a less dense crust and a more dense underlying mantle. This was followed hundreds of millions of years later by a second episode of heating—this time from internal radioactivity—that resulted in volcanic outpourings of lava. The Moon's mean density is 3.34 g/cm³ (1.93 oz/in³), close to that of Earth's mantle. Because of the Moon's small size and mass, its surface gravity is only about one-sixth of Earth's; it retains so little atmosphere that the molecules of any gases present on the surface move with-out collision.

In the absence of an atmospheric shield to protect the surface from bom-bardment, countless bodies ranging in size from asteroids to tiny particles have struck and cratered the Moon. This has formed a debris layer, or regolith, con-sisting of rock fragments of all sizes down to the finest dust. In the ancient past the largest impacts made great basins, some of which were later partly filled by the enormous lava floods. These great dark plains, called maria (Latin for "seas"), are clearly visible to the naked eye from Earth. The dark maria and the lighter highlands, whose unchanging patterns many people recognize as the "man in the moon," constitute the two main kinds of lunar territory. Lunar mountains, located mostly along the rims of ancient basins, are tall but not steep or sharp-peaked, because all lunar landforms have been eroded by the unending rain of impacts.

PRINCIPAL CHARACTERISTICS OF THE EARTH-MOON SYSTEM

In addition to its nearness to Earth, the Moon is relatively massive compared with it—the ratio of their masses is much larger than those of other natural satellites to the planets that they orbit. The Moon and Earth consequently exert a strong gravitational influence on each other, forming a system having distinct properties and behaviour of its own.

MASCONS

Mascons are regions where particularly dense lavas rose up from the mantle and flooded into basins. Lunar mascons were first identified by the observation of small anomalies in the orbits of Lunar Orbiter spacecraft launched in 1966–67. As the spacecraft passed over certain surface regions, the stronger gravity field caused the craft to dip slightly and speed up. Apollo space program scientists used the data to correct for the observed gravity irregularities in order to improve the targeting accuracy of manned Moon landings. Later scientific study of these anomalies supported the interpretation that the Moon had a complex history of heating, differentiation (sinking of denser materials and rising of lighter ones to form a deep mantle and overlying crust), and modification by impacts and subsequent huge outflows of lava. Tracking of the velocities of the Clementine, Lunar Prospector, and Kaguya spacecraft (launched 1994, 1998 and 2007, respectively) by their Doppler-shifted radio signals as they orbited the Moon provided detailed gravity maps, including mascon characteristics, of most of the lunar surface.

The Moon's larger mascons coincide with circular, topographically low impact basins where particularly dense—and thus more massive and gravitationally attractive—magma upwelled from the mantle and solidified to form dark mare plains. Examples are the Imbrium, Serenitatis, Crisium, and Nectaris basins (maria), all of which are visible at full moon with the unaided eye from Earth. The survival, over the three billion years since they were formed, of these gravity anomalies testifies to the existence of a thick, rigid lunar crust. This, in turn, implies that the Moon's initial heat source is extinct.

Although the Moon is commonly described as orbiting Earth, it is more accurate to say that the two bodies orbit each other about a common centre of mass. Called the barycentre, this point lies inside Earth about 4,700 km (2,900 miles) from its centre. Also more accurately, it is the barycentre, rather than the centre of Earth, that follows an elliptical path around the Sun in accord with Kepler's laws of planetary motion. The orbital geometry of the Moon, Earth, and the Sun gives rise to the Moon's phases and to the phenomena of lunar and solar eclipses.

The distance between the Moon and Earth varies rather widely because of the combined gravity of Earth, the Sun, and the planets. For example, in the last three decades of the 20th century, the Moon's apogee—the farthest distance that it travels from Earth in a revolution—ranged between about 404,000 and 406,700 km (251,000 and 252,700 miles), while its perigee—the closest that it comes to Earth—ranged between about 356,500 and 370,400 km (221,500 and 230,200 miles). Tidal interactions, the cyclic deformations in each body caused by the gravitational attraction of the other, have braked the Moon's spin such that it now rotates at the same rate as it revolves around Earth and thus always keeps the same side facing the planet. As discovered by the Italian-born French astronomer Gian Domenico Cassini in 1692, the Moon's spin axis precesses with respect to its orbital plane; i.e., its orientation changes slowly over time, tracing out a circular path.

In accord with Kepler's second law, the eccentricity of the Moon's orbit

PROPERTIES OF THE MOON AND THE EARTH-MOON SYSTEM			
	Moon	Earth	Approximate ratio (Moon to Earth)
mean distance from Earth (orbital radius)	384,400 km	—	—
period of orbit around Earth (sidereal period of revolution)	27.3217 Earth days	—	—
inclination of equator to ecliptic plane (Earth's orbital plane)	1.53°	23.45°	—

	MOON	EARTH	APPROXIMATE RATIO (MOON TO EARTH)
inclination of equator to body's own orbital plane (obliquity to orbit)	6.68°	23.45°	—
inclination of orbit to Earth's equator	18.28°–28.58°	—	—
eccentricity of orbit around Earth	0.0549	—	—
recession rate from Earth	3.8 cm/year	—	—
rotation period	synchronous with orbital period	23.9345 hr	—
equatorial radius	1,738 km	6,378 km	1:4
surface area	37,900,000 km²	510,066,000 km² (land area, 148,000,000 km²)	1:14
mass	0.0735×10^{24} kg	5.976×10^{24} kg	1:81
mean density	3.34 g/cm³	5.52 g/cm³	1:1.7
mean surface gravity	162 cm/sec²	980 cm/sec²	1:6
escape velocity	2.38 km/sec	11.2 km/sec	1:5
mean surface temperature	day, 380 K (224 °F, 107 °C); night, 120 K (-244 °F, -153 °C)	288 K (59 °F, 15 °C)	—
temperature extremes	396 K (253 °F, 123 °C) to 40 K (-388 °F, -233 °C)	331 K (136 °F, 58 °C) to 184 K (-128 °F, -89 °C)	—
surface pressure	3×10^{-15} bar	1 bar	1:300 trillion
atmospheric molecular density	day, 104 molecules/cm³; night, 2×105 molecules/cm³	2.5×10^{19} molecules/cm³ (at standard temperature and pressure)	about 1:100 trillion
average heat flow	29 mW/m²	63 mW/m²	1:2.2

results in its traveling faster in that part of its orbit nearer Earth and slower in the part farther away. Combined with the Moon's constant spin rate, these changes in speed give rise to an apparent oscillation, or libration, which over time allows an observer on Earth to see more than half of the lunar surface. In addition to this apparent turning motion, the Moon actually does rock slightly to and fro in both longitude and latitude, and the observer's vantage point moves with Earth's rotation. As a result of all these motions, more than 59 percent of the lunar surface can be seen at one time or another from Earth.

The orbital eccentricity also affects solar eclipses, in which the Moon passes between the Sun and Earth, casting a moving shadow across Earth's sunlit surface. If a solar eclipse occurs when the Moon is near perigee, observers along the path of the Moon's dark inner shadow (umbra) see a total eclipse. If the Moon is near apogee, it does not quite cover the Sun; the resulting eclipse is annular, and observers can see a thin ring of the solar disk around the Moon's silhouette.

The Moon and Earth presently orbit the barycentre in 27.322 days, the sidereal month, or sidereal revolution period of the Moon. Because the whole system is moving around the Sun once per year, the angle of illumination changes about one degree per day, so that the time from one full moon to the next is 29.531 days, the synodic month, or synodic revolution period of the Moon. As a result, the Moon's terminator—the dividing line between dayside and nightside—moves once around the Moon in this synodic period, exposing most locations to alternating periods of sunlight and darkness each nearly 15 Earth days long.

The sidereal and synodic periods are slowly changing with time because of tidal interactions. Tidal friction occurs between water tides and sea bottoms, particularly where the sea is relatively shallow, or between parts of the solid crust of a planet or satellite that move against each other. Tidal friction on Earth prevents the tidal bulge, which is raised in Earth's seas and crust by the Moon's pull, from staying directly under the Moon. Instead, the bulge is carried out from directly under the Moon by the rotation of Earth, which spins almost 30 times for every time the Moon revolves in its orbit. The mutual attraction between the Moon and the material in the bulge tends to accelerate the Moon in its orbit, thereby moving the Moon farther from Earth by about 3 cm (1.2 inches) per year, and to slow Earth's daily rotation by a small fraction of a second per year. Millions of years from now these effects may cause Earth to keep the same face always turned to a distant Moon and to rotate once in a day that is about 50 times longer than the present one and equal to the month of that time. This condition probably will not be stable, because of the tidal effects of the Sun on the Earth-Moon system.

View over the lunar north pole, in a mosaic made from images collected by the Galileo spacecraft as it flew by the Moon on December 7, 1992. In this image, the north pole lies just within the shadowed region about a third of the way along the terminator, starting from the top left. NASA/JPL

Extending this relationship back into the past, both periods must have been significantly shorter hundreds of millions of years ago—a hypothesis confirmed from measurements of the daily and tide-related growth rings of fossil corals. That the Moon keeps the same part of its surface always turned toward Earth is attributed to the past effects of tidal friction in the Moon. The theory of tidal friction was first developed mathematically after 1879 by the English astronomer George Darwin (1845–1912), son of the naturalist Charles Darwin.

Because the Moon's spin axis is almost perpendicular to the plane of the ecliptic (the plane of Earth's orbit around the Sun)—inclined only 1½° from the vertical—the Moon has no seasons. Sunlight is always nearly horizontal at the lunar poles, which results in permanently cold and dark environments at the bottoms of deep craters.

MOTIONS OF THE MOON

The study of the Moon's motions has been central to the growth of knowledge not only about the Moon itself but also about fundamentals of celestial mechanics and physics. As the stars appear to move westward because of Earth's daily rotation and its annual motion about the Sun, so the Moon slowly moves eastward, rising later each day and passing through its phases: new, first quarter, full, last quarter, and new again each month. The long-running Chinese, Chaldean, and Mayan calendars were attempts to reconcile these repetitive but incommensurate movements. From the time of the Babylonian astrologers and the Greek astronomers up to the present, investigators looked for small departures from the motions predicted. The English physicist Isaac Newton used lunar observations in developing his theory of gravitation in the late 17th century, and he was able to show some effects of solar gravity in perturbing the Moon's motion. By the 18th and 19th centuries the mathematical study of lunar movements, both orbital and rotational, was advancing, driven in part by the need for precise tables of the predicted positions of celestial bodies (ephemerides) for navigation. While theory developed with improved observations, many small and puzzling discrepancies continued to appear. It gradually became evident that some arise from irregularities in Earth's rotation rate, others from minor tidal effects on Earth and the Moon.

Space exploration brought a need for greatly increased accuracy, and, at the same time, the availability of fast computers and new observational tools provided the means for attaining it. Analytic treatments—mathematical modeling of the Moon's motions with a series of terms representing the gravitational influence of Earth, the Sun, and the planets—gave way to methods based on direct numerical integration of equations of motion for the Moon. Both methods required significant input based on observation, but use of the latter led to great increases in the accuracy of predictions. At the same time, optical and radio observations vastly improved—retroreflectors placed on the lunar surface by Apollo astronauts allowed laser ranging of the Moon from Earth, and new techniques of radio astronomy, including very long baseline interferometry, permitted observations of celestial radio sources as the Moon occulted them. These observations, having precisions on the order of centimetres, have enabled scientists to measure changes in the Moon's speed caused by terrestrial tidal momentum exchange, have advanced understanding of the theories of relativity, and are leading to improved geophysical knowledge of both the Moon and Earth.

THE ATMOSPHERE

Though the Moon is surrounded by a vacuum higher than is usually created in laboratories on Earth, its atmosphere is extensive and of high scientific interest. During the two-week daytime period, atoms and molecules are ejected by a variety of processes from the lunar surface, ionized by the solar wind, and then driven by electromagnetic effects as a collisionless plasma. The position of the Moon in its orbit determines the behaviour of the atmosphere. For part of each month, when the Moon is on the sunward side of Earth, atmospheric gases collide with the undisturbed solar wind;

in other parts of the orbit, they move into and out of the elongated tail of Earth's magnetosphere, an enormous region of space where the planet's magnetic field dominates the behaviour of electrically charged particles. In addition, the low temperatures on the Moon's nightside and in permanently shaded polar craters provide cold traps for condensable gases.

Instruments placed on the lunar surface by Apollo astronauts measured various properties of the Moon's atmosphere, but analysis of the data was difficult because the atmosphere's extreme thinness made contamination from Apollo-originated gases a significant factor. The main gases naturally present are neon, hydrogen, helium, and argon. The argon is mostly radiogenic; i.e., it is released from lunar rocks by the decay of radioactive potassium. Lunar night temperatures are low enough for the argon to condense but not the neon, hydrogen, or helium, which originate in the solar wind and remain in the atmosphere as gases unless implanted in soil particles.

In addition to the near-surface gases and the extensive sodium-potassium cloud detected around the Moon, a small amount of dust circulates within a few metres of the lunar surface. This is believed to be suspended electrostatically.

THE LUNAR SURFACE

With binoculars or a small telescope, an observer can see details of the Moon's near side in addition to the pattern of maria and highlands. As the Moon passes through its phases, the terminator moves slowly across the Moon's disk, its long shadows revealing the relief of mountains and craters. At full moon the relief disappears, replaced by the contrast between lighter and darker surfaces. Though the full moon is brilliant at night, the Moon is actually a dark object, reflecting only a few percent (albedo 0.07) of the sunlight that strikes it. (Some sunlight reflects from Earth to the Moon and back again. For a few days before and after a new moon, this doubly reflected sunlight, or earthshine, is powerful enough to make the whole Moon visible. At this time an observer on the Moon would see Earth as a bright body, four times the diameter of the Moon as seen from Earth, almost completely illuminated by the Sun. The phases of Earth and the Moon are complementary, so Earth is near full when the Moon is near new, and the earthshine then is strongest.)

Beginning with the Italian scientist Galileo's sketches in the early 17th century and continuing into the 19th century, astronomers mapped and named the visible features down to a resolution of a few kilometres, the best that can be accomplished when viewing the Moon telescopically through Earth's turbulent atmosphere. The work culminated in a great hand-drawn lunar atlas made by observers in Berlin and Athens. This was followed by a lengthy hiatus as astronomers turned their attention beyond the Moon until the mid-20th century, when it became apparent that human travel to the Moon might eventually be possible. In the 1950s another great atlas was compiled, this time a photographic one published in 1960 under the sponsorship of the U.S. Air Force.

Astronomers long debated whether the Moon's topographic features had been caused by volcanism. Only in the 20th century did the dominance of impacts in the shaping of the lunar surface become clear. Every highland region is heavily cratered—evidence for repeated collisions with large bodies. (The survival of similar large impact structures on Earth is relatively rare because of Earth's geologic activity and weathering.) The maria, on the other hand, show much less cratering and thus must be significantly younger. Mountains are mostly parts of the upthrust rims of ancient impact basins. Volcanic activity has occurred within the Moon, but the results are mostly quite different from those on Earth. The lavas that upwelled in floods to form the maria were extremely fluid. Evidence of volcanic mountain building as has occurred on Earth is limited to a few fields of small, low domes.

For millennia people wondered about the appearance of the Moon's unseen side. The mystery began to be dispelled with the flight of the Soviet space probe Luna 3 in 1959, which returned the first photographs of the far side. In contrast to the near side, the surface displayed in the Luna 3 images consisted mostly of highlands, with only small areas of dark mare material. Later missions showed that the ancient far-side highlands are scarred by huge basins but that these basins are not filled with lava.

View of the Moon never seen from Earth, predominantly the heavily cratered far side, photographed by Apollo 16 astronauts in April 1972. The near-side impact basin Mare Crisium is the large dark marking on the upper left limb; the two dark areas below it are Mare Marginis (nearer Crisium) and Mare Smythii. Although the far side is well scarred with giant basins, these never filled with lava to form maria. F.J. Doyle/National Space Science Data Center

EFFECTS OF IMPACTS AND VOLCANISM

The dominant consequences of impacts are observed in every lunar scene. At the largest scale are the ancient basins, which extend hundreds of kilometres across. A beautiful example is Orientale Basin, or Mare Orientale, whose mountain walls can just be seen from Earth near the Moon's limb (the apparent edge of the lunar disk) when the lunar libration is favourable. Orientale Basin appears to be the youngest large impact basin on the Moon. Its multiring ramparts are characteristic of the largest basins; they are accented by the partial lava flooding of low regions between the rings. A multiringed basin typically resembles a bull's-eye and may cover an area of many thousands of square kilometres. The outer rings of the basins are clifflike scarps that face inward. The rings probably were formed as part of the crater-forming process during impact, although some hypotheses suggest that they were formed, or were enhanced, by post-impact collapse. Transitional structures between bowl-shaped craters and multiringed basins include craters with central peaks and larger craters with central rings of peaks.

Orientale's name arises from lunar-mapping conventions. During the great age of telescopic observation in the 17th-19th centuries, portrayals of the Moon usually showed south at the top because the telescopes inverted the image. East and west referred to those directions in the sky—i.e., the Moon moves eastward and so its leading limb was east, and the portion of the basin that could be seen from Earth was accordingly called Mare Orientale. For mapping purposes lunar coordinates were taken to originate near the centre of the near-side face, at the intersection of the equator and a meridian defined by the mean librations. A small crater, Mösting A, was agreed upon as the reference point. With the Moon considered as a world, rather than just a disk moving across the sky, east and west are interchanged. Thus, Orientale, despite its name, is located at west lunar longitudes.

Smaller impact features, ranging in diameter from tens of kilometres to microscopic size, are described by the term *crater*. The relative ages of lunar craters are indicated by their form and structural features. Young craters have rugged profiles and are surrounded by hummocky blankets of debris, called ejecta, and long light-coloured rays made by expelled material hitting the lunar surface. Older craters have rounded and subdued profiles, the result of continued bombardment.

A crater's form and structure also yield information about the impact process. When a body strikes a much larger one at speeds of many kilometres per second, the available kinetic energy is enough to completely melt, even partly vaporize, the impacting body along with a small portion of its target material. On impact, a melt sheet is thrown out, along with quantities of rubble, to form the ejecta blanket around the contact site. Meanwhile, a shock travels into the subsurface, shattering mineral structures and leaving a telltale signature in the rocks. The initial cup-shaped cavity is unstable and, depending on its size, evolves in different ways. A typical end result is the great crater Aristarchus, with slumping terraces in its walls and a central peak. Aristarchus is about 40 km (25 miles) in diameter and 4 km (2.5 miles) deep.

The region around Aristarchus shows a number of peculiar lunar features, some of which have origins not yet well explained. The Aristarchus impact occurred on an elevated, old-looking surface surrounded by lavas of the northern part of the mare known as Oceanus Procellarum. These lava flows inundated the older crater Prinz, whose rim is now only partly visible. At one point on the rim, an apparently volcanic event produced a crater; subsequently, a long, winding channel, called a sinuous rille, emerged to flow across the mare. Other sinuous rilles are found nearby, including the largest one on the Moon, discovered by the German astronomer Johann Schröter in 1787. Named in his honour, Schröter's Valley is a deep, winding channel, hundreds of kilometres long, with a smaller inner channel that meanders just as slow rivers do on Earth. The end of this "river" simply tapers away to nothing and disappears on the mare plains. In some way that remains to be accounted for, hundreds of cubic kilometres of fluid and excavated mare material vanished.

The results of seismic and heat-flow measurements suggest that any volcanic activity that persists on the Moon is slight by comparison with that of Earth. Over the years reliable observers have reported seeing transient events of a possibly volcanic nature, and some spectroscopic evidence for them exists. In the late 1980s a cloud of sodium and potassium atoms was observed around the Moon, but it was not necessarily the result of volcanic emissions. It is possible that interactions of the lunar surface and the solar wind produced the cloud. In any case, the question of whether the Moon is volcanically active remains open.

Telescopic observers beginning in the 19th century applied the term *rille* (German for "furrow") to several types of trenchlike lunar features. Rilles measure about 1–5 km (0.6–3 miles) wide and as much as several hundred kilometres long. They are divided into two main types, straight rilles and sinuous rilles, which seem to have different origins. Those of the first variety are flat floored and relatively straight; they are occasionally associated with crater chains and are sometimes arranged in an echelon pattern. Some of these structures are thought to be grabens, or elongated blocks of crust that have collapsed between parallel faults. Other straight rilles, some of which have branches—for example, Rima Hyginus (the word *rima* [from Latin, "fissure"] is often used for the rilles) and the rilles on the floor of the great crater Alphonsus—appear to be tension cracks in regions where subsurface gases have driven eruptions of dark material resulting in rimless vent craters.

Sinuous rilles resemble winding river valleys on Earth. They are thought to be similar to flow channels created by lava flows on Earth, but the shape of these lunar valleys is more meandering, perhaps because ancient lunar lavas were much less viscous than those now known on Earth. In 1971 Apollo 15 astronauts explored the sinuous Hadley Rille and found a V-shaped valley filled with rubble from walls that appeared to contain exposed rock layers laid down by successive lava flows. Their observations, however, did not clarify the feature's origin. Though the Moon shows both tension and compression features (low wrinkle ridges, usually near mare margins, may result from compression), it gives no evidence of having experienced the large, lateral motions of plate tectonics marked by faults in Earth's crust.

Among the most enigmatic features of the lunar surface are several light, swirling patterns with no associated topography. A prime example is Reiner Gamma, located in the southeastern portion of Oceanus Procellarum. Whereas other relatively bright features exist—e.g., crater rays—they are explained as consequences of the impact process. Features such as Reiner Gamma have no clear explanation. Some scientists have suggested that they are the marks of comet impacts, in which the impacting body was large in size but had so little density as to produce no crater. Reiner Gamma is also unusual in that it coincides with a large magnetic anomaly (region of magnetic irregularity) in the crust.

SMALL-SCALE FEATURES

On a small-to-microscopic scale, the properties of the lunar surface are governed by a combination of phenomena—impact effects due to the arrival, at speeds up to tens of kilometres per second, of meteoritic material ranging in size down to fractions of a micrometre; bombardment by solar-wind, cosmic-ray, and solar-flare particles; ionizing radiation; and temperature extremes. Subject to no meteorological effects and unprotected by a substantial atmosphere, the uppermost surface reaches almost 400 K (127 °C, or 260 °F) during the day and plunges to below 100 K (-173 °C, or -279 °F) at

night. The top layer of regolith, however, serves as an efficient insulator because of its high porosity (large number of voids, or pore spaces, per unit of volume). As a result, the daily temperature swings penetrate into the soil to less than 1 metre (3 feet).

Long before human beings could observe the regolith firsthand, Earth-based astronomers concluded from several kinds of measurements that the Moon's surface must be very peculiar. The evidence from photometry (brightness measurements) is particularly striking. From Earth the fully illuminated Moon is 11 times as bright as one only half illuminated, and it appears bright up to the edge of the disk. Measurements of the amount of sunlight reflected back in the direction of illumination indicate the reason: on a small scale the surface is extremely rough, and light reflected from within mineral grains and deep cavities remains shadowed until the illumination source is directly behind the observer—i.e., until the full moon—at which time light abruptly reflects out of the cavities. The polarization properties of the reflected light show that the surface is rough even at a microscopic scale.

Before spacecraft landed on the Moon, astronomers had no straightforward means by which to measure the depth of the regolith layer. Nevertheless, after the development of infrared detectors allowed them to make accurate thermal observations through the telescope, they could finally draw some reasonable conclusions about the outer surface characteristics. As Earth's shadow falls across the Moon during a lunar eclipse, the lunar surface cools rapidly, but the cooling is uneven, being slower near relatively young craters where exposed rock fields are to be expected. This behaviour could be interpreted to show that the highly insulating layer is fairly shallow, a few metres at most. Though not all astronomers accepted this conclusion at first, it was confirmed in the mid-1960s when the first robotic spacecraft soft-landed and sank only a few centimetres instead of disappearing completely into the regolith.

NOTABLE SURFACE FEATURES

Prominent and noteworthy features of the lunar surface range from prominent craters such as Copernicus and Tycho to sites important in humanity's brave history of lunar exploration such as Taurus-Littrow and Hadley Rille.

Copernicus is one of the most prominent craters on the Moon. It constitutes a classic example of a relatively young, well-preserved lunar impact crater. Located at 10° N, 20° W, near the southern rim of the Imbrium Basin (Mare Imbrium) impact structure, Copernicus measures 93 km (58 miles) in diameter and is a source of radial bright rays, light-coloured streaks on the lunar surface formed of material ejected by the impact. Photographs of the crater taken from spacecraft above the Moon show terraced slumps on the crater walls that resemble

giant stairs leading to the floor, 3.8 km (2.4 miles) below the rim crest. Peaked mountains rise from the centre of the crater to a height of 800 metres (2,600 feet); they probably were formed as a result of a rebound of deep-seated rocks at the site of impact. Lunar scientists estimated that Copernicus was created less than one billion years ago.

The Fra Mauro crater appears to be heavily eroded. It was named for a 15th-century Italian monk and mapmaker. About 80 km (50 miles) in diameter, Fra Mauro lies at about 6° S, 17° W, in the Nubium Basin (Mare Nubium) impact structure. The name is also applied to the extensive surrounding region, called the Fra Mauro Formation, which lunar scientists interpret to be material ejected from the impact that formed the giant Imbrium Basin (Mare Imbrium) to the north—the largest impact basin (mare) on the Moon's near side.

A broad, shallow valley within the formation about 50 km (30 miles) north of Fra Mauro crater served as the site of the Apollo 14 manned lunar landing in February 1971. On two separate Moon walks, Apollo astronauts Alan Shepard and Edgar Mitchell collected samples of what was believed to be ejected rock; in later radiometric analysis on Earth, this material was found to have been thermally shocked about 3.9 billion years ago, presumably by the cataclysmic event that created Imbrium.

Hadley Rille is a typical sinuous rille. The feature was a primary site of exploration for the Apollo 15 lunar-landing mission. Named for the 18th-century English inventor John Hadley, the rille is located at approximately 26° N, 3° E, at the southeastern edge of the great lava-filled Imbrium Basin (Mare Imbrium) impact feature. The steep-walled valley, about 1.5 km (0.9 mile) wide and 400 metres (1,300 feet) deep, winds for more than 100 km (60 miles) across the plains of Palus Putredinis along the foot of the Apennine mountain range, a part of the Imbrium Basin's upthrown ramparts.

The rille is easily visible with a telescope from Earth under the right lighting conditions (low-angle morning or evening illumination at the site) and with good seeing (a state of low turbulence in Earth's atmosphere that allows sharp telescopic images). In July 1971 Apollo 15 astronauts drove their rover to the brink of the curving canyon and photographed possible layering in its eroded walls suggestive of stratified lava beds. Because all lunar features are covered by impact debris and no mission has yet visited the interior subsurface of a rille, the true origin of Hadley Rille and other sinuous rilles remains to be elucidated.

The Taurus-Littrow Valley region on the Moon was selected as the landing site of the Apollo 17 manned lunar mission. Located at 22° N, 31° E, it is named for the surrounding Taurus Mountains, a part of the ramparts of the Serenitatis Basin (Mare Serenitatis) impact structure, and for the nearby 30-km- (19-mile-) diameter crater Littrow.

The site was chosen because it had geologic features promising a varied collection of images, samples, and other data from both ancient highland and younger volcanic areas. In December 1972, after descending to the Moon, Apollo astronaut Eugene Cernan and geologist-astronaut Harrison Schmitt deployed their lunar rover and traveled for a total of 36 km (22 miles) on three separate excursions around the valley, retrieving samples that had come downslope from the nearby highlands and collecting specimens of the variegated, titanium-rich mare basalt rocks and soils filling the valley. They also collected samples of orange and black glass indicative of ancient volcanic "fire fountains" (eruptive gouts of lava) on the Moon.

Sample analyses conducted on Earth interpreted the highland rocks as parts of the material excavated by the enormous impact that created the Serenitatis Basin. Some rocks from the Taurus-Littrow site, which is crossed by one of the rays of material ejected from the impact that formed the comparatively young crater Tycho, suggested an age for the crater of about 100 million years. The complex geologic history of the Taurus-Littrow region makes it a prime target for future scientific landing and roving missions on the Moon.

Tycho is the most conspicuous impact crater on the Moon. It lies at the centre of the most extensive system of bright rays on the near side. The rays, which are light-coloured streaks formed of material

Apollo 17 geologist-astronaut Harrison Schmitt at the foot of a huge split boulder, December 13, 1972, during the mission's third extravehicular exploration of the Taurus-Littrow Valley landing site. NASA

ejected from the impact, dominate the southern highlands and extend for more than 2,600 km (1,600 miles) across the Moon's surface.

Tycho, located at 43° S, 11° W, in the highlands south of the Nubium Basin (Mare Nubium) impact structure, measures 85 km (53 miles) in diameter and about 4 km (2.5 miles) deep. Laboratory analysis of samples returned in 1972 by Apollo 17, whose landing site was crossed by one of Tycho's rays, suggests that the crater was formed about 100 million years ago. Because of its relatively young age, the crater retains hummocky rim deposits, terraced walls, and seemingly fresh pools of dark flowlike materials. Multispectral images from the lunar-orbiting robotic Clementine spacecraft in 1994 show that the composition of

Tycho's central peak differs from that of other parts of the crater, consistent with the idea that such features of craters result from a rebound of rocks originating at greater depths in the crust under the centre of the impact.

Lunar Rocks and Soil

The lunar regolith comprises rock fragments in a continuous distribution of particle sizes. It includes a fine fraction—dirtlike in character—that, for convenience, is called soil. The term, however, does not imply a biological contribution to its origin as it does on Earth.

Almost all the rocks at the lunar surface are igneous—they formed from the cooling of lava. (By contrast, the most prevalent rocks exposed on Earth's surface are sedimentary, which required the action of water or wind for their formation.) The two most common kinds are basalts and anorthosites. The lunar basalts, relatively rich in iron and many also in titanium, are found in the maria. In the highlands the rocks are largely anorthosites, which are relatively rich in aluminum, calcium, and silicon. Some of the rocks in both the maria and the highlands are breccias; i.e., they are composed of fragments produced by an initial impact and then reagglomerated by later impacts. The physical compositions of lunar breccias range from broken and shock-altered fragments, called clasts, to a matrix of completely impact-melted material that has lost its original mineral character. The repeated impact history of a particular rock can result in a breccia welded either into a strong, coherent mass or into a weak, crumbly mixture in which the matrix consists of poorly aggregated or metamorphosed fragments. Massive bedrock—that is, bedrock not excavated by natural processes—is absent from the lunar samples so far collected.

Lunar soils are derived from lunar rocks, but they have a distinctive character. They represent the end result of micrometeoroid bombardment and of the Moon's thermal, particulate, and radiation environments. In the ancient past the stream of impacting bodies, some of which were quite large, turned over—or "gardened"—the lunar surface to a depth that is unknown but may have been as much as tens of kilometres. As the frequency of large impacts decreased, the gardening depth became shallower. It is estimated that the top centimetre of the surface at a particular site presently has a 50 percent chance of being turned over every million years, while during the same period the top millimetre is turned over a few dozen times and the outermost tenth of a millimetre is gardened hundreds of times. One result of this process is the presence in the soil of a large fraction of glassy particles forming agglutinates, aggregates of lunar soil fragments set in a glassy cement. The agglutinate fraction is a measure of soil maturity—i.e., of how long a particular sample has been exposed to the continuing rain of tiny impacts.

Cohesiveness of lunar soil, demonstrated qualitatively in a crisply defined boot print left on the Moon by U.S. astronaut Edwin Aldrin during the Apollo 11 mission, July 1969. Aldrin photographed the print as part of a study of the nature of the soil and its compaction behaviour. This image has also become an icon of the first visit by humans to another world. NASA

Although the chemical and mineral-ogical properties of soil particles show that they were derived from native lunar rocks, they also contain small amounts of meteoritic iron and other materials from impacting bodies. Volatile substances from comets, such as carbon compounds and water, would be expected to be mostly driven off by the heat generated by the impact, but the small amounts of carbon found in lunar soils may include atoms of cometary origin.

A fascinating and scientifically important property of lunar soils is the implantation of solar wind particles. Unimpeded by atmospheric or electro-magnetic effects, protons, electrons, and atoms arrive at speeds of hundreds of kilometres per second and are driven into the outermost surfaces of soil grains. Lunar soils thus contain a collection of material from the Sun. Because of their gardening history, soils obtained from different depths have been exposed to the solar wind at the surface at different times and therefore can reveal some aspects of ancient solar behaviour. In addition to its scientific interest, this implantation phe-nomenon may have implications for long-term human habitation of the Moon in the future, as discussed in the section Lunar Resources below.

The chemical and mineral properties of lunar rocks and soils hold clues to the Moon's history, and the study of lunar samples has become an extensive field of science. To date, scientists have obtained lunar material from three sources: six U.S. Apollo Moon-landing missions (1969–72), which collectively brought back almost 382 kg (842 pounds) of samples; three Soviet Luna automated sampling mis-sions (1970–76), which returned about 300 g (0.66 pound) of material; and scien-tific expeditions to Antarctica, which have collected meteorites on the ice fields since 1969. Some of these meteorites are rocks that were blasted out of the Moon by impacts, found their way to Earth, and have been confirmed as lunar in origin by comparison with the samples returned by spacecraft.

The mineral constituents of a rock reflect its chemical composition and thermal history. Rock textures—i.e., the shapes and sizes of mineral grains and the nature of their interfaces—provide clues as to the conditions under which the rock cooled and solidified from a melt. The most common minerals in lunar rocks are silicates (including pyroxene, olivine, and feldspar) and oxides (including ilmenite, spinel, and a mineral discovered in rocks collected by Apollo 11 astronauts and named armalcolite, a word made from the first letters of the astronauts' surnames—Armstrong, Aldrin, and Collins). The properties of lunar minerals reflect the many differences between the history of the Moon and that of Earth. Lunar rocks appear to have formed in the total absence of water. Many minor mineral constituents in lunar rocks reflect the history of formation of the lunar mantle and crust, and they confirm the hypothesis that most rocks now found at the lunar surface formed under reducing conditions—i.e., those in which oxygen was scarce.

MAIN GROUPINGS

The materials formed of these minerals are classified into four main groups: (1) basaltic volcanics, the rocks forming the maria, (2) pristine highland rocks uncontaminated by impact mixing, (3) breccias and impact melts, formed by impacts that disassembled and reassembled mixtures of rocks, and (4) soils, defined as unconsolidated aggregates of particles less than 1 cm (0.4 inch) in size, derived from all the rock types. All these materials are of igneous origin, but their melting and crystallization history is complex.

The mare basalts, when in liquid form, were much less viscous than typical lavas on Earth; they flowed like heavy oil. This was due to the low availability of oxygen and the absence of water in the regions where they formed. The melting temperature of the parent rock was higher than in Earth's volcanic source regions. As the lunar lavas rose to the surface and poured out in thin layers, they filled the basins of the Moon's near side and flowed out over plains, drowning older craters and embaying the basin margins. Some of the lavas contained dissolved gases, as shown by the presence of vesicles (bubbles) in certain rock samples and by the existence of pyroclastic glass (essentially volcanic ash) at some locations. There are also rimless craters, surrounded by dark halos, which do not have the characteristic shape of an impact scar but instead appear to have been formed by eruptions.

Most mare basalts differ from Earthly lavas not only in the lack of evidence of water but also in depletion of other volatile substances such as potassium, sodium, and carbon compounds. They also are depleted of elements classified geochemically as siderophiles—elements that tend to affiliate with iron when rocks cool from a melt. (This siderophile depletion is an important clue to the history of the Earth-Moon system, as discussed in the section Origin and Evolution, below.) Some lavas were relatively rich in elements whose atoms do not readily fit into the crystal lattice sites of the common lunar minerals and are thus called incompatible elements. They tend to remain uncombined in a melt—of either mare or highland composition—and to become concentrated in the last portions to solidify upon cooling. Lunar scientists gave these lavas the name KREEP, an acronym for potassium (chemical symbol K), rare-earth elements, and phosphorus (P). These rocks give information as to the history of partial melting in the lunar mantle and the subsequent rise of lavas through the crust. Radiometric age dating reveals that the great eruptions that formed the maria occurred hundreds of millions of years later than the more extensive heating that produced the lunar highlands.

Ancient highland material that is considered pristine is relatively rare because most highland rocks have been subjected to repeated smashing and reagglomeration by impacts and are therefore in brecciated form. A few of the collected lunar samples, however, appear to have been essentially unaltered since they solidified in the primeval lunar crust. These rocks, some rich in aluminum and calcium or magnesium and others showing the KREEP chemical signature, suggest that late in its formation the Moon was covered by a deep magma ocean. The slow cooling of this enormous molten body, in which lighter minerals rose as they formed and heavier ones sank, appears to have resulted in the crust and mantle that exists today.

THE LUNAR INTERIOR

STRUCTURE AND COMPOSITION

Most of the knowledge about the lunar interior has come from the Apollo missions and from robotic spacecraft, including Galileo, Clementine, and Lunar Prospector, which observed the Moon in the 1990s. Combining all available data, scientists have created a picture of the Moon as a layered body comprising a low-density crust, which ranges from 60 to 100 km (40 to 60 miles) in thickness, overlying a denser mantle, which constitutes the great majority of the Moon's volume. At the centre there probably is a small iron-rich metallic core with a radius of about 350 km (250 miles) at most. At one time, shortly after the Moon's formation, the core had an electromagnetic dynamo like that of Earth, which accounts for the remanent magnetism observed in some lunar rocks, but it appears that such internal activity has long ceased on the Moon.

Despite these gains in knowledge, important uncertainties remain. For example, there seems to be no generally accepted explanation for the evidence that the crust is asymmetrical: thicker on the Moon's far side, with the maria predominantly on the near side. Examination of naturally excavated samples from large impact basins may help to resolve this and other questions in lunar history.

Internal Activity of the Past and Present

The idea that the lunar crust is the product of differentiation in an ancient magma ocean is supported to some extent by compositional data, which show that lightweight rocks, containing such minerals as plagioclase, rose while denser materials, such as pyroxene and olivine, sank to become the source regions for the later radioactive heating episode that resulted in the outflows of mare basalts. Whether or not there ever was a uniform global ocean of molten rock, it is clear that the Moon's history is one of much heating and melting in a complex series of events that would have driven off volatiles (if any were present) and erased the record of earlier mineral compositions.

At present all evidence points to the Moon as a body in which, given its small size, all heat-driven internal processes have run down. Its heat flow near the surface, as measured at two sites by Apollo instruments, appears to be less than half that of Earth. Seismic activity is probably far less than that of Earth,

though this conclusion needs to be verified by longer-running observations than Apollo provided. Many of the moonquakes detected seem to be only small "creaks" during the Moon's continual adjustment to gravity gradients in its eccentric orbit, while others are due to meteorite impacts or thermal effects. Quakes of truly tectonic origin seem to be uncommon. The small quakes that do occur demonstrate distinct differences from Earth in the way seismic waves are transmitted, both in the regolith and in deeper layers. The seismic data suggest that impacts have fragmented and mixed the upper part of the lunar crust in a manner that left a high proportion of void space. At depths beyond tens of kilometres, the crust behaves as consolidated dry rock.

ORIGIN AND EVOLUTION

With the rise of scientific inquiry in the Renaissance, investigators attempted to fit theories on the origin of the Moon to the available information, and the question of the Moon's formation became a part of the attempt to explain the observed properties of the solar system. At first the approach was largely founded on a mathematical examination of the dynamics of the Earth-Moon system. Rigorous analysis of careful observations over a period of more than 200 years gradually revealed that, because of tidal effects, the rotations of both the Moon and Earth are slowing and the Moon is receding from Earth.

Studies then turned back to consider the state of the system when the Moon was closer to Earth. Throughout the 17th, 18th, and 19th centuries, investigators examined different theories on lunar origin in an attempt to find one that would agree with the observations.

Lunar origin theories can be divided into three main categories: coaccretion, fission, and capture. Coaccretion suggests that the Moon and Earth were formed together from a primordial cloud of gas and dust. This scenario, however, cannot explain the large angular momentum of the present system. In fission theories a fluid proto-Earth began rotating so rapidly that it flung off a mass of material that formed the Moon. Although persuasive, the theory eventually failed when examined in detail; scientists could not find a combination of properties for a spinning proto-Earth that would eject the right kind of proto-Moon. According to capture theories, the Moon formed elsewhere in the solar system and was later trapped by the strong gravitational field of Earth. This scenario remained popular for a long time, even though the circumstances needed in celestial mechanics to brake a passing Moon into just the right orbit always seemed unlikely.

By the mid-20th century, scientists had imposed additional requirements for a viable lunar-origin theory. Of great importance is the observation that the Moon is much less dense than Earth, and the only likely reason is that the Moon contains significantly less iron. Such a large chemical difference argued against a common origin for the two bodies. Independent-origin theories, however, had their own problems. The question remained unresolved even after the scientifically productive Apollo missions, and it was only in the early 1980s that a model emerged—the giant-impact hypothesis—that eventually gained the support of most lunar scientists.

In this scenario the proto-Earth, shortly after its formation from the solar nebula about 4.6 billion years ago, was struck a glancing blow by a body the size of Mars. Prior to the impact, both bodies already had undergone differentiation into core and mantle. The titanic collision ejected a cloud of fragments, which aggregated into a full or partial ring around Earth and then coalesced into a proto-Moon. The ejected matter consisted mainly of mantle material from the colliding body and the proto-Earth, and it experienced enormous heating from the collision. As a result, the proto-Moon that formed was highly depleted in volatiles and relatively depleted in iron (and thus also in siderophiles). Computer modeling of the collision shows that, given the right initial conditions, an orbiting cloud of debris as massive as the Moon could indeed have formed.

Once a proto-Moon was present in the debris cloud, it would have quickly swept up the remaining fragments in a tremendous bombardment. Then, over a period of 100 million years or so, the rate of impacting bodies diminished, although there still occurred occasional collisions with large objects. Perhaps this was the time of the putative magma ocean and the differentiation of the ancient plagioclase-rich crust. After the Moon had cooled and solidified enough to preserve impact scars, it began to retain the huge signatures of basin-forming collisions with asteroid-sized bodies left over from the formation of the solar system. About 3.9 billion years ago, one of these formed the great Imbrium Basin, or Mare Imbrium, and its mountain ramparts. During some period over the next several hundred million years there occurred the long sequence of volcanic events that filled the near-side basins with mare lavas.

In an effort to unravel the history of this period, scientists have applied modern analytic techniques to lunar rock samples. The mare basalts show a wide range of chemical and mineral compositions reflecting different conditions in the deep regions of the mantle where, presumably because of heating from radioactive elements in the rock, primordial lunar materials were partly remelted and fractionated so that the lavas carried unique trace-element signatures up to the surface. By studying the past events and processes reflected in the mineral, chemical, and isotopic properties of these rocks, lunar scientists have slowly built a picture of a variegated Moon. Their findings have provided valuable background information for Earth- and spacecraft-based efforts to map how the content of important materials varies over the lunar surface.

Once the huge mare lava outflows had diminished, apparently the Moon's heat source had run down. The last few billion years of its history have been calm and essentially geologically inactive except for the continuing rain of impacts, which is also declining over time, and the microscopic weathering due to bombardment by solar and cosmic radiation and particles.

LUNAR EXPLORATION

EARLY STUDIES

Investigations of the Moon and some understanding of lunar phenomena can be traced back to a few centuries BCE. In ancient China the Moon's motion was carefully recorded as part of a grand structure of astrological thought. In both China and the Middle East, observations became accurate enough to enable the prediction of eclipses, and the recording of eclipses left data of great value for later scientists interested in tracing the history of the Earth-Moon system. Several early Greek philosophers saw reason to believe that the Moon was inhabited, although they did not base their conclusion on scientific principles. The Greek astronomer and mathematician Hipparchus, on the other hand, took an experimental approach: observing Earth's round shadow creeping across the Moon during a lunar eclipse, he concluded that Earth must be spherical and that the Moon was an independent world, and he correctly explained the Moon's phases and accurately estimated the distance between the two bodies. Later, Mayan calendars were constructed that reflected the results of careful observation and long-range prediction.

For centuries, knowledge about the Moon accumulated slowly, driven by astrological and navigational needs, until an outburst of progress began in the Renaissance. In the early 1600s the German astronomer Johannes Kepler used observations made by Tycho Brahe of Denmark to find empirically the laws governing planetary motion. Kepler wrote a remarkable work of science fiction, *Somnium* ("The Dream"), which describes the life of imagined inhabitants of the Moon and correctly portrays such facts as the high temperature of the Moon's sunlit side. In 1609–10 Galileo began his telescopic observations that forever changed human understanding of the Moon. Most effort hitherto had been devoted to understanding the movements of the Moon through space, but now astronomers began to focus their attention on the character of the Moon itself. Some milestones in human exploration and understanding of the Moon are given in the table.

HISTORY OF LUNAR OBSERVATION AND EXPLORATION	
TIME PERIOD	**ACCOMPLISHMENT**
prehistoric and early historic times	Basic knowledge of Moon's motion, phases, and markings is gathered and expressed in myth and legend.
500 BCE to 150 CE	Phases and eclipses are correctly explained; Moon's size and distance from Earth are measured.
Middle Ages	Lunar ephemeris is refined.
Renaissance	Laws of motion are formulated; telescopic observations begin.
19th century	Near-side lunar mapping is completed; atmosphere is proved absent; geologic principles are applied in volcanism-versus-impact debate over formation of Moon's landscape.
1924	Polarimetry studies show that lunar surface is composed of small particles.
1927–30	Surface temperatures are measured for lunar day and night and during eclipses.

TIME PERIOD	ACCOMPLISHMENT
1946	Radar echoes are reflected from Moon and detected for first time.
1950–57	Theories of Moon's formation are incorporated in efforts to explain origin of solar system; radiometric age dating is employed in meteorite research; lunar subsurface temperatures are measured by microwave radiometry; relative ages of lunar features are derived from principles of stratigraphy (study of rock layers and their chronological relationship).
1959	Luna 2 spacecraft becomes first man-made object to strike Moon; global magnetic field is found to be absent; Luna 3 supplies first far-side images.
1960	Detailed measurements of lunar surface cooling during eclipses are made from Earth.
1964	Ranger 7 transmits high-resolution pictures of Moon.
1966	Luna 9 and Surveyor 1 make first lunar soft landings; Luna 10 and Lunar Orbiter 1 become first spacecraft to orbit Moon.
1967	First measurements made of lunar surface chemistry.
1968	Mascons are discovered in analysis of data from Lunar Orbiters; Apollo 8 astronauts orbit Moon.
1969	Apollo 11 astronauts become first humans to walk on Moon; lunar samples and data are returned to Earth.
1969–74	Manned Apollo orbital and surface expeditions and automated Luna flights explore Moon's lower latitudes; Apollo program is completed.
1970s–present	Lunar studies are continued using samples returned by Apollo and Luna missions, meteorites originating from Moon, and data gathered by Earth-based mineralogical remote-sensing techniques.
1990	Galileo spacecraft collects compositional remote-sensing data during lunar flyby, demonstrating potential for future orbital geochemical missions.
1994	Orbiting Clementine spacecraft provides imagery, altimetry, and gravity maps of entire Moon.
1998–99	Orbiting Lunar Prospector spacecraft maps lunar surface composition and magnetic field; its neutron spectrometer data confirm presence of excess hydrogen at both poles, suggesting presence of water ice there.

EXPLORATION BY SPACECRAFT

FIRST ROBOTIC MISSIONS

Following the launch in 1957 of the U.S.S.R.'s satellite Sputnik, the first spacecraft to orbit Earth, it became obvious that the next major goal of both the Soviet and the U.S. space programs would be the Moon. The United States quickly prepared and launched a few robotic lunar probes, most of which failed and none of which reached the Moon. The Soviet Union had more success, achieving in 1959 the first escape from Earth's gravity with Luna 1, the first impact on the lunar surface with Luna 2, and the first photographic survey of the Moon's far side with Luna 3. After the National Aeronautics and Space Administration (NASA) was founded in 1958, the U.S. program became more ambitious technically and more scientifically oriented. Initial spacecraft investigations were geared toward studying the Moon's fundamental character as a planetary body by means of seismic observation, gamma-ray spectrometry, and close-up imaging. Scientists believed that even limited seismic data would give clues toward resolving the question as to whether the Moon was a primitive, undifferentiated body or one that had been heated and modified by physical and chemical processes such as those on Earth. Gamma-ray measurements would complement the seismic results by showing whether the Moon's interior had

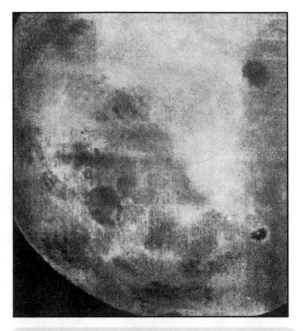

One of the first recorded views of the Moon's far side, part of a 29-photograph sequence taken by the Soviet Luna 3 spacecraft on October 7, 1959. Mare Smythii, which lies on the boundary between the near and far sides, is the circular dark patch below and left of centre, and Mare Moscoviense is the dark circle at upper right. At lower right, appearing as a dark spot with an inner white dot, is the crater Tsiolkovskiy with its central peak. NASA/Goddard Space Flight Center

sufficient radioactivity to serve as an active heat engine, and they would also give some information on the chemical composition of the lunar surface. Imaging would reveal features too small to be seen from Earth, perhaps providing information on lunar surface processes and also arousing public interest.

Among nine U.S. Ranger missions launched between 1961 and 1965, Ranger 4 (1962) became the first U.S. spacecraft to strike the Moon. Only the last three craft, however, avoided the plaguing malfunctions that limited or prematurely ended the missions of their predecessors. Ranger 7 (1964) returned thousands of excellent television images before impacting as designed, and Rangers 8 and 9 (both 1965) followed successfully. The impact locale of Ranger 7 was named Mare Cognitum for the new knowledge gained, a major example of which was the discovery that even small lunar features have been mostly subdued from incessant meteorite impacts.

After a number of failures in the mid-1960s, the Soviet Union scored several notable achievements: the first successful lunar soft landing by Luna 9 and the first lunar orbit by Luna 10, both in 1966. Pictures from Luna 9 revealed the soft, rubbly nature of the regolith and, because the landing capsule did not sink out of sight, confirmed its approximate bearing strength. Gamma-ray data from Luna 10 hinted at a basaltic composition for near-side regions. In 1965 the Soviet flyby mission designated Zond 3 returned good pictures of the Moon's far side.

In the mid-1960s the United States carried out its own soft-landing and orbital missions. In 1966 Surveyor 1 touched down on the Moon and returned panoramic television images. Six more Surveyors followed between 1966 and 1968, with two failures; they provided not only detailed television views of lunar scenery but also the first chemical data on lunar soil and the first soil-mechanics information showing mechanical properties of the top few centimetres of the regolith. Also, during 1966–67 five U.S. Lunar Orbiters made photographic surveys of most of the lunar surface, providing the mapping essential for planning the Apollo missions.

APOLLO TO THE PRESENT

After the Soviet cosmonaut Yury Gagarin pioneered human Earth-orbital flight in April 1961, U.S. President John F. Kennedy established the national objective of landing a man on the Moon and returning him safely by the end of the decade. Apollo was the result of that effort.

Within a few years the Soviet Union and the United States were heavily engaged in a political and technological race to launch manned flights to the Moon. At the time, the Soviets did not publicly acknowledge the full extent of their program, but they did launch a number of human-precursor circumlunar missions between 1968 and 1970 under the generic name Zond, using spacecraft derived from their piloted Soyuz design. Some of the Zond flights brought back colour photographs of the Moon's far side and safely carried live tortoises and other organisms around the Moon and back to Earth. In parallel with these developments, Soviet scientists began launching

Planet Earth rising above the lunar horizon, an unprecedented view captured in December 1968 by Apollo 8 astronauts as their orbit carried them clear of the far side of the Moon. NASA

In December 1968, acting partly out of concern that the Soviet Union might be first in getting people to the Moon's vicinity, the United States employed the Apollo 8 mission to take three astronauts—Frank Borman, James Lovell, and William Anders—into lunar orbit. After circling the Moon three times, the crew returned home safely with hundreds of photographs. The Apollo 9 and 10 missions completed the remaining tests of the systems needed for landing on and ascending from the Moon. On July 20, 1969, Apollo 11 astronauts Neil Armstrong and Edwin ("Buzz") Aldrin set foot on the Moon while Michael Collins orbited above them. Five more successful manned landing missions followed, ending with Apollo 17 in 1972; at the completion of the program, a total of 12 astronauts had set foot on the Moon.

Twenty years later the Soviet Union admitted that it had indeed been aiming at the same goal as Apollo, not only with a set of spacecraft modules for landing on and returning from the Moon but also with the development of a huge launch

a series of robotic Luna spacecraft designed to go into lunar orbit and then land with heavy payloads. This series, continuing to 1976, eventually returned drill-core samples of regolith to Earth and also landed two wheeled rovers, Lunokhod 1 and 2 (1970 and 1973), that pioneered robotic mobile exploration of the Moon. The Luna samples that were returned to Earth were valuable because they were collected from eastern equatorial areas far from the Apollo sites.

U.S. astronaut Edwin ("Buzz") Aldrin walking on the Moon, July 20, 1969. NASA

vehicle, called the N1, comparable to the Apollo program's Saturn V. After several launch failures of the N1, the program was canceled in 1974.

After the Apollo missions, lunar scientists continued to conduct multi-spectral remote-sensing observations from Earth and perfected instrumental and data-analysis techniques. During Galileo's flybys of Earth and the Moon in December 1990 and 1992 en route to Jupiter, the spacecraft demonstrated the potential for spaceborne multispectral observations—i.e., imaging the Moon in several discrete wavelength ranges—to gather geochemical data. As a next logical step, scientists generally agreed on a global survey of physical and geochemical properties by an automated spacecraft in polar orbit above the Moon and

Apollo 15 astronaut James B. Irwin standing in back of the lunar roving vehicle; the lunar module (LM) is at left with the modular equipment storage assembly (MESA) in front of it. Apollo 15 was launched July 26, 1971. NASA

employing techniques evolved from those used during the Apollo missions. Finally, after a long hiatus, orbital mapping of the Moon resumed with the flights of the Clementine and Lunar Prospector spacecraft, launched in 1994 and 1998, respectively.

The Clementine and Lunar Prospector spacecraft, operating in lunar polar orbits, used complementary suites of remote-sensing instruments to map the entire Moon, measuring its surface composition, geomorphology, topography, and gravitational and magnetic anomalies. The topographic data highlighted the huge South Pole–Aitken Basin, which, like the other basins on the far side, is devoid of lava filling. Measuring roughly 2,500 km (1,550 miles) in diameter and 13 km (8 miles) deep, it is the largest impact feature on the Moon and the largest known in the solar system; because of its location, its existence was not confirmed until the Lunar Orbiter missions in the 1960s. The gravity data collected by the spacecraft, combined with topography, confirmed the existence of a thick, rigid crust, giving yet more

Multispectral image of the Moon's Mare Tranquillitatis and Mare Serenitatis regions (upper left and lower right, respectively) derived from observations by the Galileo spacecraft in December 1992 during its second lunar flyby. The image was constructed from multiple exposures made at different wavelengths. The photo indicates both low and high concentrations of titanium on the planet. NASA/Goddard Space Flight Center

evidence that the Moon's heat source has expired. Both spacecraft missions hinted at the long-considered possibility that water ice exists in permanently shadowed polar craters. The most persuasive evidence came from the neutron spectrometer of Lunar Prospector.

Toward the end of the first decade of the 21st century, there was a revival of lunar exploration on the part of several spacefaring nations. In 2007 Japan

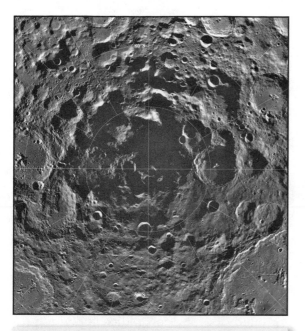

The Moon's south polar region in a mosaic of images made by the U.S. Clementine spacecraft from lunar orbit in 1994. The mosaic, which is centred on the south pole and combines the illumination received over more than two of the Moon's solar days (each about 29 Earth days), reveals the existence of appreciable permanently shadowed areas where water ice could exist. Ice deposits, if they could be mined economically, would constitute an important resource for a future manned lunar outpost. NASA/Goddard Space Flight Center

launched the Kaguya satellite, which mapped the Moon's gravity field. That same year, China launched its first lunar probe, Chang'e 1, and the U.S. search engine company Google announced a $30 million prize to the first privately funded team to land a robotic rover on the Moon. In 2008 Chandrayaan-1, the first Indian lunar probe, studied the Moon's mineralogy.

Future planned unmanned missions include other satellites in the Kaguya, Chang'e, and Chandrayaan series. Russia and the U.K. have announced probes, Luna-Glob and MoonLITE, respectively, scheduled for launch in 2014, that will study the Moon's seismic activity. The U.S. has planned three lunar probes: the Lunar Reconnaissance Orbiter (LRO, 2009), which will map the Moon; the Lunar Atmosphere and Dust Environment Explorer (LADEE, 2011), which will study the Moon's atmosphere, and the Gravity Recovery and Interior Laboratory (GRAIL, 2011), which will accurately map the Moon's gravity field. These three missions will pave the way for the return of astronauts to the Moon in 2020 as part of the Constellation program, which will carry four astronauts in Orion, the main spacecraft, and Altair, the lunar lander.

LUNAR RESOURCES

Scientists and space planners have long acknowledged that extended human residence on the Moon would be greatly aided by the use of local resources. This would avoid the high cost of lifting payloads against Earth's strong gravity. Certainly, lunar soil could be used for shielding habitats against the radiation environment. More advanced uses of lunar resources are clearly possible, but how advantageous they would be is presently unknown. For example, most lunar rocks are about 40 percent oxygen, and chemical and electrochemical methods for extracting it have been demonstrated in laboratories. Nevertheless, significant engineering advances would be needed before the cost and difficulty of operating an industrial-scale mining and oxygen-production facility on the Moon could be estimated and its advantages over transporting oxygen from Earth could be evaluated. In the long run, however, some form of extractive industry on the Moon is likely, in part because launching fleets of large rockets continuously from Earth would be too costly and too polluting of the atmosphere.

The solar wind has implanted hydrogen, helium, and other elements in the surfaces of fine grains of lunar soil. Though their amounts are small—they constitute about 100 parts per million in the soil—they may someday serve as a resource. They are easily released by moderate heating, but large volumes of soil would need to be processed to obtain useful amounts of the desired materials. Helium-3, a helium isotope that is rare on Earth and that has been deposited on the Moon by the solar wind, has been proposed as a fuel for nuclear fusion reactors in the future.

One natural resource uniquely available on the Moon is its polar environment. Because the Moon's axis is nearly perpendicular to the plane of the ecliptic, sunlight is always horizontal at the lunar poles, and certain areas, such as crater bottoms, exist in perpetual shadow. Under these conditions the surface may reach temperatures as low as 40 K (–388 °F, –233 °C). Some scientists have theorized that these cold traps may have collected volatile substances, including water ice, over geologic time, though others have expressed doubt that ice deposits could have survived there.

The Lunar Prospector spacecraft, which orbited the Moon for a year and a half, carried a neutron spectrometer to investigate the composition of the regolith within about a metre (three feet) of the surface. Neutrons originating underground owing to radioactivity and cosmic-ray bombardment interact with the nuclei of elements in the regolith en route to space, where they can be detected from orbit. A neutron loses more energy in an interaction with a light nucleus than with a heavy one, so the observed neutron spectrum can reveal whether light elements are present in the regolith. Lunar Prospector gave clear indications of light-element concentrations at both poles, interpreted as proof of excess hydrogen atoms. The observed hydrogen signature may represent the theoretically predicted deposits of water ice. However, the Kaguya spacecraft saw no evidence of water ice in a crater at the Moon's south pole where Clementine's radar had possibly detected frozen water.

A high priority for future lunar exploration is to send an autonomous robotic rover into a dark polar region to confirm the putative ice deposits, find out the form of the ice if it exists, and begin assessing its possible utility. If lunar ice can be mined economically, it can serve as a source of rocket propellants when split into its hydrogen and oxygen components. From a longer-term perspective, however, the ice would better be regarded as a limited, recyclable resource for life support (in the form of drinking water and perhaps breathable oxygen). Should this resource exist, an international policy for its conservation and management would be needed. Discovery of volatile substances anywhere on the Moon would be important both scientifically and for potential human habitation because all known lunar rocks are totally dry.

Even if no icy bonanza is discovered, the lunar polar regions still represent an important resource. Only there can be found not only continuous darkness but also continuous sunlight. A solar collector tracking the Sun from a high peak near a lunar pole could provide essentially uninterrupted heat and electric power. Also, the radiators required for eliminating waste heat could be positioned in areas of continuous darkness, where the heat could be dissipated into space.

The lunar poles also could serve as good sites for certain astronomical observations. To observe objects in the cosmos that radiate in the infrared and millimetre-wavelength regions of the spectrum, astronomers need telescopes and detectors that are cold enough to limit the interference generated by the instruments' own heat. To date, such telescopes launched into space have carried cryogenic coolants, which eventually run out. A telescope permanently sited in a lunar polar cold region and insulated from local heat sources might cool on its own to 40 K (-233 °C, or -388 °F) or lower. Although such an instrument could observe less than half the sky—ideally, one would be placed at each lunar pole—it would enable uninterrupted viewing of any object above its horizon.

CHAPTER 7

ECLIPSES

One of the most beautiful and awe-inspiring phenomena that can be seen from our vantage point in the inner solar system is that of the eclipse. To see the Sun slowly disappear as if swallowed by some enormous beast or to see the Moon dim to a blood-red hue startled ancient peoples. Today, however, we know that we do not have to resort to myth to explain these events. Eclipses are the complete or partial obscuring of a celestial body by another, and in more general terms an eclipse occurs when three celestial objects become aligned.

From the perspective of a person on Earth, the Sun is eclipsed when the Moon comes between it and Earth, and the Moon is eclipsed when it moves into the shadow of Earth cast by the Sun. Eclipses of natural satellites (moons) or of spacecraft orbiting or flying past a planet occur as the bodies move into the planet's shadow. In the universe outside the solar system, the two component stars of an eclipsing binary star move around each other in such a way that their orbital plane passes through or very near Earth, and each star periodically eclipses the other as seen from Earth.

The phenomena of occultations and transits are related to eclipses. When the apparent size of the eclipsed body is much smaller than that of the eclipsing body, the phenomenon is known as an occultation. Examples are the disappearance of a star, nebula, or planet behind the Moon or the vanishing of a natural satellite or spacecraft behind some body of the solar system. A transit occurs when, as viewed from Earth or another point in space, a relatively small body passes across the disk of a larger body, usually the Sun or a planet, eclipsing only a very small area. Mercury and Venus, for example, periodically transit the Sun, and a natural satellite may transit its planet.

PHENOMENA OBSERVED DURING ECLIPSES

LUNAR ECLIPSE PHENOMENA

The Moon, when full, may enter the shadow of Earth. The motion of the Moon around Earth is from west to east. For an observer facing south, the shadowing of the Moon begins at its left edge (if the Moon were north of the observer, as, for example, in parts of the Southern Hemisphere, the opposite would be true). If the eclipse is a total one and circumstances are favourable, the Moon will pass through the umbra, the darkest part of the shadow, in about two hours. During this time the Moon is usually not completely dark. A part of the sunlight, especially the redder light, penetrates Earth's atmosphere, is refracted into the shadow cone, and reaches the Moon. Meteorological conditions on Earth strongly affect the amount and colour of light that can penetrate the atmosphere. Generally, the totally eclipsed Moon is clearly visible and has a reddish brown, coppery colour, but the brightness varies strongly from one eclipse to another.

Before the Moon enters the umbra and after it leaves the umbra, it must pass through the penumbra, or partial shadow. When the border between umbra and penumbra is visible on the Moon, the border is seen to be part of a circle, the projection of the circumference of Earth. This is a direct proof of the spherical shape of Earth, a discovery made by the ancient Greeks. Because of Earth's atmosphere, the edge of the umbra is rather diffuse, and the times of contact between the Moon and the umbra cannot be observed accurately.

During the eclipse the surface of the Moon cools at a rate dependent on the constitution of the lunar soil, which is not everywhere the same. Many spots on the Moon sometimes remain brighter than their surroundings during totality—particularly in their output of infrared radiation—possibly because their heat conductivity is less, but the cause is not fully understood. An eclipse of the Moon can be seen under similar conditions at all places on Earth where the Moon is above the horizon.

SOLAR ECLIPSE PHENOMENA

Totality at any particular solar eclipse can be seen only from a narrow belt on Earth, sometimes only 150 km (90 miles) wide. The designation "first contact" refers to the moment when the disk of the Moon, invisible against the bright sky background, first touches the disk of the Sun. The partial phase of the eclipse then begins as a small indentation in the western rim of the Sun becomes noticeable. The dark disk of the Moon now gradually moves across the Sun's disk, and the bright area of the Sun is reduced to a crescent. On Earth the sunlight, shining through gaps in foliage and other small openings, is then seen to form little crescents of light that are images of the light source, the Sun. Toward the beginning of totality, the direct light from the Sun diminishes very quickly, and the colour changes. The sky near the zenith becomes dark, but along the horizon Earth's atmosphere still appears bright because of the narrow extent of the umbra of the Moon's shadow on Earth. The scattered light coming in from a distance beyond the umbral region produces the effect of twilight. Animals may react with fear, humans often with awe. Birds may go to roost as they do at sunset.

As the tiny, narrow crescent of sunlight disappears, little bright specks remain where depressions in the Moon's edge, the limb, are last to obscure the Sun's limb. These specks are known as Baily's beads, named for the 19th-century English astronomer Francis Baily, who first drew attention to them. The beads vanish at the moment of second contact, when totality begins. This is the climax of the eclipse. The reddish prominences and chromosphere of the Sun, around the Moon's limb, can now be seen. The brighter planets and stars become visible in the sky. White coronal streamers extend from the Sun to a distance of several solar radii. The air temperature on Earth in the path of totality falls by some degrees. The light of totality is much brighter than that of the full moon but is quite different in colour. The duration of totality is brief, typically lasting two to five minutes.

The moment of third contact occurs when the Moon's west edge first reveals the Sun's disk. Many of the phenomena of second contact appear again, in reverse order. Suddenly the first Baily's bead appears. More beads of light follow, the Sun's crescent grows again, the corona disappears, daylight brightens, and the stars and planets fade from view. The thin crescent of the Sun gradually widens, and about one and a quarter hours later the eclipse ends with fourth contact, when the last encroachment made by the Moon on the Sun's rim disappears.

During the partial phase, both before and after totality, it is absolutely essential for an observer to protect the eyes against injury by the intense brilliance of the Sun. This phase should never be viewed directly except through strong filters or a dark smoked glass.

When totality is imminent and only a small crescent of the Sun remains, so-called shadow bands can often be seen on plain light-coloured surfaces, such as floors and walls. These are striations of light and shade, moving and undulating, several centimetres wide. Their speed and direction depend on air currents at various heights, because they are caused by refraction of sunlight by small inhomogeneities in Earth's atmosphere. The phenomenon is similar to the images of water waves seen on the bottom of a sunlit swimming pool or bath.

OCCULTATIONS

The Moon occults all the objects in the sky in a 10°-wide belt centred on the ecliptic within a period of about nine years. Initially, astronomers' primary goal of observing lunar occultations of stars was to refine the parameters of the Moon's orbit. With the advent of large telescopes and fast electronics, lunar occultations have found application in measuring stellar angular diameters, detecting dust envelopes around stars, and a variety of other studies.

Lunar occultations are used extensively to determine the angular diameters of cool giant stars such as Antares and Aldebaran. An angular resolution of a few thousandths of an arc second is achievable. As a star becomes occulted, its light is diffracted around the sharp edge of the Moon and produces a characteristic oscillatory signal. From the duration and shape of the signal, astronomers can derive the diameter and effective surface temperature of the star. The event is so fast, lasting only a few milliseconds, that any distortion due to Earth's atmosphere (twinkling, or scintillation) is eliminated, which is an advantage over the alternative method of optical interferometry. The diameters of some stars determined in this way seem to vary in time, as if the stars are pulsating slowly.

Lunar occultations have also revealed dust shells around stars and helped determine their shape and structure. One class of stars studied this way are the Wolf-Rayet stars—large, massive stars that blow off a thick envelope of material from their surface in a stellar wind as they near the end of their lives. In addition, lunar occultations are useful for discovering binary stars, and systematic surveys of the sky are made for this purpose.

Arguably the most famous application of lunar occultation occurred in 1962, when the British astronomer Cyril Hazard and colleagues used the Parkes radio telescope in Australia to refine measurements of the positions in the sky of catalogued radio sources that were not identified with any known stars or galaxies. To improve the accuracy of the positions, Hazard timed the occultation of the sources by the Moon. One radio source, designated 3C 273, turned out to consist of two sources separated by 19.5 arc seconds. The signal from one component suggested it could be a star, but it had a type of radio spectrum that had never been seen before. The following year the American astronomer Maarten Schmidt identified a 12th-magnitude star at the precise location of this radio source and obtained its spectrum. The spectrum showed that the source was receding at 15 percent of the speed of light and was therefore very distant. Hazard had in fact resolved the location of the first known quasi-stellar radio source, or quasar.

All the major planets and their moons occult stars in their paths, and such occultations can occasionally yield information on planetary atmospheres. For example, variations over time in the atmosphere of Pluto have been inferred from stellar occultations. Sometimes a stellar occultation produces a stunning surprise, as occurred on March 10, 1977, when the planet Uranus was predicted to pass between Earth and a bright star. The event was observed by several teams of astronomers, who hoped to derive an accurate estimate of the diameter of the planet from their data. Unexpectedly, however, the light from the star was briefly obscured several times before and after the disk of Uranus occulted it. It was concluded that the brief changes in the star's brightness were due to the presence around Uranus of a previously unobserved system of rings, somewhat like the rings of Saturn.

Asteroids, like moons and planets, occult stars as they orbit the Sun. By timing the vanishing and reappearance of a star as an asteroid crosses it from two or more locations on Earth, astronomers can determine the asteroid's size and shape. In modern times a large community of professional and amateur scientists has cooperated in predicting and observing such occultations. For example, on Jan. 19, 1991, observers at nine locations across the United States timed the occultation of a star by Kleopatra, a main-belt asteroid. The timings determined nine different chords across the asteroid, from which was drawn a rough outline of the asteroid, showing it to have an elongated, cigar shape.

TRANSITS OF MERCURY AND VENUS

A transit of Mercury or Venus across the face of the Sun, as seen from Earth, occurs at inferior conjunction, when the planet lies between the Sun and Earth. Because the orbits of both planets, like the Moon's orbit, are inclined to the ecliptic, these planets usually pass above or below the Sun. Also like the Moon's orbit, each planet's orbit intersects the ecliptic plane in two points called nodes; if inferior conjunction occurs at a time when the planet is near a node, a transit of the Sun can occur.

For Mercury these times occur around May 8 and November 10. November transits occur at intervals of 7, 13, or 33 years, while May transits occur only at the latter two intervals. On average, Mercury transits the Sun about 13 times per century. In the transit of Mercury that took place on Nov. 15, 1999, the planet just grazed the edge of the Sun. The Transition Region and Coronal Explorer (TRACE) satellite, an Earth-orbiting solar observatory launched in 1998, recorded the event in several wavelengths. Mercury's dark disk measured only about 10 arc seconds in diameter, compared with the Sun's diameter of 1,922 arc seconds. Transits of Mercury also have occurred or will occur on May 7, 2003, Nov. 8, 2006, May 9, 2016, Nov. 11, 2019, and Nov. 13, 2032. Observers cannot see Mercury's tiny disk against the Sun without some form of magnification.

Transits of Venus occur at its nodes in December and June and generally follow a recurrence pattern of 8, 121, 8, and 105 years before starting over. Following the transits of Dec. 9, 1874, and Dec. 6, 1882, the world waited 121 years until June 8,

2004, for the next transit to occur. Dates for successive transits of Venus are June 6, 2012, and, after a 105-year interval, Dec. 11, 2117, and Dec. 8, 2125. Unlike a transit of Mercury, a transit of Venus can be watched without magnification through a suitable dark filter or as an image projected on a screen through a pinhole lens.

THE GEOMETRY OF ECLIPSES, OCCULTATIONS, AND TRANSITS

ECLIPSES OF THE SUN

An eclipse of the Sun takes place when the Moon comes between Earth and the Sun so that the Moon's shadow sweeps over the face of Earth. This shadow consists of two parts: the umbra, a cone into which no direct sunlight penetrates; and the penumbra, which is reached by light from only a part of the Sun's disk.

To an observer within the umbra, the Sun's disk appears completely covered by the disk of the Moon; such an eclipse is called total. To an observer within the penumbra, the Moon's disk appears projected against the Sun's disk so as to overlap it partly; the eclipse is then called partial for that observer. The umbral cone is narrow at the distance of Earth, and a total eclipse is observable only within the narrow strip of land or sea over which the umbra passes. A partial eclipse may be seen from places within the large area covered by the penumbra. Sometimes Earth intercepts the penumbra of the Moon but is missed by its umbra; only a partial eclipse of the Sun is then observed anywhere on Earth.

By a remarkable coincidence, the sizes and distances of the Sun and Moon are such that they appear as very nearly the same angular size (about 0.5°) at Earth, but their apparent sizes depend on their distances from Earth. Earth revolves around the Sun in an elliptical orbit, so that the distance of the Sun changes slightly during a year, with a correspondingly small change in the apparent size, the angular diameter, of the solar disk. In a similar way, the apparent size of the Moon's disk changes somewhat during the month because the Moon's orbit is also elliptical. When the Sun is nearest to Earth and the Moon is at its greatest distance, the apparent disk of the Moon is smaller than that of the Sun. If an eclipse of the Sun occurs at this time, the Moon's disk passing over the Sun's disk cannot cover it completely but will leave the rim of the Sun visible all around it. Such an eclipse is said to be annular. Total and annular eclipses are called central.

In a partial eclipse the centre of the Moon's disk does not pass across the centre of the Sun's. After the first contact, the visible crescent of the Sun decreases in width until the centres of the two disks reach their closest approach. This is the moment of maximum phase, and the extent is measured by the ratio between the smallest width of the crescent and the diameter of the Sun. After maximum phase, the crescent of the Sun widens again until the Moon passes out of the Sun's disk at the last contact.

ECLIPSES OF THE MOON

When the Moon moves through the shadow of Earth, it dims considerably but remains faintly visible. Because the shadow of Earth is directed away from the Sun, a lunar eclipse can occur only at the time of the full moon—that is, when the Moon is on the side of Earth opposite to that of the Sun. A lunar eclipse appears much the same at all points of Earth from which it can be seen. When the Moon enters the penumbra, a penumbral eclipse occurs. The dimming of the Moon's illumination by the penumbra is so slight as to be scarcely noticeable, and penumbral eclipses are rarely watched. After a part of the Moon's surface is in the umbra and thus darkened, the Moon is said to be in partial eclipse. After about an hour, when the whole disk of the Moon is within the umbra, the eclipse becomes total. If the Moon's path leads through the centre of the umbra, the total eclipse can be expected to last about an hour and three-quarters.

THE FREQUENCY OF SOLAR AND LUNAR ECLIPSES

A solar eclipse, especially a total one, can be seen from only a limited part of Earth, whereas the eclipsed Moon can be seen at the time of the eclipse wherever the Moon is above the horizon.

In most calendar years there are two lunar eclipses; in some years one or three or none occur. Solar eclipses occur two to five times a year, five being exceptional; there last were five in 1935, and there will not be five again until 2206. The average number of total solar eclipses in a century is 66 for Earth as a whole.

Numbers of solar eclipses that have taken place or are predicted to take place during the 20th to 25th centuries are:

1901–2000: 228 eclipses, of which 145 were central (i.e., total or annular);
2001–2100: 224 eclipses, 144 central;
2101–2200: 235 eclipses, 151 central;
2201–2300: 248 eclipses, 156 central;
2301–2400: 248 eclipses, 160 central;
2401–2500: 237 eclipses, 153 central.

Any point on Earth may on the average experience no more than one total solar eclipse in three to four centuries. The situation is quite different for lunar eclipses. An observer remaining at the same place (and granted cloudless skies) could see 19 or 20 lunar eclipses in 18 years. Over that period three or four total eclipses and six or seven partial eclipses may be visible from beginning to end, and five total eclipses and four or five partial eclipses may be at least partially visible. All these numbers can be worked out from the geometry of the eclipses. A total lunar eclipse can last as long as an hour and three-quarters, but for a solar total eclipse maximum duration of totality is only 7½ minutes. This difference results from the fact that the Moon's diameter is much smaller than the extension of Earth's shadow at the Moon's distance from Earth, but the Moon can be only a little greater in apparent size than the Sun.

CYCLES OF ECLIPSES

The eclipses of the Sun and the Moon occur at new moon and full moon, respectively, so that one basic time period involved in the occurrence of eclipses is the synodic month—i.e., the interval between successive new moons, as seen from Earth.

A solar eclipse does not occur at every new moon, nor does a lunar eclipse occur at every full moon, because the Moon's orbital plane is inclined to the ecliptic, the plane of the orbit of Earth around the Sun. The angle between the planes is about 5°; thus, the Moon can pass well above or below the Sun. The line of intersection of the planes is called the line of the nodes, being the two points where the Moon's orbit intersects the ecliptic plane. The ascending node is the point where the Moon crosses the ecliptic from south to north, and the descending node is where it crosses from north to south. The nodes move along the ecliptic from east to west as seen from Earth, completing a revolution in 18.6 years. The Moon's revolution from one node to the same node again (called the draconic month, 27.212220 days) takes somewhat less time than a revolution from new moon to new moon (the synodic month, 29.530589 days). For a solar or lunar eclipse to occur, the Moon has to be near one of the nodes of its orbit. The draconic month is therefore the other basic period of eclipses.

Resonance between these two periods results in an interval called the saros, after which time the Moon and the Sun return very nearly to the same relative positions. The saros was known to the ancient Babylonians. It comprises 223 synodic months—that is, 6,585.321124 days, or 241.9986 draconic months. This latter value is nearly a whole number, so the new moon is in almost the same position (i.e., very near a node) at the beginning and end of a saros. The saros lasts 18 years, 11⅓ days or 18 years, 10⅓ days if five leap years fall within the period. Thus, there is usually a close resemblance between an eclipse and the one taking place 18 years and 11 days earlier or later. Because the date differs by only about 11 days in the calendar year, the latitudes on Earth of the two eclipses will be about the same, as will the relative apparent sizes of the Sun and Moon. The saros period also comprises 238.992 anomalistic months, again nearly a whole number. In one anomalistic month, the Moon describes its orbit from perigee to perigee, the point at which it is nearest to Earth. Thus, the Moon's distance from Earth is the same after a whole number of anomalistic months and very nearly the same after one saros. The saros period is therefore extremely useful for the prediction of both solar and lunar eclipses.

Because of the extra one-third day (and thus an additional eight hours of Earth's rotation) in the saros, the eclipse recurs each time approximately 120° farther west on the surface of Earth. After three saroses, or 54 years and about a month, the longitude is repeated.

There is a regular shift on Earth to the north or to the south of successive eclipse tracks from one saros to the next. The eclipses occurring when the Moon is near its ascending node shift to the south; those happening when it is near its descending node shift to the north. A saros series of eclipses begins its life at one pole of Earth and ends it at the other. A saros series lasts between 1,226 and 1,550 years and comprises 69 to 87 eclipses. As old series finish, new ones begin; about 42 of these series are in progress at any given time.

Two consecutive saros series are separated by the inex, a period of 29 years minus 20 days—that is, 358 synodic months—after which time the new moon has come from one node to the opposite node. A group of inex periods lasts about 23,000 years, with about 70 groups coexisting at any one time, each group comprising an average of 780 eclipses. All other cycles in eclipses are combinations of the saros and the inex.

Prediction and Calculation of Solar and Lunar Eclipses

The problem of predicting eclipses may be divided into two parts. The first is to find out when an eclipse will occur; the other is to determine when and where it will be visible.

For this purpose it is convenient first to consider Earth as fixed and to suppose

an observer is looking out from its centre. To this observer, the Sun and Moon appear projected on the celestial sphere. While this sphere appears to rotate daily, as measured by the positions of the stars, around Earth's axis of rotation, the Sun's disk appears to travel slowly along the ecliptic, making a complete revolution in one year. At the same time, the Moon's disk travels along its own path, once during a lunar month. The angular diameters of the Sun's and the Moon's disks are each about 0.5° but vary slightly.

Every month, the Moon's disk moving along its path will overtake the more slowly moving Sun once, at the moment of the new moon. Usually the Moon's disk will pass above or below the Sun's disk. Overlapping of the two results in an eclipse of the Sun, which can happen only when the new moon occurs at the same time that the Sun is near the ascending node or descending node of the Moon's orbit. Because the nodes are 180° apart, eclipses occur in the so-called eclipse seasons, six months apart.

The projection of Earth's umbra is a disk at the distance of the Moon's orbit. At that distance the shadow's disk subtends an angle of about 1.4°; its centre is always opposite the Sun's disk and travels along the ecliptic. A lunar eclipse occurs whenever the shadow's disk overlaps the Moon's disk; this happens only when the shadow's disk is near one of the nodes and the Sun is near the opposite node. The Sun's passage through the lunar nodes is thus the critical time for both solar and lunar eclipses. The plane of the Moon's path is not fixed, and its nodes move slowly along the ecliptic in the direction indicated by the arrows, making a complete revolution in about 19 years. The interval between two successive passages of the Sun through one of the nodes is termed an eclipse year, and, since the Moon's node moves so as to meet the advancing Sun, this interval is about 18.6 days less than a tropical (or ordinary) year.

To the observer on Earth at the centre of the sphere, the Sun's disk will travel along the ecliptic and the Moon's disk along its designated path. The Sun is so distant compared with the size of Earth that, from all places on Earth's surface, the Sun is seen nearly in the same position as it would be from the very centre. On the other hand, the Moon is relatively near, and so its projected position on the celestial sphere is different for various places of observation on Earth. In fact, it may be displaced as much as 1° from the position in which it is seen from the centre of Earth. If the radius of the Moon's disk is enlarged by 1°, a "Moon circle" is obtained that encloses all possible positions of the Moon's disk seen from anywhere on Earth. Conversely, if any disk of the Moon's size is placed inside this Moon circle, there is a place on Earth from which the Moon is seen in that position.

Accordingly, an eclipse of the Sun occurs somewhere on Earth whenever the Moon overtakes the Sun in such a position that the Moon circle passes over the Sun's disk; when the latter is entirely covered by the Moon circle, the eclipse will be total or annular. It is evident that a solar eclipse will take place if a new moon occurs while the Sun moves through the solar node. This period is the eclipse season; it starts 19 days before the Sun passes through a lunar node and ends 19 days thereafter. There are two complete eclipse seasons, one at each node, during a calendar year. Because there is a new moon every month, at least one solar eclipse, and occasionally two, occurs during each eclipse season. A fifth solar eclipse during a calendar year is possible because part of a third eclipse season may occur at the beginning of January or at the end of December.

For a lunar eclipse the conditions are similar. If a full moon occurs within 13 days of the passage of the Sun though a lunar node—and thus of Earth's umbral disk through the opposite node—the Moon will be eclipsed. Most eclipse seasons, but not all, will thus also contain a lunar eclipse. When two eclipse seasons and a partial third season fall in a calendar year, there may be three lunar eclipses in that year. Eclipses of the Sun are evidently more frequent than those of the Moon. Solar eclipses, however, can be seen from only a very limited region of Earth, whereas lunar eclipses are visible from an entire hemisphere.

During a solar eclipse the shadow cones—the umbra and penumbra—of the Moon sweep across the face of Earth, while, at the same time, Earth is rotating on its axis. Within the narrow area covered by the umbra, the eclipse is total.

Within the wider surrounding region covered by the penumbra, the eclipse is partial.

Astronomical ephemerides, or tables, that are published annually for the year ahead provide maps tracing the paths of the more important eclipses in considerable detail, as well as data for accurate calculation of the times of contact at any given observing location on Earth. Calculations are made some years ahead in Terrestrial Time (TT), which is defined by the orbital motion of Earth and the other planets. At the time of the eclipse, the correction is made to Universal Time (UT), which is defined by the rotation of Earth and is not rigorously uniform.

Modern computers make it possible to predict solar eclipses years ahead with high accuracy. By means of the same calculational methods, eclipses can be "predicted backward" in time. The generation of the times and observational locations for ancient eclipses has been valuable in historical and scientific research.

ECLIPSE RESEARCH ACTIVITIES

SOLAR RESEARCH

During a total solar eclipse, when the Moon has fully covered the Sun's brilliant visible disk, the faint extensive outer atmosphere of the Sun, known as the corona, is revealed. Just prior to this event, the chromosphere, a thin bright red layer in the lower solar atmosphere, appears for a few seconds at the edge of the Sun's disk. Then, as the chromosphere vanishes, the corona leaps into view. Pearly white coronal streamers can be seen far beyond the Moon's dark disk, sometimes to a distance several times the Sun's radius. When the corona is made visible, astronomers can observe and record its details.

Because the corona is a million times fainter than the disk of the Sun, it cannot be seen unaided in broad daylight. In 1930 the French astronomer Bernard Lyot invented the coronagraph, a specialized telescope that produces an artificial eclipse of the Sun. Astronomers could then study the corona any day when the aureole, the bright ring around the Sun composed of light scattered by particles in Earth's atmosphere, was not especially bright. Nevertheless, the daytime sky near the Sun is at least a thousand times darker during a total eclipse than otherwise. Therefore, total eclipses continued to provide the best opportunities to study the Sun's outer atmosphere until the mid-1970s, when suborbital rocket and satellite observatories became available.

Observatories in space have several important advantages over surface-based instruments, being immune to weather and bright skies and above the distorting and filtering effects of Earth's atmosphere. On the other hand, they are exceedingly expensive and require years of development and construction. In comparison, an eclipse expedition—the establishment of a temporary observation station in the path of totality of an upcoming eclipse—is relatively cheap and highly flexible in design. Therefore, despite their limitations, surface-based observations of total solar eclipses continue to play a role in gathering new knowledge about the Sun.

Among the many important advances that were made during past total eclipses, three notable ones can serve as examples—the discovery of the element helium, experimental support for the general theory of relativity, and the discovery that the Sun's corona is exceedingly hot

DISCOVERY OF HELIUM

In 1868, while observing an eclipse whose path of totality passed over India, the French astronomer Pierre Janssen observed a bright yellow line in the spectrum of a solar prominence, a bright cloud of hot ionized gas that extends into the corona. Janssen noticed that the yellow line's wavelength was slightly shorter than that of the well-known line of sodium, and he reported his result to the British astronomer Joseph Norman Lockyer, who had missed the eclipse. Lockyer, using a powerful new spectrograph at the University of Cambridge, was able to observe the yellow line in a prominence outside a solar eclipse. Despite many attempts, he failed to identify the line with any element known on Earth and finally concluded that it corresponded to a new element, which he named helium, from the Greek word for sun. Helium was not discovered on Earth until 1895.

SUPPORT FOR THE GENERAL THEORY OF RELATIVITY

Soon after Albert Einstein's general theory of relativity was published in 1916, scientists set to conducting a number of experimental tests to verify or disprove various predictions of the theory. One prediction was that the dark (absorption) lines known as Fraunhofer lines in the spectrum of sunlight should be redshifted (i.e., shifted toward longer wavelengths) by a precise amount because of the Sun's gravitational field. Astronomers failed initially to find this shift, so in 1918 the validity of the general theory was still in some doubt.

The general theory also predicted that a ray of light emanating from a distant star and passing near the Sun should be deflected a measurable amount by the Sun's gravity. If the ray just grazes the edge of the Sun, the angular deflection should be 1.75 arc seconds, and the deflection should decrease in proportion to the distance of the ray from the Sun's edge. (For comparison, the average solar diameter is 1,922 arc seconds.) Einstein suggested that astronomers should observe this effect at a total eclipse as another test of his theory.

British astronomers, including Arthur Eddington, took up the challenge. They organized two expeditions to observe the five minutes of totality afforded by the eclipse of May 29, 1919, one in Sobral, Braz., and the other on the island of Príncipe, off the African coast. From Sobral the astronomers obtained a series of photographs on glass plates of the stars around the Sun at mid-totality. The expedition also photographed the same stars that had appeared during the eclipse but without the presence of the Sun. By comparing the relative positions of the stars on the two sets of plates, the astronomers obtained a figure of 1.98 arc seconds for the deflection of starlight at the edge of the solar disk. The expedition to Príncipe, led by Eddington, encountered clouds during the eclipse and was able to photograph only four stars on five plates. From these, Eddington derived an estimate of 1.61 arc seconds for the deflection at the edge of the Sun. The combined results from the two expeditions were close enough to the predicted 1.75 arc seconds to lend support to Einstein's theory but not to establish it unconditionally. Nevertheless, they had tremendous popular appeal and helped establish Einstein as one of the foremost physicists of his time.

Many attempts were made to improve on the accuracy of this stellar method, but with limited success. In 1974, however, astronomers at the U.S. National Radio Astronomy Observatory observed three quasars that lie in a straight line in the sky and are occulted by the Sun at some time during the year. The radiation from these radio sources was deflected by the Sun in the same manner as starlight. Their radio interferometer was capable of much higher angular precision than photography allows, and their final result was within 1 percent of the prediction of the general theory.

Temperature of the Corona

About 1930 German astronomer Walter Grotrian examined spectra of the solar corona he had obtained at a total eclipse. He noticed that, although coronal light had the same distribution of colours as light from the solar surface—the photosphere—it lacked the absorption lines observed in photospheric light. Grotrian hypothesized that coronal light consists of photospheric light that has been scattered toward Earth by free electrons in the corona. To account for the lack of absorption lines in coronal light, these free electrons had to be moving at very high speeds; that is, the corona must be very hot.

A second clue came from some strange bright lines in the corona's spectrum. Because similar lines found in the spectra of interstellar gaseous nebulae had been shown to be emitted by ionized oxygen and nitrogen under conditions of extremely low gas density and high temperature, Grotrian speculated that the bright coronal lines might have a similar origin. He wrote to Bengt Edlén, a Swedish physicist who was studying the spectra of elements at very high temperatures. With atomic data that Edlén supplied, Grotrian was able to predict the wavelengths of two of the strongest coronal lines, including one that can be produced only from ionized iron at a temperature of about a million kelvins (K). With Grotrian thus showing the way, Edlén eventually was able to identify the majority of the two dozen known coronal lines with terrestrial elements such as silicon, calcium, and iron. All these lines are emitted only at temperatures of a million K or more. They are called "forbidden" because, according to the rules of quantum mechanics, the atomic transitions from higher to lower energy states responsible for lines have only a small likelihood of occurring under normal laboratory conditions.

Since Grotrian and Edlén's work, astronomers have learned that some parts of the normal corona can attain temperatures as high as 3 or 4 million K. In comparison, the photosphere has a temperature of only 6,000 K (5,727°C, 10,340°F). Because heat cannot flow spontaneously from cooler to hotter regions, some unknown, nonthermal process must maintain the high temperature of the corona. Although astronomers have searched for this process for decades, they have yet to identify it positively. Many investigations of the corona still take place during the ideal conditions of a total solar eclipse.

LUNAR RESEARCH

Lunar eclipses can yield information about the cooling of the Moon's soil when the Sun's radiation is suddenly removed and therefore about the soil's conductivity of heat and its structure. Infrared and radio-wavelength radiation from the Moon declines in intensity more slowly than does visible light emission during an eclipse because they are emitted from below the surface, and measurements indicate how far the different kinds of radiation penetrate into the lunar soil. Infrared observations show that at many "bright spots" the soil retains its heat much longer than in surrounding areas.

Because of the absence of a lunar atmosphere, the Moon's solid surface is exposed to the full intensity of ultraviolet and particulate radiation from the Sun, which may give rise to fluorescence in some rock materials. Observations during lunar eclipses have given positive results for this phenomenon, with the appearance of abnormal bright regions in eclipse-obscured parts of the Moon

ECLIPSES IN HISTORY

Eclipses of the Sun and Moon are often quite spectacular, and in ancient and medieval times they were frequently recorded as portents—usually of disaster. Hence, it is not surprising that many of these events are mentioned in history and literature as well as in astronomical writings.

Well over 1,000 individual eclipse records are extant from various parts of the ancient and medieval world. Most known ancient observations of these phenomena originate from only three countries: China, Babylonia, and Greece. No eclipse records appear to have survived from ancient Egypt or India, for example. Whereas virtually all Babylonian accounts are confined to astronomical treatises, those from China and Greece are found in historical and literary works as well. As yet, no eclipse report before

800 BCE can be definitely dated; the earliest reliable observation is from Assyria and dates from June 15, 763 BCE. Commencing only a few decades later, numerous Babylonian and Chinese observations are preserved. Eclipses are occasionally noted in surviving European writings from the Dark Ages (for instance, in the works of the 5th-century bishop Hydatius and the 8th-century theologian and historian Saint Bede the Venerable). However, during this period only the Chinese continued to observe and report such events on a regular basis. Chinese records in the traditional style continued almost uninterrupted to modern times.

Many eclipses were carefully recorded by the astronomers of Baghdad and Cairo between about 800 and 1000 CE. Also, after about 800 CE, both European and Arabic annalists began to include in their chronicles accounts of eclipses and other remarkable celestial phenomena. Some of these chronicles continued until the 16th century and even later, although the peak period was between about 1100 and 1400. Around 1450, European astronomers commenced making fairly accurate measurements of the time of day or night when eclipses occurred, and this pursuit spread rapidly following the invention of the telescope. This discussion is confined to eclipse observations made in the pretelescopic period.

Babylonian clay tablet giving a detailed description of the total solar eclipse of April 15, 136 BCE. The tablet is a goal-year text, a type that lists astronomical data of predictive use for an assigned group of years. F. Richard Stephenson

The present-day value of ancient and medieval records of eclipses falls into two main categories: (1) chronological, depending mainly on the connection between an eclipse and a significant historical event, and (2) astronomical, especially the study of long-term variations in the length of the mean solar day.

The Sun is usually so brilliant that the casual observer is liable to overlook those eclipses in which less than about 80 percent of the solar disk is obscured. Only when a substantial proportion of the Sun is covered by the Moon does the loss of daylight become noticeable.

Hence, it is rare to find references to small partial eclipses in literary and historical works. At various times, astronomers in Babylonia, China, and the Arab lands systematically reported eclipses of small magnitude, but their vigilance was assisted by their ability to make approximate predictions. They thus knew roughly when to scrutinize the Sun. Arab astronomers sometimes viewed the Sun by reflection in water to diminish its brightness when watching for eclipses. The Roman philosopher and writer Seneca (c. 4 BCE–65 CE), on the other hand, recounts that, in his time, pitch was employed for this purpose. It is not known, however, whether such artificial aids were used regularly.

When the Moon covers a large proportion of the Sun, the sky becomes appreciably darker, and stars may appear. On those rare occasions when the whole of the Sun is obscured, the sudden occurrence of intense darkness, accompanied by a pronounced fall in temperature, may leave a profound impression on eyewitnesses. Total or near-total eclipses of the Sun are of special chronological importance. On average, they occur so infrequently at any particular location that if the date of such an event can be established by historical means to within a decade or two, it may well prove possible to fix an exact date by astronomical calculation.

The Moon even when full is much dimmer than the Sun, and lunar eclipses of quite small magnitude are thus fairly readily visible to the unaided eye. Both partial and total obscurations are recorded in history with roughly comparable frequency. As total eclipses of the Moon occur rather often (every two or three years on average at a given place), they are of less chronological importance than their solar counterparts. There are, however, several notable exceptions, as is discussed below.

LITERARY AND HISTORICAL REFERENCES

The following subsections address some aspects of how eclipses were regarded by the great ancient civilizations. When reading these accounts of long-gone people who grappled with the implications of startling and portentous events in the sky, one cannot help but be struck by the immediacy of their emotions, and one must also admire the beginnings of astronomy, of humanity's understanding, however dimly, of its place in the universe.

CHINESE

According to long-established tradition, the history of astronomy in ancient China can be traced back before 2000 BCE. The earliest relics that are of astronomical significance date from nearly a millennium later, however. The Anyang oracle bones (inscribed turtle shells, ox bones, and so forth) of the latter part of the Shang dynasty (c. 1600–1046 BCE), which were uncovered near Anyang in northeastern China, record several eclipses of both the Sun and the Moon. The following report is an example:

> On day guiyou [the 10th day of the 60-day cycle], it was inquired [by divination]: "The Sun was eclipsed in the evening; is it good?" On day guiyou it was inquired: "The Sun was eclipsed in the evening; is it bad?"

The above text provides clear evidence that eclipses were regarded as omens at this early period (as is true of other celestial phenomena). Such a belief was extremely prevalent in China during later centuries. The term translated here as "eclipse" (shi) is the same as the word for "eat." Evidently the Shang people thought that a monster actually devoured the Sun or Moon during an eclipse. Not until many centuries later was the true explanation known, but by then the use of the term shi was firmly established to describe eclipses, and so it remained throughout Chinese history. The oracle-bone text, translated above, twice gives the day of the sexagenary cycle; this cycle, which was independent of any astronomical parameter, continued in use (seemingly without interruption) until modern times. Nevertheless, as the year in which an eclipse occurred is never mentioned on the preserved oracle bones (many of which are mere fragments), dating of these observations by astronomical calculation has proved extremely difficult. In general, Shang chronology is still very uncertain.

The Shijing ("Classic of Poetry") contains a lamentation occasioned by an eclipse of the Moon followed by an eclipse of the Sun. The text, dating from the 8th century BCE, may be translated:

> The Sun was eclipsed, we found it greatly ominous . . . that this Moon is eclipsed is but an ordinary matter; but that this Sun is eclipsed—wherein lies the evil?

The different attitudes toward solar and lunar eclipses at this time is interesting. Throughout the subsequent 1,000 years or so, lunar eclipses were hardly ever reported in China—in marked contrast to solar obscurations, which were systematically observed during much of this period. The earliest of these observations are recorded in a chronicle of the Chinese state of Lu (now in Shandong Province), the birthplace of Confucius. This work, known as the Chunqiu ("Spring and Autumn [Annals]"), lists many solar eclipses between 722 and 481 BCE. On three occasions the Chunqiu describes eclipse ceremonies in which drums were beaten and oxen were sacrificed. Further, three eclipses (occurring in 709, 601, and 549 BCE) were described as total. The earliest of these, that of July 17, 709 BCE, is recorded as follows:

> Third year of Duke Huan, 7th month, day renchen [the 29th day of the cycle], the first day of the month. The Sun was eclipsed and it was total.

This is the earliest known record of a total solar eclipse from any civilization. Computation shows that this eclipse was indeed total at Qufu, the Lu capital.

From about 200 BCE (following the unification of China into a single empire), a wide variety of celestial phenomena began to be noted on a regular basis. Summaries of these records are found in astronomical treatises contained in the official histories. In many instances, a report is accompanied by a detailed astrological prognostication. For example, the *Houhanshu* ("History of the Later Han Dynasty") contains the following account under a year corresponding to 119–120 CE:

> *On the day* wuwu *[the 55th cyclical day], the 1st day of the 12th lunar month, the Sun was eclipsed; it was almost complete. On Earth it became like evening. It was 11 deg in the constellation of the Maid. The woman ruler [i.e., the empress dowager] showed aversion to it. Two years and three months later, Deng, the empress dowager, died.*

The date of this eclipse is equivalent to Jan. 18, 120 CE. On this exact day there

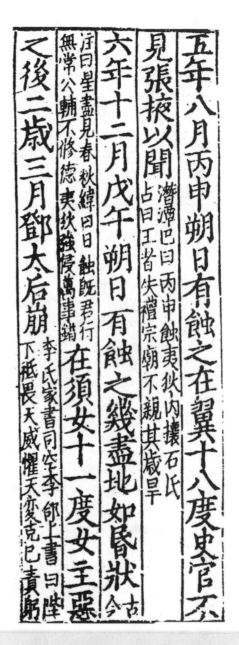

Chinese text from an astronomical treatise contained in the Houhanshu ("History of the Later Han Dynasty"), in which two solar eclipses, in 118 and 120 CE, are recorded. The second account, of the eclipse of Jan. 18, 120, notes (in the large characters) that the eclipse "was almost complete. On the Earth it became like evening." The account adds that the empress dowager was upset by it, and two years and three months later she died. F. Richard Stephenson

occurred an eclipse of the Sun that was very large in China. The above-cited text is particularly interesting because it clearly describes an obscuration of the Sun, which, though causing dusk conditions, was not quite total where it was seen. With regard to the accompanying prognostication, it should be pointed out that a delay of two or three years between the occurrence of a celestial omen and its presumed fulfillment is quite typical of Chinese astrology.

Systematic observation of lunar eclipses in China began around 400 CE, and from this period onward the official astronomers often timed the various phases of both solar and lunar eclipses with the aid of clepsydras (water clocks). Chinese astronomical techniques spread to Korea and Japan, and, especially after 1000 CE, eclipses were regularly observed independently in all three countries. However, the Chinese records are usually the most detailed.

The following account from the *Yuanshi* ("History of the Yuan Dynasty") of the total lunar eclipse of May 19, 1277 CE, follows the customary practice of quoting timings in double hours (12 to a combined day and night) and marks (each equal to $\frac{1}{100}$ of a day and night, or 0.24 hours):

14th year of the Zhiyuan reign period, 4th month, day guiyou [the 10th cyclical day], full Moon. The Moon was eclipsed. Beginning of loss at 6 marks in the hour of zi;

the eclipse was total at 3 marks in the hour of chou; maximum at 5 marks in the hour of chou; reappearance of light at 7 marks in the hour of chou; restoration to fullness at 4 marks in the hour of yin.

The three consecutive double hours *zi, chou,* and *yin* correspond, respectively, to 11 PM to 1 AM, 1 AM to 3 AM, and 3 AM to 5 AM. The measured times are equivalent to 12:34 AM (start of eclipse), 1:50 AM (beginning of totality), 2:19 AM (mid-eclipse), 2:48 AM (end of totality), and 4:05 AM (end of eclipse).

From the 3rd century CE onward, there is evidence of attempts at predicting eclipses by Chinese astronomers. Crude at first, these predictions reached their peak accuracy near the end of the 13th century, with typical timing errors of about one-fourth of an hour.

ASSYRIAN

The Assyrian Chronicle, a cuneiform tablet that preserves the names of the annual magistrates who gave their names to the years (similar to the later Athenian archons or Roman consuls), records under the year that corresponds to 763–762 BCE: "Revolt in the citadel; in [the month] Siwan [equivalent to May–June], the Sun had an eclipse." The reference must be to the eclipse of June 15, 763 BCE, the only large eclipse visible in Assyria over a period of many years. A possible allusion to the same eclipse is found in the Hebrew

Bible: "'And on that day,' says the Lord God, 'I will make the Sun go down at noon, and darken the earth in broad daylight'" (Amos 8:9). Amos was prophesying during the reign of King Jeroboam II (786–746 BCE) of Israel, and the eclipse would be very large throughout Israel.

Many references to both solar and lunar eclipses in the first half of the 7th century BCE are found among the divination reports to Assyrian kings. These tablets, which are now largely in the British Museum, were found in the royal archives at Nineveh. A text probably dating from 675 BCE carries the following account, indicating that the eclipse was regarded as an unfavourable omen:

The eclipse of the Moon which took place in Marchesvan [month VIII] began [in the east]. That is bad for Subartu. What [is wrong]? After it, Jupiter ent[ered] the Moon three times. What is being done to make its evil pass?

BABYLONIAN

Until the discovery of the late Babylonian astronomical texts in the latter half of the 19th century, the Alexandrian astronomer Ptolemy's *Almagest* (2nd century CE) was the only source of Babylonian eclipse observations. Ptolemy cites several records of lunar eclipses, the earliest in 721 BCE. Unfortunately, the dates and observational details are not in original form but have been edited, presumably

by the Greek astronomer Hipparchus (2nd century BCE). Dates have been converted to the Egyptian 365-day calendar, while times have been expressed in hours instead of the original units.

The discovery and decipherment of vast numbers of cuneiform astronomical texts at the site of Babylon in the 1870s and '80s completely revolutionized the study of Babylonian astronomy. Most of the extant texts, dating from about 747 BCE to 75 CE, are in the British Museum. Numerous day-to-day astronomical diaries contain records of celestial phenomena, including many eclipses. Although most of the tablets are very fragmentary, additional Babylonian collections of eclipse reports—abstracted from the original diaries—also survive. An example of a lunar eclipse record, dating from 80 BCE, is as follows. Time intervals, presumably measured with the aid of a water clock, are expressed in UŠ (time-degrees, equal to four minutes), while eclipse magnitudes are expressed in "fingers," each equal to 1/12 of the lunar diameter:

Year 168 [Arsacid dynasty], that is year 232 [Seleucid kingdom] . . . month I, day 13 . . . lunar eclipse . . . In 20 deg of night it made six fingers. Duration of maximal phase 7 deg of night, until it began to become bright. In 13 deg . . . 4 fingers lacking to brightness it set . . . [Began] at 40 deg before sunrise.

The date, when converted to the Julian calendar (April 11, 80 BCE), is exactly correct. Sunrise on this occasion would occur at 5:37 AM, so that the measured start of the eclipse was at 2:57 AM, and maximum phase (when half of the Moon was estimated to be in shadow) was at 4:31 AM. When the Moon set, one-third of its disk was observed to be still in shadow. Use of "fingers" to express the magnitude of an eclipse (both lunar and solar) spread to Greece and hence to the Arab world. This convention was still fairly standard among astronomers worldwide until the 20th century.

Babylonian eclipse predictions, which were based on past series of observations, were fairly accurate for this early period. Timing errors averaged about two hours, and predictions gave a useful indication of the likelihood of an eclipse to intending observers.

JEWISH

In his *Antiquities of the Jews*, the Jewish historian Flavius Josephus says the Judean king Herod died in the spring shortly after a lunar eclipse. Calculation shows that the only springtime lunar eclipses visible in Israel between 17 BCE and 3 CE took place on March 23, 5 BCE, and March 13, 4 BCE. The former was total in the mid-evening, while on the latter occasion about one-third of the Moon was in shadow around 3 AM. These two dates are conveniently close to one another, although the latter date is usually preferred by chronologists—implying that Herod died in the spring of 4 BCE.

GREEK

In a fragment of a lost poem by the 7th-century-BCE Greek poet Archilochus occur the words:

Nothing can be surprising any more or impossible or miraculous, now that Zeus, father of the Olympians, has made night out of noonday, hiding the bright sunlight, and fear has come upon mankind. After this, men can believe anything, expect anything.

This seems a clear reference to a total solar eclipse. The phenomenon has been identified as most likely the eclipse of April 6, 648 BCE, which was total in the Aegean and occurred during Archilochus's lifetime.

Fragments survive of other early Greek poetic descriptions of eclipses, and the ninth paean of Pindar, addressed to the Thebans, takes an eclipse of the Sun as its theme:

Beam of the Sun! O thou that seest from afar, what wilt thou be devising? O mother of mine eyes! O star supreme, reft from us in the daytime! Why hast thou perplexed the power of man and the way of wisdom, by rushing forth on a darksome track?

The 5th-century-BCE poet then proceeds to speculate on the meaning of this omen. Although he prays, "Change this worldwide portent into some painless blessing for Thebes," he adds, "I in no wise lament whate'er I shall suffer with the rest." This strongly suggests that Pindar, who was a Theban, had himself recently witnessed a great eclipse at his hometown. The most probable date for the eclipse is April 30, 463 BCE; modern calculations indicate that the eclipse was nearly total at Thebes.

The historian Thucydides records three eclipses during the Peloponnesian War, which began in 431 BCE and lasted for 27 years. The first of these was a solar obscuration that occurred in the summer of the first year of the war (calculated date Aug. 3, 431 BCE). On this occasion, the Sun assumed the form of a crescent in the afternoon before returning to its natural shape, and during the eclipse some stars became visible. This description agrees well with modern computations, except that no "star" apart from the planet Venus should have been seen. Seven years afterward, Thucydides noted that a "small" solar eclipse took place in the summer of the eighth year of the war (calculated date March 21, 424 BCE). Finally, a lunar eclipse occurred in the summer of the 19th year of the war (calculated date Aug. 27, 413 BCE). This last date had been selected by the Athenian commanders Nicias and Demosthenes for the departure of their armies from Syracuse. All preparations were ready, but the signal had not been given when the Moon was totally eclipsed in the evening. The Athenian soldiers and sailors clamoured against departure, and Nicias, in obedience to the soothsayers, resolved to remain thrice nine days. This delay enabled the Syracusans to capture or destroy the whole of the Athenian fleet and army.

Aug. 15, 310 BCE, is the date of a total eclipse of the Sun that was seen at sea by the tyrant Agathocles and his men after they had escaped from Syracuse and were on their way to Africa. Diodorus Siculus, a historian of the 1st century BCE, reported that "on the next day [after the escape] there occurred such an eclipse of the Sun that utter darkness set in and the stars were seen everywhere." Historians of astronomy have often debated whether Agathocles' ships sailed around the north or south coast of Sicily during the course of the journey. Modern computations of the eclipse track are still unable to resolve this issue, although they indicate that the eclipse was total over much of Sicily.

In the dialogue of the Greek author Plutarch (46–c. 119 CE) concerning the features of the Moon's disk, one of the characters, named Lucius, deduces from the phases of the Moon and the phenomenon of eclipses a similarity between Earth and the Moon. Lucius illustrates his argument by means of a recent eclipse of the Sun, which, "beginning just after noonday, made many stars shine out from many parts of the sky and tempered the air in the manner of twilight." This eclipse has been identified with one that occurred on March 20, 71 CE, which was total in

Greece. Whether Plutarch is describing a real, and therefore datable, event or is merely basing his description on accounts written by earlier authors has been disputed. However, his description is so vivid and original that it seems likely that Plutarch witnessed the eclipse himself. Later in the same dialogue, Lucius refers to a brightness that appears around the Moon's rim in total eclipses of the Sun. This is one of the earliest known allusions to the solar corona. Plutarch was unusually interested in eclipses, and his *Parallel Lives*, an account of the deeds and characters of illustrious Greeks and Romans, contains many references to both lunar and solar eclipses of considerable historical importance. There also are frequent records of eclipses in other ancient Greek literature.

Ptolemy in his *Almagest* records several lunar eclipses between 201 BCE and 136 CE. Most of these were observed at Alexandria in Egypt. For instance, the eclipse of May 1, 174 BCE, is described in the following words:

> From the beginning of the eighth hour till the end of the tenth in Alexandria there was an eclipse of the Moon which reached a maximum obscuration of 7 digits from the north; so mid-eclipse occurred 2½ seasonal hours after midnight, which corresponds to 2⅓ equinoctial hours.

The local times of beginning and end correspond to about 12:55 AM and 3:35 AM, so mid-eclipse would have been close to 2:15 AM.

ROMAN

Roman history is less replete with references to eclipses than that of Greece, but there are several interesting allusions to these events in Roman writings. Some, like the total solar eclipse said by Dio Cassius, a Roman historian of the 3rd century CE, to have occurred at the time of the funeral of Agrippina the Younger, the mother of the Roman emperor Nero, never took place. An eclipse of the Sun recorded by the historian Livy (64/59 BCE–17 CE) in a year corresponding to 190 BCE is of interest to students of astronomy and of the Roman calendar alike. Although Livy notes that the event happened in early July, the calculated date is March 14. Consequently, the Roman calendar in that year must have been more than three months out of adjustment.

What may well be an indirect allusion to a total eclipse of the Sun is recorded by Livy for a time corresponding to 188–187 BCE (the consulship of Valerius Messala and Livius Salinator during the Roman Republic):

> Before the new magistrates departed for their provinces, a three-day period of prayer was proclaimed in the name of the College of Decemvirs at all the street-corner shrines because in the daytime, between about the

third and fourth hours, darkness had covered everything.

The darkness took place some time after the election of the consuls (Ides of March), and, allowing for the confusion of the Roman calendar at this time, the total eclipse of July 17, 188 BCE, would be the most satisfactory explanation for the unusual morning darkness. Since the Sun is not mentioned in the text, the phenomenon possibly occurred on a cloudy day.

The total eclipse of the Moon on the evening of June 21, 168 BCE, has attracted much attention. This event occurred shortly before the defeat of Perseus, the last king of Macedonia, by the Romans at the Battle of Pydna. The contemporary Greek historian Polybius, in remarking on this eclipse, stated that "the report gained popular credence that it portended the eclipse of a king. This, while it lent fresh courage to the Romans, discouraged the Macedonians." Polybius added the wry comment: "So true is the saying, 'there are many empty things in war.'"

MEDIEVAL EUROPEAN

Following the close of the classical age in Europe, eclipses were in general only rarely recorded by European writers for several centuries. Not until after about 800 CE did eclipses and other celestial phenomena begin to be frequently reported again, especially in monastic chronicles. Hydatius, bishop of Chaves (in Portugal), was one of the few known chroniclers of the early Middle Ages. He seems to have had an unusual interest in eclipses, and he recounted the occurrence of five such events (involving both the Sun and the Moon) between 447 and 464 CE. In each case, only brief details are given, and Hydatius gives the years of occurrence in terms of the Olympiads (i.e., reckoning time from the first Olympic Games, in 776 BCE). During the total lunar eclipse of March 2, 462 CE (this date is known to be accurate), the Moon is said to have been "turned into blood." Statements of this kind are common throughout the Middle Ages, presumably inspired by the Hebrew Bible allusion in Joel (2:31). Similar descriptions, however, are occasionally found in non-Christian sources, as, for example, a Chinese one of 498 CE.

Given below is a selection from the vast number of extant medieval European reports of eclipses. In many cases, the date is accurately recorded, but there also are frequent instances of chronological error.

In the year 733 CE, the continuation of Bede's *Historia ecclesiastica gentis Anglorum* ("Ecclesiastical History of the English People") contains an early reference to an annular eclipse on a date corresponding to August 14. When the eclipse was at its height, "almost the whole of the Sun's disk seemed to be like a black and horrid shield." Bede was the first historian to use "AD" dates systematically.

An occultation of a bright star by the eclipsed Moon in 756 CE (actually the previous year) is the subject of an entry in the chronicle of Simeon of Durham. Although Simeon lived some four centuries after the event, he is clearly quoting an eyewitness source:

Moreover, the Moon was covered with a blood-red color on the 8th day before the Kalends of December [i.e., November 24] when 15 days old, that is, the Full Moon; and then the darkness gradually decreased and it returned to its original brightness. And remarkably indeed, a bright star following the Moon itself passed through it, and after the return to brightness it preceded the Moon by the same distance as it had followed the Moon before it was obscured.

The text gives no hint of the identity of the star. Modern computations show that the Moon was totally eclipsed on the evening of Nov. 23, 755 CE. During the closing stages of the eclipse, Jupiter would have been occulted by the Moon, as seen from England. This is an example of the care with which an observer who was not an astronomer could describe a compound astronomical event without having any real understanding of what was happening.

Several eclipses are recorded in Byzantine history, beginning in the 6th century CE. By far the most vivid account relates to the solar eclipse of Dec. 22, 968 CE. This was penned by the contemporary chronicler Leo the Deacon:

At the winter solstice there was an eclipse of the Sun such as has never happened before . . . It occurred on the 22nd day of the month of December, at the 4th hour of the day, the air being calm. Darkness fell upon the Earth and all the brighter stars revealed themselves. Everyone could see the disk of the Sun without brightness, deprived of light, and a certain dull and feeble glow, like a narrow headband, shining round the extreme parts of the edge of the disk. However, the Sun gradually going past the Moon (for this appeared covering it directly) sent out its original rays, and light filled the Earth again.

This is the earliest account of the solar corona that can be definitely linked to a datable eclipse. Although the appearance of the corona during totality is rather impressive, early descriptions of it are extremely rare. Possibly many ancient and medieval eyewitnesses of total eclipses were so terrified by the onset of sudden darkness that they failed to notice that the darkened Sun was surrounded by a diffuse envelope of light.

In a chronicle of the Norman rule in Sicily and southern Italy during the 11th century, Goffredo Malaterra records an eclipse of the Sun that, even though it caused alarm to some people, was evidently regarded by others as no more than a practical inconvenience:

> *[1084 CE] On the sixth day of the month of February between the sixth and ninth hours the Sun was obscured for the space of three hours; it was so great that any people who were working indoors could only continue if in the meantime they lit lamps. Indeed some people went from house to house to get lanterns or torches. Many were terrified.*

This eclipse actually occurred on Feb. 16, 1086 CE. It was the only large eclipse visible in southern Italy for several years around this time; hence, the chronicler had mistaken both the year and day.

The German astronomer Regiomontanus (Johannes Müller) carefully timed nine eclipses between 1457 and 1471 CE. He compared his measured times with those calculated by using the Alfonsine Tables, a set of astronomical tables compiled two centuries beforehand that allowed computation of eclipses and planetary positions. His account of the lunar eclipse of Dec. 17, 1461 CE, is as follows:

> *The Moon rose eclipsed by 10 digits of its diameter [calculated]. Indeed I merely noted 8 [digits]. Moreover, from the Alfonsine computations the end of the eclipse occurred at 1 hour and 56*

minutes after sunset. At this same end of the eclipse the altitude of the star Alhioth [Capella, or Alpha Aurigae] in the east was 38 degrees 30 minutes, whereas [the altitude of] the star Aldebaran [Alpha Tauri] was 29 degrees in the east. This was in the city of Rome.

In quoting star altitudes, Regiomontanus was following a practice favoured by medieval Arab astronomers. The local times corresponding to the two altitude measurements are respectively 5:21 PM and 5:25 PM; these compare with the Alfonsine result of 6:30 PM. Hence, the tables were more than an hour in error at this date.

MEDIEVAL ISLAMIC

Like their Christian counterparts, medieval Islamic chroniclers recorded a number of detailed and often vivid descriptions of eclipses. Usually the exact date of occurrence is given (on the lunar calendar). A graphic narrative of the total solar eclipse of June 20, 1061 CE, was recorded by the Baghdad annalist Ibn al-Jawzī, who wrote approximately a century after the event:

> On Wednesday, when two nights remained to the completion of the month Jumādā al-Ūlā [in 453 CE], two hours after daybreak, the Sun was eclipsed totally. There was darkness and the birds fell whilst flying. The astrologers claimed that one-sixth of the Sun should have

remained [uneclipsed] but nothing of it did so. The Sun reappeared after four hours and a fraction. The eclipse was not in the whole of the Sun in places other than Baghdad and its provinces.

The date corresponds exactly to June 20, 1061 CE, on the morning of which there was a total eclipse of the Sun visible in Baghdad. The duration of totality is much exaggerated, but this is common in medieval accounts of eclipses. The phenomenon of birds falling from the sky at the onset of the total phase was also noticed in Europe during several eclipses in the Middle Ages.

Two independent accounts of the total solar eclipse of 1176 CE are recorded in contemporary Arab history. Ibn al-Athīr, who was aged 16 at the time, described the event as follows:

In this year [571 CE] the Sun was eclipsed totally and the Earth was in darkness so that it was like a dark night and the stars appeared. That was the forenoon of Friday the 29th of the month Ramaḍān at Jazīrat Ibn ʿUmar, when I was young and in the company of my arithmetic teacher. When I saw it I was very much afraid; I held on to him and my heart was strengthened. My teacher was learned about the stars and told me, "Now, you will see that all of this will go away," and it went quickly.

The date of the eclipse is given correctly, apart from the weekday (actually Sunday), and is equivalent to April 11, 1176 CE. Calculation shows that the whole of the Sun would have been obscured over a wide region around Jazīrat Ibn ʿUmar (now Cizre, Turkey). Farther south, totality was also witnessed by the Muslim leader Saladin and his army while crossing the Orontes River near Ḥamāh (in present-day Syria). The chronicler ʿImād al-Dīn, who was with Saladin at the time, noted that "the Sun was eclipsed and it became dark in the daytime. People were frightened and stars appeared." As it happens, ʿImād al-Dīn dates the event one year too early (570 CE); the only large eclipse visible in this region for several years was that of 1176 CE.

Lunar and solar eclipses are fairly frequently visible on Earth's surface 15 days apart, and from time to time such a pair of eclipses may be seen from one and the same location. Such was the case in the summer of 1433 CE, but this occurrence caused some surprise to the contemporary Cairo chronicler al-Maqrīzī:

On Wednesday the 28th of Shawwāl [i.e., June 17], the Sun was eclipsed by about two-thirds in the sign of Cancer more than one hour after the afternoon prayer. The eclipse cleared at sunset. During the eclipse there was darkness and some stars appeared ... On Friday night the 14th of Dhū ʾl-Qaʿda [July 3], most of the Moon was eclipsed. It rose eclipsed from the eastern horizon. The eclipse cleared in the time of the nightfall prayer. This is a rarity—the occurrence of a lunar eclipse 15 days after a solar eclipse.

The description of the loss of daylight produced by the solar eclipse is much exaggerated, but otherwise the account is fairly careful.

Medieval Arab astronomers carefully timed the various phases of eclipses by measuring the altitude of the Sun (in the case of a solar eclipse) or of the Moon or a bright star (for a lunar obscuration). These altitude measurements were later converted to local time. For instance, the lunar eclipse of April 22, 981 CE, was recorded by the Cairo astronomer Ibn Yūnus:

> *This lunar eclipse was in the month of Shawwāl in the year 370 of al-Hijrah [i.e., 370 CE] on the night whose morning was Friday . . . We gathered to observe this eclipse at Al-Qarāfah [a district of Cairo] in the Mosque of Ibn Nasr al-Maghribī. We perceived the beginning of this eclipse when the altitude of the Moon was approximately 21 deg. About one-quarter of the Moon's diameter was eclipsed. The Moon cleared completely when about ¼ of an hour remained to sunrise.*

As seen from Cairo, the Moon would reach an altitude of 21° at 3:32 AM. The time when the eclipse ended corresponds to 5:09 AM.

Certain Arab astronomers used timings of the same lunar eclipse at two separate locations to determine the difference in longitude between the two places. Plans were made for joint observation at the two places based on prediction of the eclipse. For instance, from timings of the lunar eclipse of July 5, 1004 CE, at Ghazna (now Ghaznī, Afghanistan) and Jurjāniyyah (now Kunya-Urgench, Turkm.), the Persian scholar al-Bīrūnī estimated the longitude difference between the two cities as 10.2°. The correct figure is 9.3°. This technique was later widely adopted in Europe

USES OF ECLIPSES FOR CHRONOLOGICAL PURPOSES

Several examples of the value of eclipses in chronology are mentioned above in passing. No one system of dating has been continuously in use since ancient times, although some, such as the Olympiads, persisted for many centuries. Dates were frequently expressed in terms of a king's reign; years were also named after officials of whom lists have been preserved (for instance, the Assyrian Chronicle mentioned above). In such cases, it is important to be able to equate certain specific years thus defined with years before the Common Era (BCE). This correspondence can be made whenever the date of an eclipse is given in an ancient record. In this regard, eclipses have distinct advantages over other celestial phenomena such as comets: in addition to being frequently recorded in history, their dates of occurrence can be calculated exactly.

Chinese chronology can be confirmed accurately by eclipses from the 8th century BCE (during the Zhou dynasty) onward. The *Chunqiu* chronicle, mentioned above, notes the occurrence of 36 solar eclipses between 722 and 481 BCE—the earliest surviving series of solar eclipse observations from any part of the world. The records give the date of each event in the following form: year of the ruler, lunar month, and day of the 60-day cycle. As many as 32 of the eclipses cited in the *Chunqiu* can be identified by modern calculations. Errors in the recorded lunar month (typically amounting to no more than a single month) are fairly common, but both the year and the recorded day of the sexagenary cycle are invariably correct.

The chronology of Ptolemy's canon list of kings—which gives the Babylonian series from 747 to 539 BCE, the Persian series from 538 to 324 BCE, the Alexandrian series from 323 to 30 BCE, and the Roman series from 30 BCE onward—is confirmed by eclipses. The eclipse of 763 BCE, recorded in the Assyrian Chronicle, makes it possible to carry the chronology back with certainty through the period covered by that eponym canon to 893 BCE. Identifiable eclipses that were recorded under named Roman consuls extend back to 217 BCE. The lunar eclipse seen at Pydna in Macedonia on June 21, 168 BCE, and the solar eclipse observed at Rome on March 14, 190 BCE, can be used to determine months in the Roman calendar in the natural year. Furthermore, eclipses occasionally help to fix the precise dates of a series of events, such as those associated with the Athenian disaster at Syracuse in 413 BCE.

The late Babylonian astronomical texts occasionally mention major historical events, as, for example, the dates when Xerxes and Alexander the Great died. To illustrate the potential of this material for chronological purposes, the date of the death of Xerxes may be accurately fixed by reference to eclipses. On a tablet that lists lunar eclipses at 18-year intervals occurs the following brief announcement between two eclipse records: "Month V, day 14 [?], Xerxes was murdered by his son." Unfortunately, the cuneiform sign for the day of the month is damaged, and a viable reading could be anything from 14 to 18. The year is missing, but it can be deduced from the 18-year sequence as 465 BCE. This identification is confirmed by calculating the dates of the two eclipses stated to have occurred in the same year that Xerxes died. The first of these happened when the Moon was in the constellation of Sagittarius, while the second took place on the 14th day of the eighth lunar month. For many years both before and after 465 BCE, no such combination of eclipses can be found; it occurs only in 465 BCE itself. The dates deduced for the two eclipses are June 5 and November 30 of that year. Mention of an intercalary sixth month on the same tablet enables the date of the death of Xerxes to be fixed as some time between August 4 and 8 in 465 BCE.

USES OF ECLIPSES FOR ASTRONOMICAL PURPOSES

Ancient and medieval observations of eclipses are of the highest value for investigating long-term variations in the length of the day. Early investigators such as the English astronomer Edmond Halley deduced from eclipse observations that the Moon's motion was subject to an acceleration. However, not until 1939 was it conclusively demonstrated (by the British astronomer Harold Spencer Jones) that only part of this acceleration was real. The remainder was apparent and was a consequence of the practice of measuring time relative to a nonuniform unit, namely, the rotation of Earth. Time determined in this way is termed Universal Time. For astronomical purposes, it is preferable to utilize an invariant time frame such as Terrestrial Time (the modern successor to Ephemeris Time)—defined by the motion of the Sun, Moon, and planets.

Lunar and solar tidal friction, occurring especially in the seas and oceans of Earth, is now known to be responsible for a gradual decrease in the terrestrial rate of rotation. Apart from slowing down Earth's rotation, lunar tides produce a reciprocal effect on the Moon's motion, causing a gradual increase in the mean distance of the Moon from Earth (at about 3.8 cm [1.5 inches] per year) and a consequent real retardation of its motion. Hence, the length of the month is slowly increasing (at about 0.04 sec in a century).

These changes in the Moon's orbit can now be accurately fixed by lunar laser ranging, and it seems likely that they have proceeded at an essentially constant rate for many centuries. The history of Earth's rotation, however, is complicated by effects of nontidal origin, and in order to obtain maximum information it is necessary to utilize both modern and ancient observations. Telescopic observations reveal fluctuations in the length of the day on timescales of several decades, and these fluctuations are mainly attributed to interactions between the fluid core of Earth and the surrounding solid mantle. Ancient and medieval observations also suggest the presence of longer-term variations, which could be produced by alterations in the moment of inertia of Earth resulting from both the ongoing rise of land that was glaciated during the Pleistocene Ice Age (which ended around 10,000 years ago) and the sea-level changes associated with the freezing and melting of polar ice.

Records of large solar eclipses preserved in literary and historical works have made an important contribution to the study of past variations in Earth's rate of rotation. In recent years, major advances have also come from the analysis of timings of lunar and solar eclipses by ancient Babylonian and medieval Chinese and Arab astronomers. Although many Babylonian texts are fragmentary, about 120 usable timings of eclipse contacts are accessible (including measurements at different phases of the same eclipse).

These observations date primarily from between about 700 and 50 BCE. By comparison, only a handful of similar Greek measurements are preserved, and these are less precise. Approximately 80 eclipse timings by Chinese astronomers are preserved in Chinese history. These are from two main periods: between 400 and 600 CE and later from 1000 to 1300 CE. In addition, almost 50 measurements of eclipse times by medieval Arab astronomers are extant; these date from between about 800 and 1000 CE and are mainly contained in the Hakemite Tables compiled by Ibn Yūnus about 1005 CE. Unfortunately, there are very few timings between 50 BCE and 400 CE and again from 600 to 800 CE.

Tidal computations indicate a steady increase in the length of the mean solar day by about 1/40 sec every millennium. Nontidal causes produce smaller effects, generally in opposition to the main trend. Although the rate of change in the length of the day is minute, the loss of energy by Earth is huge. In measuring changes in Earth's rate of spin, the long timescale covered by ancient observations is an important asset. Approximately one million days, each marginally shorter than at present, have elapsed since the earliest reliable eclipse observations were made, about 700 BCE. The contribution of individual small increments is summative. As a result, present-day computations of ancient eclipses that make no allowance for any increase in the length of the day may be as much as five or six hours ahead of the observed time of occurrence. In the case of total solar eclipses, the path of the Moon's shadow across Earth's surface may appear to be displaced by thousands of kilometres.

The technique of using ancient observations to investigate changes in the rate of Earth's rotation is well illustrated by a total solar eclipse observed by Babylonian astronomers on a date corresponding to April 15, 136 BCE. This event is recorded on two damaged tablets, a composite translation of which follows:

> At 24 degrees after sunrise, there was a solar eclipse beginning on the southwest side. After 18 degrees it became total such that there was complete night. Venus, Mercury, and the normal stars were visible. Jupiter and Mars, which were in their period of disappearance, were visible in that eclipse. [The shadow] moved from southwest to northeast. [Time interval of] 35 degrees for obscuration and clearing up.

This is an exceptionally fine account of a total solar eclipse and is by far the best preserved from the ancient world. The Babylonians were able to detect a number of stars, as well as four planets, during the few minutes of darkness. Modern calculations confirm that Jupiter and Mars were too near the Sun to be observed under normal circumstances; Jupiter was very close to the solar disk.

As noted above, time intervals were expressed by the Babylonians in degrees, each equivalent to 4 minutes of time. Hence, the eclipse is recorded as beginning 96 minutes after sunrise (or about 7:10 AM), becoming total 72 minutes later and lasting from start to finish for 140 minutes. Computations that make no allowance for changes in the length of the day displace the track of totality far to the west and imply that this eclipse was barely visible at Babylon, with as little as 15 percent of the Sun being covered. Furthermore, the computed time of onset is around noon rather than in the early morning—a difference of 3.4 hours. In order to best comply with the record, it is necessary to assume that the length of the day has increased by about $\frac{1}{30}$ sec in the intervening two millennia or so.

Numerous eclipses of both the Sun and the Moon were timed by the Babylonian astronomers with similar care, and analysis of the available records closely confirms the above result for the change in the length of the day. Although the timing device used is likely to have been of low precision, many eclipse observations were made fairly close to the reference moments of sunrise or sunset. For these the measured intervals would be so short that clock errors may be presumed to be small.

The many Arab and Chinese observations of both lunar and solar eclipses during the Middle Ages enable further variations in Earth's spin to be traced. The following observations of the lunar eclipse of Sept. 17, 1019 CE, made by al-Bīrūnī at Ghazna attest to the quality of some of these more recent data:

When I observed it, the altitude of Capella [Alpha Aurigae] above the eastern horizon was slightly less than 60 degrees when the cut at the edge of the Full Moon had become visible; the altitude of Sirius [Alpha Canis Majoris] was [then] 17 degrees, that of Procyon [Alpha Canis Minoris] was 22 degrees and that of Aldebaran [Alpha Tauri] was 63 degrees, where all altitudes are measured from the eastern horizon.

All four stellar measurements are in agreement that the eclipse began at around 2:15 AM, but calculations that make no allowance for any change in the length of the day indicate a time approximately 0.5 hour later. Observations such as these reveal that around 1000 CE the length of the day was about $\frac{1}{65}$ sec shorter than at present.

Combining the various results obtained from analysis of ancient and medieval data, it is possible to show that over the last 2,700 years the rate of increase in the length of the day has varied markedly. This emphasizes the importance of nontidal effects in producing changes in the rate of Earth's rotation period. In sum, the history of Earth's rotation is extremely complex.

CHAPTER 8

MARS

Glowering as a conspicuous red object in the night sky is Mars, the fourth planet in the solar system. Mars is designated by the symbol ♂ and is the seventh largest planet in size and mass in the solar system.

Sometimes called the Red Planet, Mars has long been associated with warfare and slaughter. It is named for the Roman god of war. As long as 3,000 years ago, Babylonian astronomer-astrologers called the planet Nergal for their god of death and pestilence. The planet's two moons, Phobos (Greek: "Fear") and Deimos ("Terror"), were named for two of the sons of Ares and Aphrodite (the counterparts of Mars and Venus, respectively, in Greek mythology).

In recent times Mars has intrigued people for more substantial reasons than its baleful appearance. The planet is the second closest to Earth, after Venus, and it is usually easy to observe in the night sky because its orbit lies outside Earth's. It is also the only planet whose solid surface and atmospheric phenomena can be seen in telescopes from Earth. Centuries of assiduous studies by earthbound observers, extended by spacecraft observations since the 1960s, have revealed that Mars is similar to Earth in many ways. Like Earth, Mars has clouds, winds, a roughly 24-hour day, seasonal weather patterns, polar ice caps, volcanoes, canyons, and other familiar features. There are intriguing clues that billions of years ago Mars was even more Earthlike than today, with a denser, warmer atmosphere and much more water—rivers, lakes,

Mars (Tharsis side), in a composite of images taken by the Mars Global Surveyor spacecraft in April 1999. The northern polar cap and encircling dark dune field of Vastitas Borealis are visible at the top of the globe. NASA/JPL/Malin Space Science Systems

flood channels, and perhaps oceans. By all indications Mars is now a sterile frozen desert, but close-up images of seemingly water-eroded gullies suggest that at least small amounts of water may have flowed on or near the planet's surface in geologically recent times and may still exist as a liquid in protected areas below the surface. The presence of water on Mars is considered a critical issue because without water life as it is presently understood cannot exist. If microscopic life-forms ever did originate on Mars, there remains a chance, albeit a remote one, that they may yet survive in these hidden watery niches. In 1996 a team of scientists reported what they concluded to be evidence for ancient microbial life in a piece of meteorite that had come from Mars, but most scientists have disputed their interpretation.

Since at least the end of the 19th century, Mars has been considered the most hospitable place in the solar system beyond Earth both for indigenous life and for human exploration and habitation. At that time, speculation was rife that the so-called canals of Mars—complex systems of long, straight surface lines that very few astronomers had claimed to see in telescopic observations—were the creations of intelligent beings. Seasonal changes in the planet's appearance, attributed to the spread and retreat of vegetation, added further to the purported evidence for biological activity. Although the canals later proved to be illusory and the seasonal changes geologic rather than biological, scientific and public interest in the possibility of Martian life and in exploration of the planet has not faded.

During the past century Mars has taken on a special place in popular culture. It has served as inspiration for generations of fiction writers from H.G. Wells and Edgar Rice Burroughs in the heyday of the Martian canals to Ray Bradbury in the 1950s and Kim Stanley Robinson in the '90s. Mars has also been a central theme in radio, television, and film, perhaps the most notorious case being Orson Welles's radio-play production of H.G. Wells's novel *War of the Worlds*, which convinced thousands of unwitting listeners on the evening of Oct. 30, 1938, that beings from Mars were invading Earth. The planet's mystique and many real mysteries remain a stimulus to both scientific inquiry and human imagination to this day.

BASIC ASTRONOMICAL DATA

Mars moves around the Sun at a mean distance of 228 million km (140 million miles), or about 1.5 times the distance of Earth from the Sun. Because of Mars's relatively elongated orbit, the distance between Mars and the Sun varies from 206.6 million to 249.2 million km (128.4 million to 154.8 million miles). Mars orbits the Sun once in 687 Earth days, which means that its year is nearly twice as long as Earth's. At its closest approach, Mars is less than 56 million km (35 million miles) from Earth, but it recedes to almost 400 million km (250 million miles) when the two planets are on opposite sides of the solar system.

Mars is easiest to observe when it and the Sun are in opposite directions in the sky—i.e., at opposition—because it is then high in the sky and shows a fully lighted face. Successive oppositions occur about every 26 months. Oppositions can take place at different points in the Martian orbit. Those best for viewing occur when the planet is closest to the Sun, and so also to Earth, because Mars is then at its

PLANETARY DATA FOR MARS

mean distance from Sun	227,941,040 km (1.5 AU)
eccentricity of orbit	0.093 399
inclination of orbit to ecliptic	1.850 20°
Martian year (sidereal period of revolution)	686.980 Earth days
visual magnitude at mean opposition	-2.01
mean synodic period*	779.94 Earth days
mean orbital velocity	24.1 km/s
equatorial radius	3,396.2 km
north polar radius	3,376.2 km
south polar radius	3,382.6 km
surface area	1.44 × 108 km²
mass	6.418 × 10²³ kg
mean density	3.94 g/cm³
mean surface gravity	372 cm/s²
escape velocity	5.022 km/s
rotation period (Martian sidereal day)	24 h 37 min 22.663 s
Martian mean solar day (sol)	24 h 39 min 36 s
inclination of equator to orbit	24.936°
mean surface temperature	210 K (-82 °F, -63 °C)
typical surface pressure	0.006 bar
number of known moons	2

*Time required for the planet to return to the same position in the sky relative to the Sun as seen from Earth.

brightest and largest. Close oppositions occur roughly every 15 years.

Mars spins on its axis once every 24 hours 37 minutes, making a day on Mars only a little longer than an Earth day. Its axis of rotation is inclined to its orbital plane by about 25°, and, as for Earth, the tilt gives rise to seasons on Mars. The Martian year consists of 668.6 Martian solar days, called sols. Because of the elliptical orbit, southern summers are shorter (154 Martian days) and warmer than those in the north (178 Martian days). The situation, however, is slowly changing such that 25,000 years from now the northern summers will be the shorter and warmer ones. In addition, the obliquity, or tilt, of the axis is slowly changing on a roughly one-million-year timescale. During the present epochs the obliquity may range from close to 0, at which times Mars has no seasons, to as high as 45°, when seasonal differences are extreme. Over hundred-million-year time-scales the obliquity may reach values as high as 80°.

Mars is a small planet, larger than only Mercury and slightly more than half the size of Earth. It has an equatorial radius of 3,396 km (2,110 miles) and a mean polar radius of 3,379 km (2,100 miles). The mass of Mars is only one-tenth the terrestrial value, and its gravitational acceleration of 3.72 metres/sec² (12.2 feet/sec²) at the surface means that objects on Mars weigh a little more than a third of their weight on Earth's surface. Mars has only 28 percent of the surface area of Earth, but, because more than two-thirds of Earth is covered by water, the land areas of the two planets are comparable.

EARLY TELESCOPIC OBSERVATIONS

Mars was an enigma to ancient astronomers, who were bewildered by its apparently capricious motion across the sky—sometimes in the same direction as the Sun and other celestial objects (direct, or prograde, motion), sometimes in the opposite direction (retrograde motion). In 1609 the German astronomer Johannes Kepler used the superior naked-eye observations of the planet by his Danish colleague Tycho Brahe to empirically deduce its laws of motion and so pave the way for the modern gravitational theory of the solar system. Kepler found that the orbit of Mars was an ellipse along which the planet moved with nonuniform but predictable motion. Earlier astronomers had based their theories on the older Ptolemaic idea of hierarchies of circular orbits and uniform motion.

The earliest telescopic observations of Mars in which the disk of the planet was seen were those of the Italian astronomer Galileo in 1610. The Dutch scientist and mathematician Christiaan Huygens is credited with the first accurate drawings of surface markings. In 1659 Huygens made a drawing of Mars showing a major dark marking on the planet now known as Syrtis Major. The Martian polar caps were first noted by the Italian-born French astronomer Gian Domenico Cassini about 1666.

Visual observers subsequently made many key discoveries. The rotation period of the planet was discovered by Huygens in 1659 and measured by Cassini in 1666 to be 24 hours 40 minutes—in error by only 3 minutes. The tenuous Martian atmosphere was first noted in the 1780s by the German-born British astronomer William Herschel, who also measured the tilt of the planet's rotation axis and first discussed the seasons of Mars. In 1877

Asaph Hall of the U.S. Naval Observatory discovered that Mars has two natural satellites. Telescopic observations also documented many meteorological and seasonal phenomena that occur on Mars, such as various cloud types, the growing and shrinking of the polar caps, and seasonal changes in the colour and extent of the dark areas.

The first known map of Mars was produced in 1830 by Wilhelm Beer and Johann Heinrich von Mädler of Germany. The Italian astronomer Giovanni Virginio Schiaparelli prepared the first modern

THE CANALS OF MARS

In the late 19th and early 20th centuries, several astronomers observed apparent systems of long, straight linear markings on the surface of Mars. These were the subject of much controversy and influenced popular thinking about the possibility of life beyond Earth.

The Italian astronomer and statesman Giovanni Virginio Schiaparelli reported observing about 100 of these markings, beginning in 1877, and described them as *canali* (Italian: "channels"), a neutral term that implied nothing about their origin. Other observers (e.g., Schiaparelli's fellow countryman Pietro Angelo Secchi in 1858) had earlier noted similar markings, but Schiaparelli's writings first drew wide attention to the subject. About the turn of the 20th century the American astronomer Percival Lowell, who had established an observatory in Flagstaff, Ariz., specifically to observe Mars, became the champion of those who believed the markings to be bands of vegetation, kilometres wide, bordering irrigation ditches, or canals, dug by intelligent beings to carry water from the polar caps. Lowell and others described canal networks studded with dark intersections called oases and covering much of the surface of the planet. Occasionally the lines were perceived as doubled; i.e., two parallel lines became visible where only a single canal had been seen before. Lowell produced ever-more-elaborate maps of the Martian canals until his death in 1916.

Most astronomers could see no canals, and many doubted their reality. Experiments with untrained observers showed that disconnected features in diagrams or drawings might be perceived as straight-line networks when viewed at the proper distance. Telescopic photography through Earth's atmosphere offered no solution, because the lines were barely discernible by the human eye and beyond the recording capability of the camera. The controversy was finally resolved only when close-up images of the Martian surface were taken from spacecraft, beginning with Mariner 4 (1965) and Mariners 6 and 7 (1969). These showed many craters and other features but nothing resembling networks of long linear channels, either natural or artificial.

astronomical map of Mars in 1877, which contained the basis of the system of nomenclature still in use today. The names on his map are in Latin and are formulated predominantly in terms of the ancient geography of the Mediterranean area.

MARS AS SEEN FROM EARTH

To the Earth-based telescopic observer, the Martian surface outside the polar caps is characterized by red-ochre-coloured bright areas on which dark markings appear superimposed. In the past, the bright areas were referred to as deserts, and the majority of large dark areas were originally called *maria* (Latin: "oceans" or "seas"; singular *mare*) in the belief that they were covered by expanses of water. No topography can be seen from Earth-based telescopes. What is observed are variations in the brightness of the surface or changes in the opacity of the atmosphere.

Surface Features

The dark markings cover about one-third of the Martian surface, mostly in a band around the planet between latitudes 10° and 40° S. Their distribution is irregular, and their gross pattern has been observed to change over timescales of tens to hundreds of years. The northern hemisphere has only three such major features—Acidalia Planitia, Syrtis Major, and a dark

collar around the pole—which were once considered to be shallow seas or vegetated regions. It is now known that many of Mars's dark areas form and change as winds move dark sand around the surface or sweep areas free of bright dust. Many of the bright areas are regions of dust accumulation. The canals that figured so prominently on maps made from telescopic observations around the turn of the 20th century are not visible in close-up spacecraft images. They were almost certainly imaginary features that observers thought they saw while straining to make out objects close to the limit of resolution of their telescopes. Other features, such as the "wave of darkening" and the "blue haze" described by early observers at the telescope, are now known to result from a combination of the viewing conditions and changes in the reflective properties of the surface.

Polar Regions

For telescopic observers the most striking regular changes on Mars occur at the poles. With the onset of fall in a particular hemisphere, clouds develop over the relevant polar region, and the cap, made of frozen carbon dioxide, begins to grow. The smaller cap in the north ultimately extends to 55° latitude, the larger one in the south to 50° latitude. In spring the caps recede. During summer the northern carbon dioxide cap disappears completely, leaving behind a small water-ice cap. In the south a small residual cap

Mars (Syrtis Major side), photographed by the Earth-orbiting Hubble Space Telescope on March 10, 1997. Among the sharpest images ever taken from Earth's vicinity, it shows the bright and dark features long familiar to telescopic observers. The north polar cap at the top has lost much of its annual frozen carbon dioxide layer, revealing the small permanent water-ice cap and dark collar of sand dunes. NASA/JPL/David Crisp and the WFPC2 Science Team

scientist, George J. Stoney, questioned this theory and suggested that the caps might consist of frozen carbon dioxide, but evidence to support the idea was not available until Dutch American astronomer Gerard Kuiper's 1947 detection of carbon dioxide in the atmosphere.

In 1966 American scientists Robert Leighton and Bruce Murray published the results of a numerical model of the thermal environment on Mars that raised considerable doubt about the water-ice hypothesis. Their calculations indicated that, under Martian conditions, atmospheric carbon dioxide would freeze at the poles, and the growth and shrinkage of their model carbon dioxide caps mimicked the observed behaviour of the actual caps. The model predicted that the seasonal caps were relatively thin, only a few metres deep near the poles and thinning toward the equator. Although based on simplifications of the actual conditions on Mars, their results were later confirmed by thermal and spectral measurements taken by the twin Mariner 6 and 7 spacecraft when they flew by Mars in 1969.

TRANSIENT ATMOSPHERIC PHENOMENA

Early telescopic observers noted instances in which Martian surface features were temporarily obscured. They observed both white and yellow obscurations that were correctly interpreted as due to condensed gas and dust,

composed of carbon dioxide ice and water ice lingers over the summer.

The composition of the seasonal polar caps was the subject of debate for nearly 200 years. One early hypothesis—that the caps were made of water ice—can be traced to English astronomer William Herschel, who imagined them to be just like those on Earth. In 1898 an Irish

respectively. Telescopic observers also noted periodic disappearances of all dark markings, usually around southern summer. Again they were correctly interpreted as the result of global dust storms. Spacecraft observations have confirmed that hazes, clouds, and fogs commonly veil the surface.

THE ATMOSPHERE

Basic Atmospheric Data

The Dutch American astronomer Gerard P. Kuiper ascertained from telescopic observations in 1947 that the Martian atmosphere is composed mainly of carbon dioxide. The atmosphere is very thin, exerting less than 1 percent of Earth's atmospheric pressure at the surface. Surface pressures range over a factor of 15 because of the large altitude variations in Mars's topography. Only small amounts of water are present in the atmosphere today. If it all precipitated out, it would form a layer of ice crystals only 10 micrometres (0.0004 inch) thick, which could be gathered into a solid block of ice not much larger than a medium-sized terrestrial iceberg. Despite the small amount of water present, the atmosphere is near saturation, and water-ice clouds are common.

Low-lying clouds and fogs are often observed within topographic depressions—i.e., valleys or craters. Thin clouds are common at the morning terminator (the dividing line between the lit and unlit portions of the planet's disk), and orographic clouds, produced when moist air is lifted over elevated terrain and cooled, form around prominent topographic features such as craters and volcanoes. In winter, westward-moving spiral-shaped storm systems, similar to those on Earth, are seen regularly at midlatitudes. Most of these clouds—in particular, the white clouds seen by the early observers—are composed of water ice.

Dust storms are common on Mars. They can occur at any time but are most frequent in southern spring and summer, when Mars is passing closest to the Sun and surface temperatures are at their highest. Most of the storms are regional in extent and last a few weeks. Every second or third year, however, the dust storms become global. At their peak, dust is carried so high in the atmosphere that only the summits of the loftiest volcanoes—up to 21 km (13 miles) above the planet's mean radius—are visible.

Although too small to be observed from Earth, dust devils have been seen from Mars orbit and at the various spacecraft landing sites. Narrow tracks, thought to be caused by dust devils, are also visible in high-resolution images taken from orbit.

The characteristic temperature in the lower atmosphere is about 200 K (-70 °C, or -100 °F), which is generally colder than the average daytime surface temperature of 250 K (20 °C, or -10 °F). These values are in the same range as those experienced on Earth in Antarctica during winter. In summer above a very dark surface, daytime temperatures can peak at about 290 K (17 °C, or 62 °F). Above the turbulent layer close to the surface, temperature decreases with elevation at a rate of about 1.5 K (−270 °C, or −460 °F) per km (about 2.4 K [−270 °C, or −455 °F] per mile) of altitude.

Unlike that of Earth, the atmosphere of Mars experiences large seasonal variations in pressure as carbon dioxide, the main constituent, "snows out" at the winter pole and returns directly to a gas (sublimes) in the spring. Because the southern winter cap is more extensive than the northern, atmospheric pressure reaches a minimum during southern winter when the southern cap is at its largest. The pressure varies annually by 26 percent as some 7.9 trillion metric tons of carbon dioxide leave and reenter the atmosphere seasonally. This is equivalent to a thickness of at least 23 cm (9 inches) of solid carbon dioxide (dry ice) or several metres of carbon dioxide snow averaged over the vast area of the seasonal polar caps.

COMPOSITION AND SURFACE PRESSURE

Carbon dioxide constitutes 95.3 percent of the atmosphere by weight, nine times the quantity now in Earth's much more massive atmosphere. Much of Earth's carbon dioxide, however, is chemically locked in sedimentary rocks; the amount in the Martian atmosphere is less than a thousandth of the terrestrial total. The balance of the Martian atmosphere consists of molecular nitrogen, water vapour, and noble gases (argon, neon, krypton, and xenon). There are also trace amounts

COMPOSITION OF THE MARTIAN ATMOSPHERE	
GAS	PERCENTAGE BY WEIGHT
carbon dioxide (CO_2)	95.32
molecular nitrogen (N_2)	2.7
argon (Ar)	1.6
molecular oxygen (O_2)	0.13
carbon monoxide (CO)	0.07
water vapour (H_2O)	0.03
neon (Ne)	0.00025
krypton (Kr)	0.00003
xenon (Xe)	0.000008

of gases that have been produced from the primary constituents by photochemical reactions, generally high in the atmosphere; these include molecular oxygen, carbon monoxide, nitric oxide, and small amounts of ozone.

The lower atmosphere supplies gas to the planet's ionosphere, where densities are low, temperatures are high, and components separate by diffusion according to their masses. Various constituents in the top of the atmosphere are lost to space, which affects the isotopic composition of the remaining gases. For example, because hydrogen is lost preferentially over its heavier isotope deuterium, Mars's atmosphere contains five times more deuterium than Earth's.

Although water is only a minor constituent of the Martian atmosphere (a few molecules per 10,000 at most), primarily because of low atmospheric and surface temperatures, it plays an important role in atmospheric chemistry and meteorology. The Martian atmosphere is effectively saturated with water vapour, yet there is no liquid water present on the surface. The temperature and pressure of the planet are so low that water molecules can exist only as ice or as vapour. Little water is exchanged daily with the surface despite the very cold nighttime surface temperatures.

Water vapour is mixed uniformly up to altitudes of 10–15 km (6–9 miles) and shows strong latitudinal gradients that depend on the season. The largest changes occur in the northern hemisphere. During

Seasonal water-ice ground frost on Mars, in a photograph taken by the Viking 2 lander at its high-latitude (48° N) landing site in Utopia Planitia on May 18, 1979. NASA/JPL

summer in the north, the complete disappearance of the carbon dioxide cap leaves behind a water-ice cap. Sublimation of water from the residual cap results in a strong north-to-south concentration gradient of water vapour in the atmosphere. In the south, where a small carbon dioxide cap remains in summer and only a small amount of water ice has been detected, a strong water vapour gradient does not normally develop in the atmosphere.

The atmospheric water vapour is believed to be in contact with a much larger reservoir in the Martian soil.

Subsurface layers of ice are thought to be ubiquitous on Mars at latitudes poleward of 40°; the very low subsurface temperatures would prevent the ice from subliming. The 2001 Mars Odyssey spacecraft confirmed that ice is present within a metre of the surface at latitudes higher than 60°, and the Phoenix lander found ice below the surface at 68° N, but it is not known how deep the ice layer extends. In contrast, at low latitudes ice is unstable, and any ice present in the ground would tend to sublime into the atmosphere.

Isotopic measurements suggest that larger amounts of carbon dioxide, nitrogen, and argon were present in the atmosphere in the past and that Mars may have lost much of its inventory of volatile substances early in its history, either to space or to the ground (i.e., locked up chemically in rocks). Mars may once have had a much thicker atmosphere that was lost to the surface through chemical reactions, which formed carbonates, and to space through large asteroid impacts, which blew off atmospheric gases.

ATMOSPHERIC STRUCTURE

The vertical structure of the Martian atmosphere—that is, the relation of temperature and pressure to altitude—is determined partly by a complicated balance of several energy-transport mechanisms and partly by the way energy from the Sun is introduced into the atmosphere and lost by radiation to space.

Two factors control the vertical structure of the lower atmosphere—its composition of almost pure carbon dioxide and its content of large quantities of suspended dust. Because carbon dioxide radiates energy efficiently at Martian temperatures, the atmosphere can respond rapidly to changes in the amount of solar radiation received. The suspended dust absorbs large quantities of heat directly from sunlight and provides a distributed source of energy throughout the lower atmosphere.

Surface temperatures depend on latitude and fluctuate over a wide range from day to night. At the Viking 1 and Pathfinder landing sites (both about 20° N latitude), the temperatures at roughly human height above the surface regularly varied from a low near 189 K (-84 °C, or -119 °F) just before sunrise to a high of 240 K (-33 °C, or -28 °F) in the early afternoon. This temperature swing is much larger than that which occurs in desert regions on Earth. The variation is greatest very close to the ground and occurs because the thin, dry atmosphere allows the surface to radiate its heat quickly during the night. During dust storms this ability is impaired, and the temperature swing is reduced. Above altitudes of a few kilometres, the daily variation is damped out, but other oscillations appear throughout the atmosphere as a result of the direct input of solar energy. These temperature and pressure oscillations, sometimes called tides because they are regular, periodic, and synchronized with the position of the Sun, give the Martian atmosphere a very complex vertical structure.

The cooling of the atmosphere with altitude at a rate of 1.5 K per km continues upward to about 40 km (25 miles), at which level (called the tropopause) the temperature becomes a roughly constant 140 K (–130 °C, or –210 °F). This rate, measured by the Viking (and later Pathfinder) spacecraft as they descended through the atmosphere, was unexpectedly low; scientists had anticipated it to be near 5 K per km. This rate is significantly lower than that expected for clear air because of the large amount of suspended dust.

Above 100 km (60 miles), the structure of the atmosphere is determined by the tendency of the heavier molecules to concentrate below the lighter ones. This diffusive separation process overcomes the tendency of turbulence to mix all the constituents together. At these high altitudes, absorption of ultraviolet light from the Sun dissociates and ionizes the gases and leads to complex sequences of chemical reactions. The top of the atmosphere has an average temperature of about 300 K (27 °C, or 80 °F).

METEOROLOGY AND ATMOSPHERIC DYNAMICS

The global pattern of atmospheric circulation on Mars shows many superficial similarities to that of Earth, but the root causes are very different. Among these differences are the atmosphere's ability to adjust rapidly to local conditions of solar heat input; the lack of oceans, which on Earth have a large resistance to temperature changes; the great range in altitude of the surface; the strong internal heating of the atmosphere because of suspended dust; and the seasonal deposition and release of a large part of the Martian atmosphere at the poles.

Near-surface winds at the Viking and Pathfinder landing sites were usually regular in behaviour and generally light. Average speeds were typically less than 2 metres/sec (4.5 miles/hour), although gusts up to 40 metres/sec (90 miles/hour) were recorded. Other observations, including streaks of wind-blown dust and patterns in dune fields and in the many varieties of clouds, have provided additional clues about surface winds.

Global circulation models, which incorporate all the factors understood to influence the behaviour of the atmosphere, predict a strong dependence of winds on the Martian seasons because of the large horizontal temperature gradients associated with the edge of the polar caps in the fall and winter. Strong jet streams with eastward velocities above 100 metres/sec (225 miles/hour) form at high latitudes in winter. Circulation is less dramatic in spring and fall, when light winds predominate everywhere. On Mars, unlike on Earth, there is also a relatively strong north-south circulation that transports the atmosphere to and from the winter and summer poles. The general circulation pattern is occasionally unstable and exhibits large-scale wave motions and instabilities: a regular series of rotating high- and low-pressure systems was clearly seen in the pressure and wind records at the Viking lander sites.

Smaller-scale motions and oscillations, driven both by the Sun and by surface topography, are ubiquitous. For example, at the Viking and Pathfinder landing sites, the winds change in direction and speed throughout the day in response to the position of the Sun and the local slope of the land.

Turbulence is an important factor in raising and maintaining the large quantity of dust found in the Martian atmosphere. Dust storms tend to begin at preferred locations in the southern hemisphere during the southern spring and summer. Activity is at first local and vigorous (for reasons yet to be understood), and large amounts of dust are thrown high into the atmosphere. If the amount of dust reaches a critical quantity, the storm rapidly intensifies, and dust is carried by high winds to all parts of the planet. In a few days the storm has obscured the entire surface, and visibility has been reduced to less than 5 percent of normal. The intensification process is evidently short-lived, as atmospheric clarity begins to return almost immediately, becoming normal typically in a few weeks.

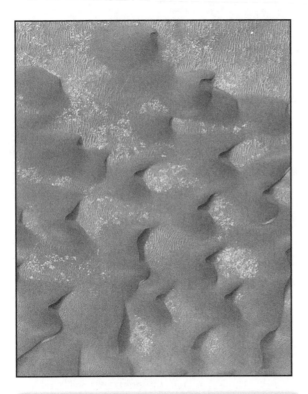

A field of sand dunes on the floor of Mars's Kaiser Crater, shown in a high-resolution image from the Mars Global Surveyor spacecraft. Wind features on several scales are apparent. NASA/JPL/Malin Space Science Systems

CHARACTER OF THE SURFACE

The character of the Martian terrain has been well established from spacecraft photography and altimetry. Almost the entire planet has been photographed from orbit at a resolution of 20 metres (66 feet) and selected areas at resolutions as high as 20 cm (8 inches). In addition, the

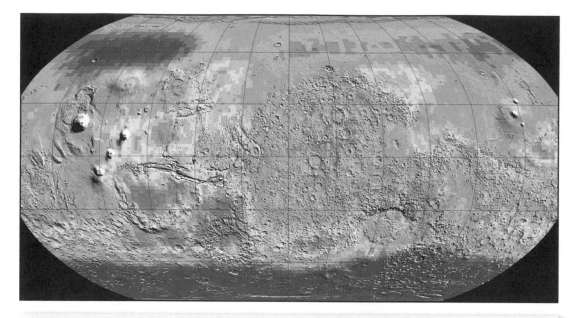

Global map of Mars in epithermal (intermediate-energy) neutrons, created from data collected by the 2001 Mars Odyssey spacecraft. Odyssey mapped the location and concentrations of epithermal neutrons knocked off the Martian surface by incoming cosmic rays. Viewing this and similar images, scientists have surmised that high levels of hydrogen are present, which is suggestive of large reservoirs of water ice below the surface. NASA/JPL/University of Arizona/Los Alamos National Laboratories

laser altimeter on Mars Global Surveyor has measured surface elevations for the entire planet averaged over a circle 300 metres (1,000 feet) across to a vertical accuracy of 1 metre (3.3 feet).

Many maps have been made to illustrate topography, geology, temperature, mineral distributions, and a variety of other data. After Mariner 9 the prime meridian on Mars—the equivalent of the Greenwich meridian on Earth—was defined as passing through a small crater named Airy-0 within the larger crater

Airy. Longitude was measured in degrees that increase to the west of this meridian completely around the planet. Later some scientists expressed a preference for a coordinate system with longitude that increases to the east of the prime meridian. Consequently, maps of Mars were published with either or both of these systems.

Despite its small size, Mars has significantly more relief than Earth. The lowest point on the planet, within the Hellas impact basin, is 8 km (5 miles)

below the reference level. The highest point, at the summit of the volcano Olympus Mons, is 21 km (13 miles) above the reference level. The elevation range is thus 29 km (18 miles), compared with about 20 km (12.4 miles) on Earth—i.e., from the bottom of the Mariana Trench to the top of Mount Everest. Because Mars has no oceans, a reference level for elevations had to be defined in terms other than sea level. In the early 1970s the elevation at which the atmospheric pressure is 6.1 millibars (about 0.006 of the sea-level pressure on Earth) was set as the reference. When Mars Global Surveyor acquired more-accurate elevation data, a better reference was needed, and the planet's mean radius of 3,389.51 km (2,106.14 miles) was chosen.

One of the most striking aspects of the Martian surface is the contrast between the southern and northern hemispheres. Most of the southern hemisphere is high-standing and heavily cratered, resembling the battered highlands of the Moon. Most of the northern hemisphere is low-lying and sparsely cratered. The difference in mean elevation between the two hemispheres is roughly 6 km (3.7 miles). The topographic boundary between the hemispheres is not parallel to the equator but roughly follows a great circle inclined to it by about 30°. In some places the boundary is broad and irregular; in other places there are steep cliffs. Some of the most intensely eroded areas on Mars occur along the boundary. Landforms there include outflow channels, areas of collapse called chaotic terrain, and an enigmatic mix of valleys and ridges known as fretted terrain. Straddling the boundary in the western hemisphere is the Tharsis rise, a vast volcanic pile 4,000 km (2,500 miles) across and 8 km (5 miles) above the reference level at its centre. It stands 12 km (7.5 miles) above the northern plains and more than 2 km (1.2 miles) above the surrounding cratered southern highlands. On or near the Tharsis rise are the planet's largest volcanoes. Conspicuously absent in either hemisphere are the types of landforms that on Earth result from plate tectonics—for example, long linear mountain chains similar to the Andes, oceanic trenches, or a global system of interconnected ridges.

The hemispheric dichotomy most likely formed when a large asteroid collided with Mars very early in its history. The resulting northern hemisphere impact crater measures roughly 8,500 by 10,700 km (5,300 by 6,600 miles) across; the object that crashed into Mars would have been more than 2,000 km (1,200 miles) across. Gravity data acquired by Mars Global Surveyor suggest that the Martian crust is much thicker under the southern highlands than under the northern plains.

SOUTHERN CRATERED HIGHLANDS

The number of very large craters in the southern highlands implies a substantial

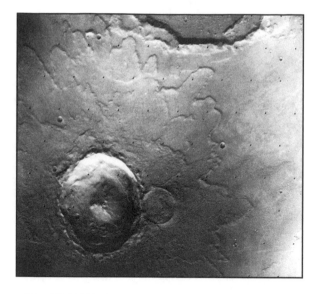

Yuty Crater on Mars, in a photograph by the Viking 1 orbiter. About 18 km (11 miles) in diameter, the impact scar is an example of a rampart crater. Seen from above, its lobes of ejected material, which are bordered with a low ridge, or rampart, give the appearance of an enormous mud splash. The mud is conjectured to have formed from a mixture of impact debris and water that was present under the Martian surface. NASA

age for the surface. Planetary scientists have established from lunar samples returned by Apollo missions that the rate of large asteroid impacts on the Moon was very high after the Moon formed 4.5 billion years ago and then declined rapidly between 3.8 billion and 3.5 billion years ago. Surfaces that formed before the decline are heavily cratered; those that formed after are less so. Mars very

likely had a similar cratering history. Thus, the southern highlands almost certainly survive from more than 3.5 billion years ago.

The southern terrain possesses several distinctive types of craters—huge impact basins; large, partially filled craters with shallow, flat floors and eroded rims; smaller, fresh-looking bowl-shaped craters like those on the Moon; and rampart and pedestal craters. Hellas, the largest impact basin on Mars, is 8 km (5 miles) deep and about 7,000 km (4,350 miles) across, including the broad elevated ring surrounding the depression. Most of the craters measuring tens to hundreds of kilometres across are highly eroded in contrast to much smaller craters that formed on the younger plains, which are barely eroded. The contrast indicates that erosion rates were much higher on early Mars. It is one piece of evidence that the climate on early Mars was very different from what it has been for most of the planet's subsequent history.

Most Martian craters look different from those on the Moon. A rampart crater is so named because the lobes of ejecta—the material thrown out from the crater and extending around it—are bordered with a low ridge, or rampart. The ejecta apparently flowed across the ground, which may indicate that it had a mudlike consistency. Some scientists have conjectured that the mud formed from a mixture of impact debris and

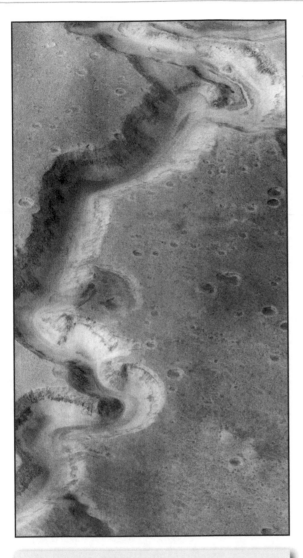

Part of the meandering canyon Nanedi Vallis on Mars, imaged by the Mars Global Surveyor spacecraft on January 8, 1998. Sited on a cratered plain near the east end of Valles Marineris, the channel is one of a number of Martian valley networks that resemble drainage systems on Earth formed by flowing water. NASA/JPL/Malin Space Science Systems

water that was present under the surface. Around a pedestal crater, the ejected material forms a steep-sided platform, or pedestal, with the crater situated inside its border. The pedestal appears to have developed when wind carved away the surface layer of the surrounding region while leaving intact that portion protected by the over-lying ejecta.

High-resolution Viking images revealed an additional characteristic of the ancient southern terrain—the pervasive presence of networks of small valleys that resemble terrestrial drainage systems created by flowing water. Examples include Nirgal Vallis, located in the southern hemisphere north of the Argyre impact basin, and Nanedi Vallis, located just north of the equator near the east end of Valles Marineris. Scientists have proposed two alternative mechanisms for their forma-tion—either the runoff of rainfall on the surface or erosion by the outflow of groundwater that seeped onto the sur-face. In either case, warm climatic conditions may have been required for their formation. A major surprise of the Mars Global Surveyor mission was observation of small fresh-appearing gullies on steep slopes at high latitudes. These features strongly resemble water-worn gullies in Earth's desert regions. They probably formed by the melting of ice driven from the poles and deposited at lower latitudes during periods of high obliquity.

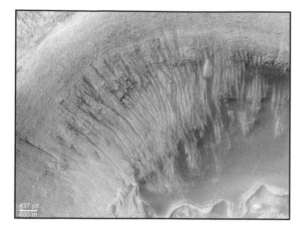

Gullies on the steep north wall of a Martian impact crater on the floor of Newton Crater, in a high-resolution composite image obtained by Mars Global Surveyor in early 2000. The many narrow, fresh-appearing channels appear to have been cut by fluid flow in perhaps hundreds of separate events. NASA/JPL/Malin Science Space Systems

SPARSELY CRATERED PLAINS

The smaller number of impact craters on the plains compared with the southern highlands indicates that they formed after the decline in impact rates between 3.8 and 3.5 billion years ago. The plains can be divided into two broad areas: the volcanic plains of Tharsis composed largely of lava flows and the northern plains. The northern plains have remarkably little relief. They encompass all the terrain within 30° of the pole except for the layered terrains immediately around the pole. Three broad lobes extend to

lower latitudes. These include Chryse Planitia and Acidalia Planitia (centred on 30° W longitude), Amazonis Planitia (160° W), and Utopia Planitia (250° W). The only significant relief in this huge area is a large ancient impact basin, informally called the Utopia basin (40° N, 250° W).

Several different types of terrain have been recognized within the northern plains. In knobby terrain, numerous small hills are separated by smooth plains. The hills appear to be remnants of an ancient cratered surface now almost completely buried by younger material that forms the plains. Various plains have a polygonal fracture pattern that resembles landforms found in permafrost regions on Earth. Others have a peculiar thumbprintlike texture, possibly indicative of the former presence of stagnant ice.

The origin of the low-lying northern plains remains controversial. Parts appear to be formed of lava, like the lunar maria. But some scientists have proposed that they were formerly occupied by ocean-sized bodies of water that were fed by large floods and that the surface of the plains is composed of sediments.

SURFACE COMPOSITION

Results from the Mars Exploration Rovers and from spectrometers on orbiting spacecraft show that the ancient highlands are compositionally distinct from the younger plains. The rover Spirit landed on a basalt plain that may be typical of plains. The rocks on the plains are mostly typical basalts with only thin alteration rinds high in sulfur, chlorine, and other volatile elements. The rinds probably formed by interaction of the basalts with acid fogs. The rover then traveled into the older Columbia Hills, where the rocks are very different. They are mostly basalts and impact breccias, but many are pervasively altered and rich in sulfates and hydrated minerals. Soils consisting almost entirely of sulfates or silica are also present. Many of the rocks appear to have been permeated by warm volcanic fluids or to have been weathered as a result of warm surface conditions. This mix of rocks and soils may be typical of the highlands in general. The results from orbit tell a similar story. Globally, the plains consist mostly of primary, unaltered basaltic minerals such as olivine and pyroxene. In contrast, alteration minerals such as clays are common throughout the ancient cratered terrain. The results indicate that surface conditions changed dramatically around 3.7 billion years ago. Prior to that time, warm and wet conditions were common and resulted in extensive rock alteration; after that time such conditions were rare, and rock alteration was minor.

VALLEYS AND LAKES

Most of the ancient cratered terrain is dissected by networks of dry valleys, mostly 1–2 km (0.6–1.2 miles) across and up to 2,000 km (1,200 miles) long. In outline they resemble terrestrial river systems. The valleys almost certainly formed by slow erosion of running water. Many local lowlands have a valley entering and a valley leaving, indicating that the lowland formerly contained a lake. Layered deposits, possibly deposited in lakes, commonly underlie these areas, and deltas are commonly observed where valleys enter the lowlands. Valley networks are rare, although not absent, in the younger, more sparsely cratered areas. Discovery of the valleys in the 1970s was a surprise because of the difficulty of having liquid water at the surface under present conditions. Their common presence in the heavily cratered terrain is another indicator that conditions on early Mars were much warmer and wetter than they are today.

OUTFLOW CHANNELS AND OCEANS

Large flood channels, termed outflow channels, are observed incised into the Martian surface in several areas. The channels are much larger than the valley networks, generally being tens of kilometres across and hundreds of kilometres long. Most emerge full-sized from rubble-filled depressions and continue downslope into the northern plains or the Hellas basin in the south. Many of the largest drain from the south and west into Chryse Planitia. These are true channels in that they were once completely filled with flowing water, as opposed to most river valleys, which have never been close

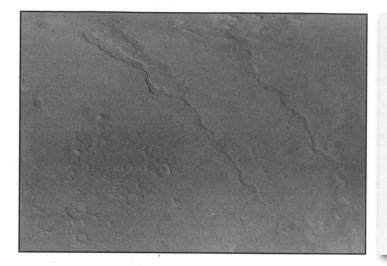

Three outflow channels located near the eastern edge of the giant impact basin Hellas, in a view obtained by Mars Global Surveyor on September 13, 2000. The channels are roughly 1 km (0.6 mile) deep and vary along their courses from about 40 km (25 miles) to about 8 km (5 miles) in width. NASA/JPL/Malin Space Science Systems

to full but contain a much smaller river channel. The peak discharges of the floods that cut the larger outflow channels are estimated to have been a hundred to a thousand times the peak discharge of the Mississippi River—truly enormous events. Some of the floods appear to have formed by catastrophic release of water from lakes. Others formed by explosive eruptions of groundwater. The outflow channels are younger than the valley networks and probably mostly formed when conditions were similar to those that prevail today. Recent discovery of very young outflow channels suggests that they could form today by eruption of groundwater from below the kilometre-thick permanently frozen ground.

VALLES MARINERIS

Close to the equator, centred on 70° W longitude, are several enormous interconnected canyons collectively called Valles Marineris. Individual canyons are roughly 200 km (125 miles) across. At the centre of the system, several canyons merge to form a depression 600 km (375 miles) across and as much as 9 km (5.6 miles) deep—about five times the depth of the Grand Canyon. The entire system is more than 4,000 km (2,500 miles) in length, or about 20 percent of Mars's circumference, almost the width of the United States. At several places within the canyons are thick, sulfate-rich sedimentary sequences, which suggest that lakes may have formerly occupied the canyons. Some of the lakes may have drained catastrophically to the east to form large outflow channels that start at the canyons' eastern end. In contrast to the Grand Canyon, which formed by erosion, the Valles Marineris formed mainly by faulting, although they have been enlarged by erosion.

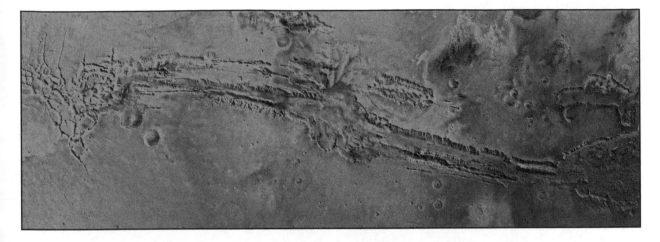

Valles Marineris, the largest canyon system on Mars, shown in a composite of images taken by the Viking 1 and 2 orbiters. NASA/JPL/Caltech

THARSIS AND ELYSIUM

The canyons of Valles Marineris terminate to the west near the crest of the Tharsis rise, a vast bulge on the Martian surface more than 8,000 km (5,000 miles) across and 8 km (5 miles) high at its centre. Near the top of the rise are three of the planet's largest volcanoes—Ascraeus Mons, Arsia Mons, and Pavonis Mons—which tower 18, 17, and 14 km (11.2, 10.5, and 8.7 miles), respectively, above the mean radius. Just off the rise to the northwest is the planet's tallest volcano, Olympus Mons. To the north is the largest volcano in areal extent, Alba Patera. It is 2,000 km (1,250 miles) across but only 7 km (4.3 miles) in height. Between these giant landforms are several smaller volcanoes and lava plains. Tharsis itself is a vast pile of volcanic rock, and although it had largely formed by 3.7 billion years ago, it has been a centre of volcanic activity ever since.

The presence of the Tharsis rise has caused stresses within, and deformation of, the crust. A vast system of fractures radiating from Tharsis and compressional ridges arrayed around the rise are evidence of this process. The radial faulting around Tharsis appears to have contributed to the formation of the Valles Marineris system.

Another volcanic rise is located in the northern region of Elysium at about 215° W longitude. The Elysium rise is much smaller than Tharsis, being only 2,000 km across and 6 km (3.7 miles) high, and is also the site of several volcanoes.

OLYMPUS MONS

The largest volcano in the solar system and the highest point on Mars is the imposing mountain Olympus Mons. Centred at 19° N, 133° W, Olympus Mons consists of a central edifice almost 22 km (14 miles) high and 700 km (400 miles) across. Around its perimeter an outward-facing cliff ascends as high as 10 km (6 miles) above the surrounding area. At the summit is an 85-km- (53-mile-) diameter crater, or caldera, comprising several mutually intersecting craters. For comparison, the largest volcano on Earth, Mauna Loa, Hawaii, measures 120 km (75 miles) across at its widest extent and rises 9 km (5.6 miles) above the ocean floor. Broad, gradually sloping flanks and the presence of numerous long flows and lava channels identify Olympus Mons as a shield volcano and suggest that it was built up from eruptions largely of fairly fluid basaltic lava. Its tremendous size has been attributed to the stability of the Martian crust and to a long accumulation time, possibly more than a billion years.

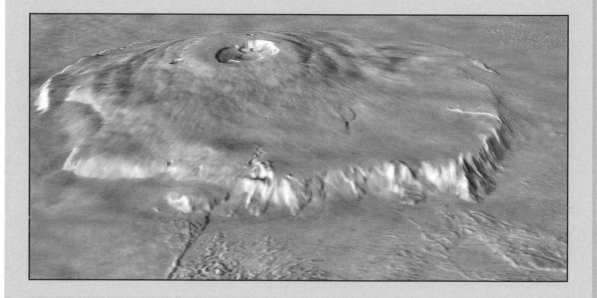

Olympus Mons, the highest point on Mars, in a computer-generated oblique view made by combining photos obtained by the Viking mission in the 1970s with topographic data gathered by Mars Global Surveyor a quarter century later. NASA/JPL/MOLA Science Team

Polar Sediments, Ground Ice, and Glaciers

At each pole is a stack of finely layered water-ice-rich sediments about 3 km (2 miles) thick and only a few tens of millions of years old. The layering is exposed around the periphery of the sediments and in valleys that spiral out from the poles. In winter the sediments are covered with carbon dioxide frost, but they are exposed in summer. At the north pole they extend southward to 80° latitude. At the south pole their extent is less clearly defined, but they appear to extend farther from the pole than in the north. The layering is believed to result from variations in the proportion of dust and ice, probably caused by changes in the tilt of the rotational axis (obliquity). At high obliquities water ice is driven off from the poles, probably causing the residual water-ice caps to disappear entirely and the ice to be deposited at lower latitudes. At low obliquities the water-ice caps are at their maximum. Obliquity variations also affect the incidence of dust storms and deposition of dust at the poles. The deposits have a young age because they have all accumulated since the last period of high obliquity when the previous sediments were removed. One peculiarity of the sediments at the north pole is that they are surrounded by, and perhaps rest upon, a vast dune field rich in the sulfate mineral gypsum.

Under present conditions, at latitudes higher than 40°, ground ice is permanently stable at depths roughly 1 metre (3 feet) or more below the surface because temperatures there never get above the frost point. Above 60° latitude the ice is shallow enough to have been detected from orbit. Ice was also found just below the surface by the Phoenix lander at 68° N. At latitudes higher than

Avalanches near Mars's north pole in an image taken by the Mars Reconnaissance Orbiter, Feb. 19, 2008. Science@NASA

40° are numerous surface features suggestive of the presence of abundant ground ice. These include polygonally fractured ground similar to that found in terrestrial permafrost regions and a general softening of the terrain probably caused by ice-abetted flow of the near-surface materials. Possibly the most striking characteristic of the 40°–60°-latitude bands indicative of ice is the presence of debris aprons at the base of most steep slopes. Materials shed from the slopes appear to have flowed tens of kilometres away from the slopes, and ground-penetrating radar shows that the aprons contain large fractions of ice.

During periods of high obliquity, ice driven from the poles accumulated on the surface at lower latitudes, possibly to form glaciers. Modeling of atmospheric circulation suggests that the preferred sites for ice accumulation during these periods are the western slopes of the Tharsis volcanoes and northeast of the Hellas basin. All these locations are rich in flow features and morainelike landforms, which suggests that glaciers were indeed formerly present.

The north polar region also contains the largest area of sand dunes on Mars. The dunes, which occupy the northern part of the plain known as Vastitas Borealis, form a band that almost completely encircles the north polar remnant cap. Interlayering of sand and seasonal carbon dioxide snow can be seen in some locations, indicating that the dunes are active on at least a seasonal timescale.

Notable Surface Features

Several surface features on Mars are notable for their distinctive topography. Others have been studied in depth by probes from Earth. The subsections that follow describe some of these features in greater detail.

Chryse Planitia

Chryse Planitia is a flat lowland region in the northern hemisphere that was chosen for the landing sites of the U.S. Viking 1 and Mars Pathfinder planetary probes. The Viking 1 lander, which touched down at 22.48° N, 47.97° W, on July 20, 1976, revealed that Chryse Planitia is a rolling, boulder-strewn plain with scattered dusty dunes and outcrops of bedrock. Mars Pathfinder confronted a similar scene when it landed at 19.33° N, 33.22° W, on July 4, 1997.

The surface rocks of Chryse Planitia are believed to be eroded remnants of basaltic lavas carried to the site by large floods during Mars's early history. Analysis of the dusty soil by Viking and Pathfinder lander instruments showed the principal constituent materials (in oxide forms by weight) to be silicon (SiO_2; 46 percent), iron (Fe_2O_3; 18 percent), aluminum (Al_2O_3; 8 percent), magnesium (MgO; 7 percent), calcium (CaO; 6 percent), sulfur (SO_3; 5.4 percent), sodium (Na_2O; 2 percent), and potassium (K_2O; 0.3 percent). This composition is consistent with igneous rocks formed from magmas that interacted with subsurface ice. The rocks were later affected by weathering and leaching processes that stained their surfaces with reddish iron oxide minerals and concentrated certain sulfates (and possibly carbonates) in the surface soil.

Hellas

The enormous impact basin Hellas in the southern hemisphere of Mars is the planet's largest recognizable impact feature. Centred at roughly 40° S, 290° W, Hellas measures about 7,000 km (4,400 miles) across, including the broad elevated ring surrounding the depression, and 8 km (5 miles) deep. Its floor, covered with partly eroded sediments, is the lowest place on Mars. The basin was probably created by collision with an asteroid very early in Mars's history, not long after the planet formed.

Nirgal Vallis

Nirgal Vallis is a sinuous, branching valley located north of the Argyre impact basin, at about 28° S, 42° W. It is about 400 km (250 miles) long and about 5 km (3 miles) wide. Its name derives from the Babylonian word for Mars. First seen in Mariner 9 spacecraft images, the valley has numerous tributaries and appears to have been cut by slow erosion of running water. The source of the water, whether from rainfall, snowfall, or groundwater seepage, is controversial. Also contentious is the origin of gullies on the valley's steep walls that were

photographed by the Mars Global Surveyor spacecraft. Some scientists have proposed that they are the result of recent groundwater seepage; others have suggested that they were created by flows of dry or gas-lubricated debris.

Syrtis Major

Syrtis Major is a distinctive dark marking centred near 290° W and 10° N, which extends some 1,500 km (930 miles) north from the planet's equator and spans 1,000 km (620 miles) from west to east. It was noticed as early as 1659, for it appears in a drawing of Mars of that date by Christiaan Huygens. It is an extensive regional slope elongated north to south that drops 4 km (2.5 miles) from its western boundary (Aeria) to its eastern edge (Isidis). Assiduously observed for more than a century because of its seasonal and long-term variability, especially near its eastern boundary, Syrtis Major was first considered a shallow sea. Later its variability was attributed to vegetation. Close-up photographs and data returned by the U.S. Mariner and Viking planetary probes during the 1960s and '70s enabled investigators to determine that the changes are caused by wind blowing sand and dust across the surface. In the early 1980s detailed topographical maps, prepared from Earth-based spectroscopic and radar observations as well as from the space-probe photographs, indicated that Syrtis Major includes a high-altitude bulge rising to 6 km (3.7 miles) at 310° W.

UTOPIA PLANITIA

The northern lava plain Utopia Planitia was selected as the landing site of the U.S. Viking 2 planetary probe. Photographs transmitted from the Viking 2 lander, which touched down at 47.97° N, 225.74° W, on Sept. 3, 1976, depicted a boulder-strewn plain that superficially resembles the Viking 1 landing site in Chryse Planitia. Soil-sample analyses conducted by the landers show that the soils at the two sites are nearly identical in composition, which is probably the result of a mixing of windblown dust from wide regions of the planet. The Utopia plain differs from the Chryse area in that it has a system of shallow troughs, which may be associated with ice-wedge activity as a result of permafrost. Vesicular boulders—i.e., those with small gas-formed pits, indicative of a volcanic origin—observed by the lander at the Utopia site may be either local lavas or rocks ejected from the nearby impact crater Mie.

Images from the Viking 2 lander showed the persistence of a thin layer of white ground frost, composed of water ice, for about 100 days during each of the two Martian winters observed. The frost is probably first precipitated together with carbon dioxide, which then sublimes in the sunlight, leaving only the water portion.

VASTITAS BOREALIS

Vastitas Borealis is a nearly level lowland plain that surrounds the north pole of the planet Mars and extends southward to about latitude 50°. The plain lies 4–5 km (2.5–3 miles) below the planet's mean radius. In some places it is characterized by numerous low hills of roughly equal size that may be remnants of an ancient cratered surface now almost completely buried by younger material. Elsewhere it has a polygonal fracture pattern reminiscent of those seen in permafrost regions on Earth. The northern part of the plain is covered with a vast dune field that almost completely encircles the pole.

The origin of Vastitas Borealis is controversial. Spacecraft images have made it clear that enormous flood channels, called outflow channels, once transported large volumes of water into this region from the higher elevations to the south. Some scientists have suggested that the smooth, almost level surface of the plain is the result of the deposition of sediments from an ocean formed by the floodwater and covering most of the northern plains; they point to linear features (interpreted as shorelines) and terraces around low hills as supporting evidence. Others question that the level surface and linear features are the result of marine processes; they suggest that the floodwater occupied only a small fraction of the northern plains.

THE INTERIOR

The interior of Mars is poorly known. Planetary scientists have yet to conduct a successful seismic experiment via spacecraft that would provide direct information on internal structure and so must rely on indirect inferences. The moment of inertia of Mars indicates that it has a central core with a radius of 1,300–2,000 km (800–1,200 miles). Isotopic data from meteorites determined to have come from Mars demonstrate unequivocally that the planet differentiated—separated into a metal-rich core and rocky mantle—at the end of the planetary accretion period 4.5 billion years ago. The planet has no detectable magnetic field that would indicate convection (heat-induced flow) in the core today. Large regions of magnetized rock have been detected in the oldest terrains, however, which suggests that very early Mars did have a magnetic field but that it disappeared as the planet cooled and the core solidified. Martian meteorites also suggest that the core may be more sulfur-rich than Earth's core and the mantle more iron-rich.

Mars is almost certainly volcanically active today, although at a very low level. Some Martian meteorites, which are all volcanic rocks, show ages as young as a few hundred million years, and some volcanic surfaces on the planet are so sparsely cratered that they must be only tens of millions of years old. Thus, Mars was volcanically active in the geologically recent past, which implies that its mantle is warm and undergoing melting locally.

Mars's gravitational field is very different from Earth's. On Earth, excesses and deficits of mass in the surface crust, corresponding to the presence of large mountains and ocean deeps, respectively, tend to be offset by compensating masses at depth (isostatic compensation). Thus, the pull of gravity on Earth is the same on high mountains as it is over the ocean. This is also true for Mars's oldest terrains, such as the Hellas basin and the southern highlands. The younger terrains, such as the Tharsis and Elysium domes, however, are only partly compensated. Associated with both of these regions are gravity highs—that is, places where the measured gravity is significantly higher than elsewhere because of the large mass of the domes. (These areas are similar to the mascons that have been detected and mapped on Earth's Moon.)

Because the gravity over the southern highlands is roughly the same as that over the low-lying northern plains, the southern highlands must be underlain by a thicker crust of material that is less dense than the mantle below it. Estimates of the thickness of the Martian crust range from only 3 km (2 miles) under the Isidis impact basin, which is just north of the equator and east of Syrtis Major, to more than 90 km (60 miles) at the south end of the Tharsis rise.

METEORITES FROM MARS

Scientists have identified more than 50 meteorites that have come from Mars. Suspicions about their origin were first raised when meteorites that appeared to be volcanic rocks were found to have ages of about 1.3 billion years instead of the 4.5 billion years of all other meteorites. These rocks had to have come from a body that was geologically active in the comparatively recent past, and Mars was the most likely candidate. The rocks also have similar ratios of oxygen isotopes, which are distinctively different from those of Earth rocks, lunar rocks, and other meteorites. A Martian origin was finally proved when it was found that several of them contained trapped gases with a composition identical to that of the Martian atmosphere as measured by the Viking landers. The rocks are thought to have been ejected from the Martian surface by large impacts. They then went into solar orbit for several million years before falling on Earth. Claims in the mid-1990s of finding evidence for past microscopic life in one of the meteorites, called ALH84001, have been viewed skeptically by the general science community.

MARTIAN MOONS

Little was learned about the two moons of Mars, Phobos and Deimos, after their discovery by American astronomer Asaph Hall in 1877 until orbiting spacecraft

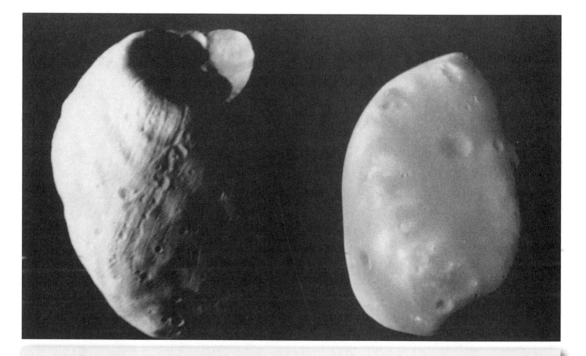

The Martian moons, Phobos (left) and Deimos (right), photographed by the Viking orbiters. Deimos's smooth surface is contrasted with the grooved, pitted, and cratered surface of Phobos. The prominent cavity on the end of Phobos is the crater Stickney. The images are not to scale; Phobos is about 75 percent larger than its companion. NASA/Malin Space Science Systems

observed them a century later. Viking 1 flew to within 100 km (60 miles) of Phobos and Viking 2 to within 30 km (20 miles) of Deimos. The Viking spacecraft discovered that both moons are irregular chunks of rock, roughly ellipsoidal in shape. Phobos and Deimos are not visible from all locations on the planet because of their small size, proximity to Mars, and near-equatorial orbits.

Phobos

Phobos is the inner and larger of Mars's two moons. It is a small, irregular rocky object with a crater-scarred, grooved surface.

A roughly ellipsoidal body, Phobos measures 26.6 km (16.5 miles) across at its widest point. It revolves once around Mars every 7 hours 39 minutes at an exceptionally close mean distance—9,378 km (5,827 miles)—in a nearly circular orbit that lies only 1° from the planet's equatorial plane. Phobos is so near to Mars that without internal strength it would be torn apart by gravitational (tidal) forces. Because the satellite's orbital period is less than the rotational period of Mars (24 hours 37 minutes), Phobos moves from west to east in the Martian sky. The long axis of Phobos constantly points toward Mars; as with Earth's Moon, it has a rotational period

MOONS OF MARS		
PROPERTY	DEIMOS	PHOBOS
mean distance from centre of planet (orbital radius)	23,459 km	9,378 km
orbital period (sidereal period)	1.262 44 Earth days	0.318 91 Earth days
mean orbital velocity	1.4 km/s	2.1 km/s
inclination of orbit to planet's equator	1.79°	1.08°
eccentricity of orbit	0.0005	0.0151
rotation period*	sync.	sync.
radial dimensions	7.5 × 6.1 × 5.2 km	13.3 × 11.1 × 9.3 km
area	525 km²	1,625 km²
mass	1.8×10^{15} kg	1.08×10^{16} kg
mean density	1.8 grams/cm³	1.9 grams/cm³
escape velocity	6 metres/s	10 metres/s
albedo	0.07	0.06

*sync. = synchronous rotation; the rotation and orbital periods are the same.

Phobos, the inner and larger of the two moons of Mars, in a composite of photographs taken by the Viking 1 orbiter in October 1978 from a distance of about 600 km (370 miles). The most prominent feature is the impact crater Stickney, which is almost half as wide as the moon itself. Also visible are linear grooves that appear to be related to Stickney and chains of small craters. NASA/NSSDC

suggesting that Phobos may be a captured asteroid-like object. Remarkable linear grooves, typically 100 metres (330 feet) wide and 20 metres (65 feet) deep, cover much of the surface. There is strong evidence that they are associated with the formation of the largest crater on Phobos. This structure, known as Stickney, measures about 10 km (6 miles) across. Precise observations of Phobos's position over the past century suggest that tidal forces from Mars are slowly pulling the satellite toward the planet. If such is the case, it may collide with Mars, possibly in less than 100 million years.

DEIMOS

Deimos is the outer and smaller of Mars's two moons. It is an irregular rocky object having a cratered surface covered with a thick layer of fine debris.

Roughly ellipsoidal in shape, Deimos measures about 15 km (9 miles) in its longest dimension. It revolves once around Mars every 30 hours 18 minutes at a mean distance of 23,459 km (14,577 miles) in a circular orbit that lies within 2° of Mars's equatorial plane. The satellite's long axis is always directed toward Mars; as with Earth's Moon, it has a rotational period equal to its orbital period and so keeps the same face to the planet. Tidal forces are causing Deimos to recede from the planet.

In spite of its tiny gravity, only about a thousandth that of Earth, Deimos has retained considerable amounts of fine regolith on its surface. It thus appears smooth because its craters lie partially

equal to its orbital period and so keeps the same face to the planet.

The heavily cratered surface of Phobos is covered with a very dark gray regolith (unconsolidated rocky debris) that reflects only about 6 percent of the light falling on it—about one-half that of the Moon's surface. This fact and the satellite's low mean density (1.9 g/cm³[1.1 oz/in³]) are consistent with the composition of carbonaceous chondrite meteorites,

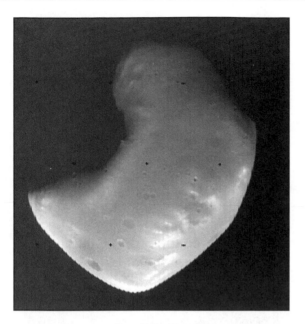

Deimos, the outer and smaller of the two known moons of Mars, photographed by the Viking 2 orbiter in October 1977 from a distance of about 1,400 km (870 miles). Although scarred with impact craters, Deimos appears smoother than its companion moon, Phobos, because it is covered with a thick layer of fine rocky debris (regolith). NASA/Goddard Space Flight Center

buried under this loose material. The largest crater, located near the satellite's south pole, is about 2.5 km (1.6 miles) wide. The surface of Deimos is gray and very dark; its reflectance is only 7 percent—about half that of the Moon's surface. This fact and the satellite's low mean density (less than 2 g/cm³ [1.16 oz/in³]) indicate a carbonaceous composition and suggest that Deimos may be a captured asteroid-like object.

SPACECRAFT EXPLORATION

Since the beginning of the space age, Mars has been a focus of planetary exploration for three main reasons: (1) it is the most Earthlike of the planets; (2) other than Earth, it is the planet most likely to have developed indigenous life; and (3) it will probably be the first extraterrestrial planet to be visited by humans. Between 1960 and 1980 the exploration of Mars was a major objective of both the U.S. and Soviet space programs. U.S. spacecraft successfully flew by Mars (Mariners 4, 6, and 7), orbited the planet (Mariner 9 and Vikings 1 and 2), and placed lander modules on its surface (Vikings 1 and 2). Three Soviet probes (Mars 2, 3, and 5) also investigated Mars, two of them reaching its surface. Mars 3 was the first spacecraft to soft-land an instrumented capsule on the planet, on Dec. 2, 1971; it landed during a planetwide dust storm and returned data for about 20 sec.

Mariner 9, the first spacecraft to orbit another planet, was placed around Mars in November 1971 and operated until October 1972. It returned a wide variety of spectroscopic, radio-propagation, and photographic data. Some 7,330 pictures covering 80 percent of the surface demonstrated a history of widespread volcanism, ancient erosion by water, and reshaping of extensive areas of the surface by internal forces.

The central theme of the Viking missions was the search for extraterrestrial life. No unequivocal evidence of biological activity was found, but the various

A portion of rock outcropping within a small crater in the Meridiani Planum region of Mars, shown in an image made by the Mars Exploration Rover Opportunity in late January 2004. The outcropping varies in height from 30 to 45 cm (12 to 18 inches) along the crater. As interpreted by rover mission scientists, the rock layers apparently were laid down as deposits at the bottom of a body of flowing salt-water, probably on the shoreline of an ancient salty sea. NASA/JPL/Cornell University

instruments on the two orbiters and two landers returned detailed information concerning Martian geology, meteorology, and the physics and chemistry of the upper atmosphere. Vikings 1 and 2 were placed into orbit during June and August 1976, respectively. Lander modules descended to the surface from the orbiters after suitable sites were found. Viking 1 landed in the region of Chryse Planitia on July 20, 1976, and Viking 2 landed 6,500 km (4,000 miles) away in Utopia Planitia on Sept. 3, 1976.

In 1988 Soviet scientists launched a pair of spacecraft, Phobos 1 and 2, to orbit Mars and make slow flyby observations of its two satellites. Phobos 1 failed during the yearlong flight, but Phobos 2 reached Mars in early 1989 and returned several days of observations of both the planet and Phobos before malfunctioning.

Amid failures of several U.S. spacecraft missions to Mars in the 1990s, Mars Pathfinder successfully set down in Chryse Planitia on July 4, 1997, and deployed a robotic wheeled rover called Sojourner on the surface. This was followed by Mars Global Surveyor, which reached Mars in September 1997 and systematically mapped various properties of the planet from orbit for several years beginning in March 1999. These included Mars's gravity and magnetic fields, surface topography, and surface mineralogy. The spacecraft also carried cameras for making both wide-angle and detailed images of the surface at resolutions down to 1.5 metres (5 feet). Mars Odyssey safely entered Mars orbit in October 2001 and started mapping other properties, including the chemical composition of the surface, the distribution of near-surface ice, and the physical properties of near-surface materials.

A wave of spacecraft converged on Mars in late 2003 and early 2004 with mixed outcomes. Nozomi, launched by Japan in 1998 on a leisurely trajectory, was the first to reach the vicinity of the planet, but malfunctions prevented it from being put into Mars orbit. In mid-2003 the European Space Agency's Mars Express was launched on a half-year journey to the Red Planet. Carrying instruments to study the atmosphere, surface, and subsurface, it entered Mars orbit on December 25; however, its lander, named Beagle 2, which was to examine the rocks and soil for signs of past or present life, failed to establish radio contact after presumably having descended to the Martian surface the same day. Within weeks of its arrival, the Mars Express orbiter detected vast fields of water ice as well as carbon dioxide ice at the south pole and confirmed that the southern summer remnant cap, like the northern one, contains permanently frozen water. It also detected large sulfur-rich deposits, mainly in Valles Marineris, and clay minerals in the heavily cratered terrains.

Also launched in mid-2003 was the U.S. Mars Exploration Rover mission, which comprised twin robotic landers, Spirit and Opportunity. Spirit touched down in Gusev Crater (15° S, 175° E) on Jan. 3, 2004. Three weeks later, on Jan. 24, Opportunity landed in Meridiani Planum (2° S, 6° W), on the opposite side of the planet. The six-wheeled rovers, each equipped with cameras and a suite of instruments that included a microscopic imager and a rock-grinding tool, analyzed the rocks, soil, and dust around their landing sites, which had been chosen because they appeared to have been affected by water in Mars's past. Both rovers found evidence of past water; perhaps the most dramatic was the discovery by Opportunity of rocks that appeared to have been laid down at the shoreline of an ancient body of salty water.

In 2005 the U.S. launched the Mars Reconnaissance Orbiter, carrying an imaging system with a resolution of 20 cm (8 inches), a spectrometer to determine surface composition, and a ground-penetrating radar. The spectrometer revealed that clay minerals and other alteration products indicative of a warm distant past are common in the ancient cratered terrains, while the radar determined the thickness of the ice at the poles and detected glaciers elsewhere.

In 2008 the U.S. probe Phoenix landed in the north polar region of Mars. Phoenix carried a small chemical laboratory to study the arctic soil. It found water ice underneath the surface of Mars.

THE QUESTION OF LIFE ON MARS

From the beginnings of telescopic observations of Mars, people have speculated about whether life could have started on the planet and what that life might be like. Early observers were concerned mostly with intelligent life, but the focus now is on life's origin, microbial communities, and limits to their survival.

Views on the prospects for life on Mars have varied greatly in recent decades. In the 1960s the possibility that changes seen at the telescope could have a biological cause led to Mariner 9's attempts to monitor surface changes in 1972 and to the launching of the Viking landers to Mars in 1975. The Viking spacecraft had an array of sophisticated experiments to detect metabolism and organic molecules. The negative results from these experiments resulted in considerable pessimism that continued through the 1980s for the prospects for life.

However, several factors subsequently contributed to a more optimistic view. The first is recognition that life can survive in a far wider range of conditions than was formerly thought possible, including near deep-sea vents at temperatures well over 1,000 °C (1,800 °F), in basaltic rocks deep below the surface, and in very saline and acid environments. The second is the discovery that on Earth life started very quickly, possibly before the end of heavy bombardment, which possibly indicates that the origin of life is not an extremely low-probability event but rather will follow if the right conditions are present. The third is mounting evidence that conditions on early Mars, when life arose on Earth, were Earthlike. A fourth factor is recognition that Earth and Mars exchange materials. As indicated above, more than 50 pieces of Mars have been found on Earth, despite the difficulty of distinguishing Mars rocks from Earth rocks. It is more difficult to get Earth rocks to Mars. Nevertheless, during the period of heavy bombardment, when life may have already started on Earth and conditions on Mars were Earthlike, pieces of Earth may have been transported to Mars. Thus, life may have originated independently on Mars or been seeded from Earth.

In 1996 the scientific world was shocked when a group of scientists announced that they had found evidence of life in a Martian meteorite. In support of their conclusion, they listed (1) bacteria-like objects in electron microscope imagery, (2) detection of hydrocarbons, (3) mineral assemblages that were not produced in chemical equilibrium, and (4) magnetic particles similar to those produced by some terrestrial bacteria. The announcement triggered a vigorous scientific debate into the validity of the claims. The scientific consensus now is that there are plausible abiological explanations for all the observations and that the claims are likely invalid.

Despite this setback, the main driver of the Mars exploration program is still the search for life. Because liquid water is so essential for life, the initial focus has been on the search for evidence of warm conditions that would enable the persistence of liquid water. The evidence for such conditions, at least on early Mars, is now compelling, and the exploration thrust will likely shift to search for more direct evidence such as organic remains and isotopic signatures. It could be argued that the best strategy is to look for fossil remains from the early period in Mars's history when conditions were more Earthlike. But the Martian meteorite debate and disagreements about early terrestrial life point to the difficulty of finding compelling evidence of microbial fossil life. Alternatively, it could be argued that the best strategy is to look for present-day life in niches such as warm volcanic regions, in the hope that if life ever started on Mars, it would survive where conditions were hospitable.

GLOSSARY

accretion Growth by gradual buildup.

annulus A ringlike structure or marking.

barycentre The center of mass of two or more bodies that orbit around each other.

chromosphere An incandescent, transparent layer of gas that surrounds a star.

coalesce To grow together to form a united whole.

convection Heat transfer, via liquid or gas, from one region to another.

dipole A pair of electric charges or magnetic poles that are of equal magnitude but opposite sign or polarity, separated by a distance.

ecliptic plane The plane of Earth's orbit.

escarpment A steep slope that results from erosion or faulting, separating two relatively level areas of differing elevations.

faculae Large bright spots on the Sun's photosphere, usually near sunspots.

grabens Depressions on a planet's surface that are bounded by fault lines.

interstellar Between or among the stars.

lithosphere Where Earth's uppermost mantle and the crust act mechanically as a single rigid layer.

lobate Having curved or scalloped edges.

magnetosphere A region surrounding Earth in which charged particles are trapped and their behavior is dominated by the planet's magnetic field.

mascons Areas where particularly dense lavas rose up from the mantle and flooded into basins.

micrometeorites A tiny particle of meteoric dust, especially one that falls to the surface of Earth or the Moon.

nebula A mass of interstellar dust or gas, visible as luminous patches or areas of darkness, depending on the way radiation is absorbed.

penumbra The grayish outer portion of a sunspot or the outer part of the shadow cast by Earth or the Moon during an eclipse.

photosurface The portion of the Sun seen in ordinary light; face of the Sun as viewed from Earth.

planetesimals Small bodies thought to have orbited the sun during the formation of the planets.

precess Move in a gyrating fashion.

prograde Direct motion of the planets around the Sun.

regolith An insulating debris layer made of dust and rock fragments ejected from distant impacts on a planet's surface.

retrograde Moving backward or in an order that is opposite the usual.

solar constant The average density of solar radiation measured outside Earth's atmosphere and at Earth's mean distance from the Sun.

spicules Streams of plasma that appear in the Sun's chromosphere.

subduction A geologic process in which one edge of one crustal plate is forced below the edge of another.

superior conjunction The position of a celestial body when it is on the opposite side of the Sun from Earth.

tenuous Long and thin.

tessarae Geologic regions of Venus that resemble mosaic tiles.

transit Event when a small astronomical body passes in front of a larger astronomical body.

tropopause The topmost portion of the troposphere.

troposphere The region on Earth where nearly all water vapour exists and essentially all weather occurs.

vulcanoids A hypothetical remnant population of asteroid-sized objects orbiting the Sun inside Mercury's orbit.

FOR FURTHER READING

Adams, W. Clifford. *Sunspots*. Overland Park, KS: Leathers Publishing, 2006.

American Association for the Advancement of Science, ed. *Exploring the Inner Solar System: Expecting the Unexpected*. Washington, DC: American Association for the Advancement of Science, 2006.

Benestad, Rasmus E. *Solar Activity and Earth's Climate*. Berlin, Ger.: Springer Praxis, 2006.

Cashford, Jules. *The Moon: Myth and Image*. Jackson, TN: Basic Books, 2003.

Cattermole, Peter. *Building Planet Earth: Five Billion Years of Earth History*. Cambridge, Eng.: Cambridge University Press, 2000.

Clark, Pamela. *Dynamic Planet: Mercury in the Context of its Environment*. Berlin, Ger.: Springer, 2007.

Gaz, Stan. *Sites of Impact: Meteorite Craters Around the World*. New York, NY: Princeton Architectural Press, 2009.

Grego, Peter. *Venus and Mercury, and How to Observe Them*. Berlin, Ger.: Springer, 2008.

Hanlon, Michael. *The Real Mars*. New York, NY: Carroll & Graf Publishers, 2004.

Hartmann, William K. *A Traveler's Guide to Mars*. New York, NY: Workman Publishing, 2003.

Miller, Ron. *Mars (Worlds Beyond)*. Minneapolis, MN: Twenty-First Century Books, 2004.

Oxlade, Chris. *Mercury, Mars, and Other Inner Planets*. New York, NY: Rosen Publishing Group, 2008.

Renfield, R.K. *Venus*. New York, NY: Rosen Publishing Group, 2004.

Schrijver, Carolus J., and Cornelius Zwaan. *Solar and Stellar Magnetic Activity*. Cambridge, Eng.: Cambridge University Press, 2008.

Sheehan, William, and John Westfall. *The Transits of Venus*. Amherst, NY: Prometheus Books, 2004.

Spangenburg, Ray. *A Look at Mars* (Out of This World). London, Eng.: Franklin Watts, 2000.

Spence, Pam. *Sun Observer's Guide*. Buffalo, NY: Firefly Books, 2004.

Woolfson, Michael. *The Formation of the Solar System*. London, Eng.: Imperial College Press, 2007.

Zanda, Brigitte, and Monica Rotaru, eds. *Meteorites: Their Impact on Science and History*. Cambridge, Eng.: Cambridge University Press, 2001.

INDEX